Two banks of

(Les Deux Rives)

Fernand Vandérem

(Translator: George Raffalovich)

Alpha Editions

This edition published in 2024

ISBN : 9789362511539

Design and Setting By
Alpha Editions
www.alphaedis.com
Email - info@alphaedis.com

As per information held with us this book is in Public Domain.
This book is a reproduction of an important historical work. Alpha Editions uses the best technology to reproduce historical work in the same manner it was first published to preserve its original nature. Any marks or number seen are left intentionally to preserve its true form.

Contents

PREFATORY NOTE..- 1 -
CHAPTER I ....- 2 -
CHAPTER II...- 10 -
CHAPTER III ....- 20 -
CHAPTER IV ....- 32 -
CHAPTER V ....- 46 -
CHAPTER VI ....- 59 -
CHAPTER VII..- 68 -
CHAPTER VIII ....- 84 -
CHAPTER IX ....- 94 -
CHAPTER X ....- 113 -
CHAPTER XI ....- 123 -
CHAPTER XII..- 131 -
CHAPTER XIII ....- 146 -
CHAPTER XIV ....- 160 -
CHAPTER XV ....- 169 -
CHAPTER XVI ....- 183 -
CHAPTER XVII...- 196 -
CHAPTER XVIII..- 209 -
CHAPTER XIX ....- 228 -

PREFATORY NOTE

Two Banks of the Seine, by Fernand Vandérem, belongs to the class of literature immortalized by Alphonse Daudet. In it we catch the slightly ironic but good-natured tone familiar to those who have read *Sapho*; and we perceive the author applying objective psychology to life—Parisian life. For M. Vandérem is not only Gallic, but vitally Parisian. His attitude towards men and women is sophisticated; but his art is always fresh and true. He is a realist who does not disdain to make use of romance when it suits his purpose.

Two Banks of the Seine is an interesting story wherein the life of the Latin Quarter and that of the upper classes are brought into sharp contrast. This supplies the author with ample material suitable to his peculiar bent. He handles his material with clear vision, often with delicate sympathy, and never without humor. The men and women in the book are sketched with a sure pen, and are put and kept in motion by a firm hand. They are made to move about briskly before us and to speak with the accents of life. Like all great novelists, M. Vandérem is more interested in character and human relationships than in plot. His book is not so much a novel in the ordinary sense as a comedy of manners.

Our author knows his Parisian well. He has studied him in the home and in the street; at work and at play. Few contemporary novelists afford us a clearer insight into the workings of the mind of the elusive Parisian, or a more intimate knowledge of his temperament.

M. Vandérem has written a number of novels besides *Two Banks of the Seine*; it is sufficient to mention here his *Charlie* and his *La Victime*, works of unusual merit.

BARNET J. BEYER.

26TH FEBRUARY, 1919.

CHAPTER I

THE carriage stopped at the gate of the Collège de France; Mme. Chambannes alighted briskly. She did not take the trouble to close the door and, swinging her muff, hurried through the somber courtyard, where three pigeons wandered in the security that silence and solitude ensured them.

Through the panes of the glass door M. Pageot, first usher of the Collège, watched her approach, his thick mustache slightly lifted in a smile of sympathy.

"Another one!" he thought, remembering all the fashionable ladies whom he had seen come in during the last hour. This one, moreover, was very dainty. Her small, fine, although bold, face, her astrakhan jacket and purple velvet toque with border of astrakhan to match, the curls of which mingled with her own brown hair, an aigrette of white feathers perched on the side, reminded him, reverence apart and minus the whiskers, of an old lithograph which hung above his bed, *Murat, Future King of Naples, at the Battle of Eylau.*

It was therefore with an eager hand that he opened the door for her.

"What is it you wish, madame?"

"If you please, where is the lecture on Egyptology?"

"M. Rainda lecture? There, you are facing the hall."

She was rushing forward when M. Pageot held her back with a calm gesture. "It is useless, madame! The hall is full, overcrowded.... Moreover, you will not miss much, for it will be over in five minutes...."

"Thank you," acknowledged Mme. Chambannes, regretfully, adding, after a pause, "Did you happen to see a tall, fair lady in a blue costume ... with a strapped jacket?"

Pageot tried to recollect.

"See her? See her?... Why, surely I saw her; but, madame, there are so many of them! Upon my word, I do not remember having seen so many people at an opening lecture during the whole fifteen years that I have been an usher of the Collège...." Carelessly he straightened his light nickel chain, and added in the competent tone of one who knew, "I suppose they came on account of his book on Cleopatra...."

Mme. Chambannes nodded assent. At that moment the doors of the lecture hall swung back under the pressure of the departing audience and the huge hall suddenly resounded with a church-like sonorousness.

"Here, perhaps, is your friend in blue," said Pageot, indicating a lady who was one of the first to come out.

Mme. Chambannes hurried to stop Mme. de Marquesse, who exclaimed:

"You!... Well, I cannot say you are early! Yet I only came here to please you!"

"A letter I was expecting from Gerald," apologized her friend. "I tell you about it later.... I was quite upset, I assure you.... Well, tell me, was it at least all right inside there? Was it worth the trouble?... Did he speak of Cleopatra?... Was he very shocking?"

Mme. de Marquesse assumed a roguish expression.

"I do know.... You are asking too much.... I am like the little girl in the play.... I saw nothing, I heard nothing.... Standing, with rows of men in front of me and the smell of perspiration!... I wo be caught again.... Or else I shall send my footman to book my seats in good time...."

"How dreadful!"

"Oh, well, it might have been worse," replied Mme. de Marquesse protectively.... "Goodness gracious! What a child you are, little Zozé! Here or elsewhere you will meet M. Raindal again.... There is nothing lost.... And all this because M. de Meuze turned your head with his blarney!..."

"This has nothing to do with M. de Meuze!"

"With whom, then?... Is it Gerald?... If it is the father, then it must be the son.... Do you really think that notorieties carry any weight with him?... How naïve you are!"

"Why not!" demanded Mme. Chambannes sarcastically. "With such ideas, in three months I shall succeed in having a salon like the Pums or the Silberschmidts.... Thank you!... My system is not so absurd.... I know what I am doing!" Then she added more cordially, "Shall we watch them come out?"

"If you like," replied Mme. de Marquesse. And they stood at one side in the narrow passage through which the audience filed out.

It was obviously a public meant for show, a delegation of that brilliant civic guard with which Paris keeps its successful glories surrounded. There were people from the literary salons, the "large circulation revues," the conservative periodicals that have none but authentic illustrations after the title-page; there were academicians, famous as well as obscure, thinkers, men with dreamy minds and men with reflective ones, jugglers of ideas, men who dug up questions and men who solved problems. There were the established mistresses of the tables where discussion takes place, plus their lively retinue of little women, little men, little young men, little old men, the whole flight of those who prattle, cackle, and giggle on the heights of art as sparrows do on the branches of trees; there were pretty faces, dull with powder, peeping out of soft sable collars; inquisitive silhouettes with military mustaches; voices that were disciplined in the practice of the correct phrase; brows that were furrowed by years of study or the persistent search for the witty word; smiles, furs, and whiffs of perfume. They called to each other; they bowed to each other; they exchanged the opinions they had or even those they were going to have—all this before the amazed eyes of a few outsiders who spoke their names in low, respectful voices.

Mme. Chambannes seemed especially delighted with the spectacle. She had never been seriously tempted to belong to this élite. Fate had directed her aims elsewhere, towards a simpler, a more human and tender object; and thither, despite contrary appearances, all her actions tended. But to witness the gossip, the coquetries and friendly encounters of those well-known people who were so often mentioned in the society columns, afforded her a naïve delight, a joy of the eye and of the mind which gave her miniature face quite a serious look of attention.

Suddenly she made an involuntary movement of surprise and touched Mme. de Marquesse.

"Do look at this one!"

Her glance indicated a poorly clad girl who was coming towards them, in a jacket of green cloth with marten revers which seemed even more worn than the dusty tulle bonnet pinned awry on her head. The girl, who had the haughty gait and the somewhat bitter, aggressive expression which fatigue, pride, and masculine worries often give to women of science, gave the two women an almost hostile look as she passed them, and approached the usher.

"Pageot, has my father come out?" she asked in a tone of authority.

The usher quickly removed his skull cap.

"No, mademoiselle.... Shall I tell him that mademoiselle...."

"Thank you, Pageot.... You will please tell him that I am waiting for him outside, near the gate...."

"Very well, mademoiselle!" and the usher ran to open the door for her. "Do you know who she is?" he added mysteriously, as he turned back to Mme. Chambannes. "You do know?... It is Mlle. Thérèse Raindal, M. Rainda daughter!"

Outside, Mlle. Raindal began to pace back and forth in front of the ancient gate, walking briskly up and down the pavement, her neck shrunk in her shoulders and her shoulders hunched forward like those of a sentry struggling against the cold. At intervals she would stop and throw a searching glance towards the steps at the end of the courtyard. Through the window could be seen the meditative face of Pageot, which had at that distance and in the thick ochreous air of that dark November afternoon, almost the complexion of a yellow-fever patient. But as M. Raindal was not yet in sight, Thérèse took up her sentry walk again, her elbows close to her body, her hands crossed inside her plush muff.

Gradually, as she paced back and forth, the line of her lips, almost as thin as a thread of rose silk, paled and all but vanished in a pouting expression. She was thinking of the approaching evening ordeal, the forced introduction which had been arranged for her at the house of M. Lemeunier de Saulvard, of the Department of Moral Sciences,—an introduction to an unknown man who would be presented to her at a dance, a "possible husband," the man who would have a right to her kisses, to her flesh, and would thereafter spend all his nights beside her. One more to reject! The ninth one in ten years! "A young savant of the greatest merit," Saulvard had written; "one of our rising hopes in Assyriology, M. Pierre Boerzell...." M. Boerzell! M. Boerzell! She repeated the harsh, barbarous name. Well, that "hope" would be no less sadly handicapped in the matter of good looks than the others before him! Probably something like the podgy little man carrying a barriste case who was coming in her direction on the other side of the street! Instinctively she stopped to take a good look at the passer-by, her lips wickedly pursed and her eye aflame as at the sight of prey. Then, with lips relaxed in a disdainful smile, she turned about, and shrugging her shoulders, murmured:

"Yes, probably one of that type!"

She was suffering. As the wind bit her face, it seemed to her that something icy was gripping her heart. She remembered that other one—the man she had once lost—the runaway and defaulting fiancé, Albert Dastarac. Ten years had passed since then, but there were still nights when, in her maidenly dreams, she fancied that she felt his maddening embraces and the lingering fragrance of his lips.

Who could have foreseen that the young *agrégé* of history would prove so perfidious? That wheedling southerner, that seductive *Albârt*, as his deep bass voice sounded his name! He was so caressing, so passionate; the director of the Normal School had praised him so much! Even now while she waited outside the gate in that icy mist, Thérèse Raindal could not believe in the actuality of that past betrayal; she could not explain it to herself or even understand it. Images, daily called back to her memory, were so familiar and recent! She fancied she was beside Albârt in her fathe drawing-room in the rue Notre-Dame-des-Champs. Once more she saw his impudent profile, like that of a classical bandit, his splendid frame, his straight legs, his huge brown eyes with scarcely any white to be seen, and the fine black mustache which he curled with his tapering fingers, coppered by the use of tobacco. How he had made love to her during those eight days of their engagement!

She was flat-chested; her mouth was bloodless, small, and narrowed as if drawn together by a cord; her complexion was dulled by that greenish tan which one acquires when shut away from the sun, amidst dusty books, in over-heated libraries or in the feverish air of lecture halls. Albârt seemed to notice none of all those defects of which she was more conscious than anyone else and which often made her secretly unhappy. He saw nothing but her charms. He was always enraptured with her pale, straight nose chiselled like an antique, with her fierce gray eyes crowned with black velvet,—like those of Minerva, he would say,—with the massive coils of her brown hair, which he wanted to take down and bathe his face in. And the tenderness of his words matched his ability to flatter.

Ceaselessly, ardently, and without reason, he called her, as in an invocation or a prayer, "*Oh, ma Theresoun! Oh, ma chato!*" For her he sang slow Provençal songs, mournful as the tunes played by distant hunting-horns, which Mme. Raindal, who was also from the South, accompanied as best she could on the piano, quiveringly singing the chorus with him. Or, when he was alone with the young girl, he would sit at her feet on a stool of blue satin while she talked about the future,—how she would regulate the hours of his work, help him in his career, and push him on to the highest attainments. Then suddenly, wildly, he would throw himself upon her and press her in his arms murmuring, "*Ma Theresoun!*" The stone-like biceps of his arm would roll against her flesh, his scented mustache would be close to her face, his fragrant lips meet hers, and she would throw back her head, her eyelids closed, with a longing to yield, to let the sweet balm of his kisses permeate all her being.

Then one morning an embarrassed letter had come from Albârt. Family matters compelled him to put off the wedding and to leave at once for St. Gaudens, his native town. The young gentleman apologized, whined, protesting his sorrow. Three weeks later, M. Raindal had taken his daughter to the Luxembourg, as one would lead a convalescent to take a little rest in the spring air of the gardens; there Thérèse saw her fiancé, the spruce and lively Dastarac, with a young girl on his arm, a short, thin, sickly creature, the third daughter of M. Gaussine, professor of the Sumarian language at the Sorbonne, who was walking behind them.

"Come along, child," murmured M. Raindal, trying to lead his daughter away. "Yes, they are to be married. I only heard of it yesterday!... Maître Gaussine has a reputation for getting good positions for his sons-in-law.... This is what must have attracted our rascal.... Come on, l explain to you...."

But she had stood still, unable to move, although she could hardly keep from screaming aloud in her pain. She had been on the verge of fainting. What an outrageous memory! Then came the ghastly days in her room, still impregnated with the rogu perfume,—the long hours of day dreams, when she had taken her vows of renunciation, swearing henceforth to devote herself to a life of study as others are driven by despair into religion!

In spite of her work, however, and of the long years that had passed since then, she had been unable to dismiss from her mind, no matter how much learning she had crowded it with, the tenacious image of the charming Albârt, who, notwithstanding the offices of his father-in-law, was said to be buried miles away from Paris, in an obscure Lycée of Provence.

Thérèse was still dazzled by the memory of his caresses, as were those mortals of antiquity whom a god had loved. He remained her mourned husband, the masterful lord of her secret life; and when they wanted to marry her, to give her to another man, it was always he who came between, who took her back, resurrecting in her austere frame his Theresoun of old, his captivated Theresoun. Invisible to all others, but present to her, he would seem to be there, hand on hip, his knee bent in that swaggering attitude of bravado, murmuring with sneering lips, "But look, *ma chato*, look, compare us!... Is it possible ... after me?" It was true; how could she stoop—betray him! And so in a few brusque words the new suitor was always dismissed.

"So you do want him, child?" M. Raindal would ask pitifully, only to be met with a refusal so sharp and angry, and like a blow that it left him dazed, reduced him to silence, and effectively prevented any further argument.

"Well, dear, are we ready?... I was delayed by a newspaper man, a reporter who interviewed me on Cleopatra, the English in Egypt ... and I do know what.... Tell me, you did not feel too impatient?"

Thérèse started on hearing the jovial voice of her father.

"No, no, I was thinking; I was working, walking up and down."

"Good! I am glad of it...." And as one does to a friend or a colleague, he took her arm and rapidly led her towards the Boulevard St. Michel.

People turned to look as they passed, puzzled by the strange couple: this officer of the Légion onneur, an old gentleman with a white beard, and a girl who looked like a school teacher, walking arm in arm tenderly. Some attempted a guess; some instinctively smiled, moved by vague sympathetic ideas. Sometimes students who knew the master by sight purposely stared at him to win a glance for themselves, or even, moved by respect, saluted him.

M. Raindal perceived this homage only confusedly. He was now concentrating all his attention on questioning Thérèse to ascertain her exact opinion of his opening lecture. Was she satisfied? Had it gone well? It was not too long? And the peroration, what had she thought that? Had he done right in dismissing those loungers and snobs who had dared to invade his lecture hall, his own quiet little chapel?

"Oh, yes!" Thérèse replied. "Although I might say you were a little too severe and scornful."

"Never enough so!... It may be good for the Sorbonne to have all those fine ladies and their tame cats.... But as for us, we want none but workers, true apprentices...."

Then he digressed into a diffuse commentary on the duties, the dignity, and the aim of the Collège de France. Science! Le Collège de France! There lay his faith, his church, and he had no other! Thérèse knew by heart the order and the verses of these fiery litanies, and let him proceed without interruption.

"Never mind, child," he concluded, out of breath. "They have had their warning. I think we shall not see them again.... Moreover, this affluence has its reasons.... It is another miracle of our *Cleopatra*."

"Oh, *our* Cleopatra!" Thérèse protested.

"Yes, yes, ours. I maintain the word...."

Following the natural bent which leads one to talk of oneself, he recalled the phases of his disconcerting triumph: fame that had come in a night, the whole press, the reviews, and the salons working together to make him famous; five thousand copies sold in three weeks; articles every night, every morning ... everywhere—those papers which fell into line later proving more ardent than the first ones, thus seeking in the fervor of their adhesion an excuse for the shame of their delay; letters, interviews, requests for articles, portraits and autographs. Success, in one word,—that imperial investiture, with its long, endless offerings, delirious praetorians, and even the intolerant enthusiasm that forces the jealous to wait, which Paris sometimes gives to its elect.

And to whom did M. Raindal owe it all? Who had suggested to him the subject of this book three years ago? Who had thought of a *Life of Cleopatra*, written from the national Egyptian point of view, and deriving its inspiration from indigenous documents and the popular sentiments of the period? And then who had helped him to the very end, faithfully seconded him in the heavy task? Who had classified the material, copied the papyri, transcribed the inscriptions, and read the proofs over and over, one by one, with the exception of the Latin notes? Who had....

"But, I say, where are you leading me now!" he exclaimed, abandoning the tone of friendly custody which he had assumed in reciting his eulogy of her.

Thérèse smiled tenderly.

"There you are, father; tha what you get for exaggerating.... One forgets everything, one does know where one is any more.... I am leading you to the *Bon Marché*, where I am going to buy gloves for to-night...."

"Ah, yes, the dance!" M. Raindal sighed, as if he had already received the customary blow of a refusal. Then he went on: "Well, no! I must leave you.... I am going to climb up to your Uncle Cyprie; I want to inquire how his rheumatism is to-day and whether he is coming to dine with us to-night...."

Before the Church of St. Germain-des-Prés, they stopped in the midst of the melancholy crowd standing about the street-car office and shook hands firmly, like two comrades.

"Au revoir, dear, I see you a little later."

"Au revoir, father."

Thérèse crossed the street, while M. Raindal gathered up his leather case, which was slipping from his elbow, and slowly and with deliberation, as if weighed down by his thoughts, ventured into the rue Bonaparte.

CHAPTER II

M. CYPRIEN RAINDAL lived on the sixth floor of an old house that stood at the corner of the rue Vavin and the rue ssas, in an apartment made up of two large rooms, the windows of which gave him a limitless vista over the yoke-elm trees of the Luxemburg. He was a thick-set, sanguine man, about forty-five years old, and wore his hair close-cropped, like soldiers in the African colonies. By temperament he was irritable and rebellious. As early as 1860 his elder brother had secured him a place in the Ministry of Industry, from which, however, had it not been for the same powerful intervention of Eusèbe Raindal, he would several times have been dismissed.

Born at the unfortunate period of their fathe life, when M. Raindal had been put out of the University for being an accomplice of Barbès and was reduced to coaching at two francs a lesson, it seemed as if the son had inherited a taste for political opposition. He had detested in turn each government which his functions compelled him to serve, the second empire, M. Thiers, the Seize-Mai, and the subsequent rule of "opportunism." Finally, in 1889, when the trunks of General Boulanger were seized, a card bearing Cyprie name was found therein upon which he had written the cordial exhortation, "Bravo, general! Forward! The whole country stands with you!"

Cyprien Raindal was on the eve of being promoted; but called to the office of the Minister, his lips already shaping words of gratitude, he received instead the notification of his dismissal. The blow struck him as he was breathing the very spirit of peace; it was like an unexpected insult, like a blow upon the cheek that had been offered for a kiss. Murmuring threats and words of rage, he had returned to his desk, and then had rushed out to order new visiting-cards, on which appeared under his name, *ancien sous-chef de bureau au Ministère de ndustrie*, and one of these he had himself nailed up on the door of his apartment. But his vengeance had stopped there. The official mind within him forbade his persisting in what was almost the usurpation of a title, and he finally decided to burn the rest of the deceptive cards. Moreover, in spite of the affair, his brother was endeavoring to secure him the benefit of his pension,—three thousand francs, without which he would have been plunged into the most undignified misery. He waited, holding himself in check for a few weeks, and only began to express himself with freedom when his pension had been officially liquidated.

When that was done, however, the fury of his opinions and the violence of his language burst forth terribly, like explosives that have been too long compressed. Thirty years of exasperation, hitherto repressed by the necessity of existing and the fear of his superiors, rushed out through his lips in avalanches that seemed to be inexhaustible. He wished at first to reduce his hatred to a formula, to justify his discontent with some sort of principles, and he inclined towards socialism. Unfortunately, however, he was lost in questions of capital and wages; statistics bored him and political economy upset him with its systems, which were always either unstable or denied by rival experts. By taste, if not by conviction, he was bourgeois; by education he was, like his brother, non-religious; by force of habit he was a waster of red-tape. What he needed was a more human and less subversive doctrine, theories easy to master, morality rather than figures, and sentiment rather than deduction.

Thus, gradually and by himself, he had built up a social creed which allowed him elbow room, as would a suit of clothes made to order. Firmly persuaded that he was the victim of injustice, he longed to see justice enthroned. The punishment of evildoers, the death or exile of the thieves, a general return to honest life and the crushing of iniquity—these he wished to see in the first place. Later? Well, one would see about the rest. Let the people obtain that much purification, and they would settle the remainder in the best way possible. M. Raindal, junior, was not one of those swaggering dreamers who promise to destroy and rebuild society as if it were the hut of a road-mender. He knew how powerful was tradition, how necessary the family, and he appreciated the indispensable charm of freedom. Before doing away with that, let Frenchmen think about clearing the country from the vermin that infested it. If the chance offered itself, Uncle Cyprien would not refuse his help. He declared himself ready to go with them any day that the "comrades" would proceed en masse to seize in their own mansions the prevaricators, the Jews, and the pillars of the church whose coalition kept down France as with a three-pronged fork. It was his own comparison, and he repeated it readily with much bragging about getting his head broken and breaking the heads of many others.

His reading of the newspapers of the opposition had thoroughly fitted him for a place in the ranks of those sincere justice-lovers whom the death of the rebel general had left without a head but not without a hope. Instinctively he turned towards the pamphleteers who denounced the enemies of the weak or supported the victims against their oppressors. By a curious anomaly he had in turn discovered within himself all the hatreds, no matter how incongruous, with which these masters stirred up the flames. Rochefort had helped him to find in his heart the hatred of all politicians; with Paul Bert or his disciples he had discerned in himself a hatred for the priests and all devout Catholics; with Drumont, hatred for Jews and exotics. He was always reading the articles and the books of these pamphleteers and could quote whole passages from memory. His conversation showed this; it was discordant with the most diverse insults. The words *chequard* (grafter), *repu* (bloated), *panamist* (one compromised in the Panama scandals), *calotin* (priest-ridden), *cafard* (canting rascal), *ratichon* (bigot), joined to those of *youtre* (Jew), *youpin* (Jew), or *rasta* (short for *rastaquouère* and meaning an exotic mongrel or Levantine) vibrated all at once like the "sustained bass" of his indignations. His virulence when he discussed sociology in the presence of strangers was a cause of deep grievance to his family.

When he heard the bell of his apartment he jumped from the little green rep-covered couch where he was dozing and, slightly limping and holding his back with one hand, he opened the door. A smile lit his face the moment he recognized M. Raindal.

"I am very glad to see you!" exclaimed Cyprien, after the two brothers had kissed as usual. "Come this way.... I had so many things to read to you...."

"And how are you?" asked M. Raindal, as he followed him. "How do you feel now? Are you coming to dine to-night?"

"Why, yes, indeed; I shall certainly come." And, entering the room in which he used to receive, Cyprien affectionately laid his hand on his brothe shoulder and said, "Now, sit down and listen to this."

Hastily he began a search among the newspapers which littered his couch. They were unfolded, crumpled or piled up so that only odd letters from their large titles could be seen. All those scattered newspapers were a sick ma debauch, a fond indulgence—a luxury, a treat he offered himself when he was kept at home by rheumatism. Otherwise he only read the papers at the café or at the brasserie, and in small doses—perhaps two or three aggressive sheets, which gave a delightful sensation of warmth to his brain after lunch, as the small glass of cognac he usually took burned his throat. When at last he had sorted them and found the three which he sought he flourished them with a rattling noise.

"Here is something!" he said. "Rich and delightful!... Enough to amuse me and to make you swell with pride.... First of all, of course, what amuses me...."

He read the first article in victorious tones. In discreet but pitiless terms the writer announced as imminent the arrest of a senator, an ex-minister and deputy, well-known for his intrigues, his accommodating complacency towards the banking interests and his clerical tendencies; and the government was congratulated for that forthcoming show of energy.

"You see," Uncle Cyprien said, when he had finished reading, "I do know who it is.... I thought about it for hours.... I could find the name ... and yet, I must admit the news caused me to pass a very pleasant day.... It is high time that all those scoundrels were swept out.... One more in jail! I score one!..." He smiled at his own merriment and added, with his two hands on his knees:

"Well, what do you think about it? It is getting serious! All these rotten gatherings are bursting open!"

M. Raindal hesitated. He wished to avoid controversy or, at least, to adjourn it and to thrash the matter out only after his brother had read the other articles. Trained by his profession and by personal inclination to consider things through the immensity of time, in the infinite span of past and future centuries, he was not so much indifferent to his own time as disdainful of it. Whenever his brother goaded him into discussing politics he felt more scared and ill at ease than if he had had to argue upon a matter of taboo with a savage chief of Polynesia in the latte own language.

"Of course! To be sure!...." he declared. "We are living in a troubled period.... There are many abuses.... How can it be helped?... Concussion is the plague of democracies.... Polybius said so...."

"Ah, leave me alone with your Polybius!" Uncle Cyprien interrupted, shaking his head as if to disentangle himself from his brothe aphorisms. "Why not simply tell me that we are governed by rogues?... It will be truer and quicker...."

Then he felt somewhat ashamed of having thus chided his illustrious elder brother whom he worshiped in the depths of his tormented soul.

"Oh, well, do get angry.... I your fault, after all.... You get on my nerves with your vague, high-sounding sentences.... See, to earn my forgiveness ... the portrait of M. Eusèbe Raindal, the man of the day, the famil standard, the glory of the French Egyptology, with the history of his life from the most remote times to our own days! Tara! Tara! Ta-ta-ta-ta!..." He gave his brother the second newspaper and marched round the room sounding through his rounded fingers a triumphal march, as in the days gone by, at the office, he had celebrated the success of some colleague.

M. Rainda eyes stared at the paper which his long-sightedness compelled him to hold at ar length.

Yes, that coarse-printed, ill-reproduced portrait, that was himself, his own strong nose, his white beard and benevolent face—a true senato face, as uncle Cyprien assured him.

Below his biography were spread out dates and yet more dates, all the titles of his books, one after the other, giving no more inkling of his life, his ideas, the joys and sorrows of his manhood than the milestones on the road or the posts at the crossings give one any idea of the places one goes through. To him, however, these dry figures and words were as alive as his own human flesh. His lips trembled in a nervous smile. Vanity overflowed from his heart to his face. He blushed with shame as if he felt directed towards him the stares of the crowd which, this very day, was looking at his features. However, his innate sense of propriety caused him to collect himself, and he said calmly:

"Entirely correct! I am much obliged to you. I carry it home...."

He rose to take his leave. A gesture from Cyprien caused him to resume his seat.

"Wait! Wait!... Tha not all. Now comes the unpleasant part!... You are insulted in the *Fléau*, a filthy rag written by *calotins* and read by all the rich Jews.... Here, listen to this!... It is awful!"

Cyprien began to read in a voice that trembled with sarcasm but even more with anger:

ACADEMIC INDISCRETIONS

The commission that is to bestow the Vital-Gerbert prize of fifteen thousand francs upon the best history book of the year will shortly meet at the French Academy. If one is to believe the rumors, the fight will be a hot one as there are several candidates. We are assured that one of them is M. Eusèbe Raindal, of the Institute, the author of that *Life of Cleopatra* which a certain section of the press has much boomed within the last month. M. Rainda candidacy, however, meets with serious opposition in academic circles. Several members consider the success of his book to be largely due to the obscene details which abound in it and which have attracted a special class of readers. Without desiring in any way to prejudice this delicate controversy, we are nevertheless compelled to admit that this book is one of the most immoral productions which have for a long time been published by a member of the Institute. The footnotes especially, although written in Latin, show signs of a revolting indecency. The author may claim in his defense that he has merely translated Egyptian pamphlets of the period and that, moreover, he has translated them only into Latin. It is nevertheless a fact that, wittingly or otherwise, he has given publicity to a mass of veritable filth. We know that history has its rights and the historian his duties. But M. Raindal will have some difficulty in establishing that it was his duty as a historian to show us Cleopatra coughing out disgusting words in the most abject surrenders of her love-making or going one better in the shameless expressions of debauchery than a female Nero. We think it is for other works, that treat of wider questions, and from a social and lofty point of view, that the academic prizes should be reserved. The "Immortals" of the Academy must decide whether we are right or wrong. To prove our contention they have this year only the difficulty of selection.

Cyprien kneaded the paper into a ball and threw it on the floor.

"Well," he concluded, "a pretty savage attack!... It has no importance whatsoever since, as I told you, only Jews read this letter.... However, if you were to authorize me, I should be very glad to go and pull the ears of the sneak who let his pen...."

M. Rainda face had grown pale with suffering as his brother had proceeded with his reading. He lifted his hand with a philosophical gesture and murmured in a voice that he had not yet steadied:

"No use.... These are the little come-backs of fame.... And then, I know the source!"

"Who?"

"I am sure that it was inspired, if not written, by my colleague and competitor Saulvard.... Lemeunier de Saulvard, of the Sciences Morales.... I recognize his hand.... He wants the prize for his *History of the Freed Men in the Roman Empire*.... I am in his way.... He gets someone to vilify me.... It is a classical method.... One can only be sorry for the wretch and smile...."

M. Raindal gave a painful smile, but his throat was obstructed by that rage, like bitter gall, which one feels under patent injustice. He spat out the word:

"Obscene!"

He paused awhile, then, his voice relieved, he repeated:

"Obscene!... No, I had never heard that in the course of my career; yet I have seen much jealousy, smallness of mind and calumny among members of my profession.... If you knew what sewers run under what is called the pure regions of science!... And the filth that is poured down in them! Obscene!... After a career like mine!... The scoundrels!"

He laughed disdainfully.

"Ha! ha!... To call a man obscene who led an almost pure, blameless youth!... A man who has worked twelve hours a day for the last forty years.... It is all they have found.... See! I am laughing!... It is too amusing! It is too funny for words!"

His brother Cyprien remained silent so as to allow full swing to this revolt, the vehemence of which was a delight to his own instincts. He pressed his brothe hand.

"Tha right! Tha the way to speak.... I can see you are a true Raindal. You do not like to be goaded.... You kick.... Tha right! I hope when you meet that person...."

"I am seeing him to-night," M. Raindal said, putting a sudden damper on his eagerness.

"To-night?" the ex-official muttered with surprise. "How?... Where?..."

"At his house.... He is giving a dance...."

"And you are going?"

"Well, yes!... A marriage for Thérèse.... A young man, a young savant, is to be introduced to us."

Cyprien laid a hand on the polished dome of his head and said dreamily:

"Ah! ah! A match for my nephew." (He always called Thérèse his nephew because of her masculine ways.) "Good! That is a reason.... Well, I have an idea that my nephew will not accept that young savant.... However, you are right; one has to see.... But be cautious! Your Saulvard seems to me utterly worthless ... and I would not be inclined to trust anything that came from that quarter...."

M. Raindal rose to his feet.

"Do worry. I shall look out.... Besides, you are wrong.... When his ambitions are not concerned Saulvard is not such a bad fellow...."

Cyprien whistled incredulously:

"Phew!... That may be.... Well, see you later ... seven lock."

And he accompanied his brother to the top of the steps.

The lamp-posts were lit outside when M. Raindal reached his home in the rue Notre-Dame-des-Champs.

Rapidly he put on his brown smoking-jacket and his felt slippers, and passed quietly through the dark hall towards his study. Two large rectangular oak tables, face to face as in a bank, almost filled the room. Thérèse was sitting at one of them, writing by the light of an oil lamp. The green cardboard shade threw back on her the crude light which her bowed forehead reflected in spots.

"Already at work!" M. Raindal exclaimed.

He took her head between his two hands as one does with a little girl and kissed her with a recrudescent selfish tenderness, with that need for a closer contact which those who are dear to us inspire after we have suffered from the wickedness of others.

She released herself with a smile, and said gently:

"Let me alone, father!... I am reading the proofs of your article for *La Revue*. They are coming for them at 5.30. You can see that there is no time to lose."

"Quite right! I obey," M. Raindal said.

He sat facing her at the other table and took up some papers on which he began to make notes. Everything was dark about the room with the exception of a few golden threads shining in the texture of the gold curtains and the thin yellow circle which the lamp threw on the ceiling. The only sounds were the somewhat halting breathing of M. Raindal, the crackling of the coke in the fireplace, and now and then a neighboring bell giving out at long intervals a few isolated, mournful sounds. Suddenly the master exclaimed:

"What about your mother?... Has she come home yet?"

"No," Thérèse replied, "but she will not be long.... She cannot be much longer."

And without ceasing to write, she added with a slight touch of sarcasm:

"It seemed to me.... No, I ought not to tell you.... Well, since I have begun, let it go!... I thought before I came in that I saw Mother entering the Church of St. Germain-des-Prés!"

"Again!" M. Raindal murmured with a tone of commiseration.... "That is at least the second time since this morning.... It is deplorable!"

Thérèse smiled and looked at her father.

"What can you expect?... It makes her happy and soothes her!"

M. Raindal made a melancholy grimace.

He, a philosophical and contemptuous atheist, whose only faith was in science, whom religious faith, even on the part of his friends, irritated as a proof of lack of understanding—had he not done everything he could in the past to bring to his wife that calm happiness which he enjoyed? If Mme. Raindal had not forgotten, she better than anyone else could testify to the patience and abnegation with which he had done so!...

It had been an unpleasant surprise. Mlle. Desjannières was so gay and merry, so childish, despite her twenty years; her father, a Marseilles barrister, who had chanced to seek his fortune in Egypt, was such a brilliant talker, such a good fellow, a singer of such catchy tunes! No one could have suspected the secret fervor at work in the mind of the girl. Well, M. Raindal had not minded because he was in love with his fiancée. He would take care of her, cure her of it! On the very day that had followed their wedding in Alexandria, and later in Paris where they had settled, he had begun the cure and pursued it methodically. Every day he had discussed it with his wife for hours, preached to her and reasoned with her. She had lent herself willingly to the régime and tried in her tenderness to surmount her fears. After three months, one morning, she threw herself on her knees before her husband, weeping and crying for mercy. She begged him to put a stop to the martyrdom, to let her return to the confessional. In presence of her affliction, M. Raindal had been compelled to agree.

She was moved by a superhuman force, an unconquerable fear, the dread of the punishments which follow sin. An old Provençal maid, a kind of Domestic Dante, had inoculated her when she was quite young with the germs of the sickness. In the evenings she had described to her, as if she had been there herself, the lurid sights, the burning horrors, the eternal pangs which torment the sinners in the lands of Hell, the pains of damnation, the torments of the senses, the howls, the moans, the diabolical contortions. And as the child grew up, her soul became gradually narrower at the flame of those tales, more sensitive, more fearful of sins. The slightest of them weighed upon her as an irremissible fault, a thorny burden that choked her heart. She must needs at once rush to a priest, unload before his indulgence that weight of anguish which was heavier than a load of lead. Often as she emerged from a sanctuary she was halted by a scruple, by the semblance of a neglect which brought her hastily back to implore once more the help of the priest as he left the sacred enclosure. And since her marriage, for the last thirty-two years, she had been living thus, forever urged toward churches by new torments of her conscience, hiding her terrors when at home, unable to dominate them when outside, dreading the sarcasm of her family and weeping over their damnation.

"Her happiness! Her peace of mind!" M. Raindal was grunting as he wrote.... "If only she had had the energy to trust me with them."

Just then the doorbell rang hurriedly twice.

"Hark!" the master said. "Here comes your mother.... I am anxious to hear what she has to say...."

Mme. Raindal stood on the threshold. A long quilted silk cape, lined with minever and slightly worn about the shoulders, encased her form. All out of breath, she panted:

"Wait!"

Her hand went under the cape and lay over her heart to suppress its beating. She explained:

"I climbed the stairs too fast."

"Sit down! Rest yourself!" M. Raindal said calmly.

"No, no! It is passed! I feel better!"

She unhooked her cape and went to kiss her husband, then her daughter. Her cheeks carried the frost of the wind outside; they were cold as a window pane; she was still panting as she bent over each of them.

"Where have you been, to return so late?" M. Raindal inquired, without lifting his eyes from his work.

She protested.

"So late!... But it is not 'so late'!... It is not more than 5.15.... I went to Guerbois, to order a pie for to-night.... Cyprie coming to dinner, is he?"

"Oh, yes ... Cyprie coming."

She did not dwell on the matter. She was choking with a new fear; she had almost sinned by telling an untruth. She poked the red lumps of coke and lowered the wick of the smoking lamp. Then, feeling the weight of the silence which was pregnant with irony and with suspicion perhaps, she left the room, her cheeks now suddenly aflame, her breast heavy with sighs.

Thérèse and her father simultaneously raised their heads and exchanged a knowing smile.

"Did you hear that?... her pie?..."

He shrugged his shoulders quite discouraged. The young girl murmured with compassion:

"Poor mother!... She is so kind!..."

CHAPTER III

AT about a quarter to six, Uncle Cyprien went to his small dark kitchenette to polish his shoes before going out.

He intended to go to the Klapproth Brasserie in the rue Vavin to join his old friend, Johann Schleifmann, and talk for an hour with him while drinking an *apéritif*.

People who knew the younger M. Rainda antisemitism were surprised at his intimacy with that Galician Jew.

But when he was asked about it, Cyprien showed not the slightest embarrassment. Far from it! He eyed his inquirer from head to foot, shrugged his shoulders and then informed him—if he cared to know—that Schleifmann was the best man in the world. He had associated with him for ten years and never had had any cause to complain of him. These inquiries, moreover, seemed to him futile, because, he could vouch for it, Schleifmann, although a Jew, was as "much of an anti-semite as you or I."

Cyprien voiced an exaggeration when he said this, or at least, he was misinterpreting his frien feelings.

Schleifmann could not be classified among those cautious Jews who deny their Jewry through fear of prejudice, or because they cringe before the majority, or through worldly or professional self-interest.

His anti-semitism, on the contrary, was made up of sheer love for his race and atavistic pride. If he appeared anti-semitic, it must have been in the fashion of a Jeremiah, an Isaiah or an Amos. In sooth, the bitter spirit of the ancient prophets animated his heart. He cursed the men of his religion merely because they were shirking the destinies of Israel and let themselves be corrupted by trifling vanities instead of ruling the world by the influence of thought. This Semitic pride had even been the cause of all the difficulties of his adventurous life.

He was a Doctor of Philosophy of Lemberg University who early in life had neglected the ancient Mosaic law in order to embrace the more recent creed which was spreading over the world—socialism. According to him, the Jews had been the initiators of that new faith as they had been of the other one. Karl Marx and Lassalle were to him the modern messengers of Jehovah upon earth, sent to bring forth the new gospel and the economic religion of the future. He considered their books as almost holy and rejoiced at seeing once more the divine Jewish supremacy asserted by their writings. He was affiliated with the principal socialist groups of the city and carried on an active propaganda in the poor districts. Three months in a fortress and ten years' exile put a sudden stop to his zeal, if not to his convictions.

While in prison he had carefully thought out the place where he would seek asylum on leaving. Life would be very painful to him in Austria or in Germany, where he would be watched by the police and exposed to the attacks of the anti-semites. He decided upon a temporary stay in France where he went towards the end of 1882.

He thought he would make a living by teaching German, philosophy or the natural sciences. Warm letters of introduction had been given him by Viennese Jews to their relatives and fellow-Jews of Paris. Thus he rapidly obtained a certain amount of patronage which placed him beyond want and even earned him comfort.

Soon, however, and of his own free will, Schleifmann was to lose that comfort owing to an idealistic ambition and a mania to put his ideas into effect and to bring the Jews back to their hereditary duties.

He had noticed in Eastern Europe the contagious progress of anti-semitism and was deeply convinced that the anti-Jewish microbe would pursue its unrelenting march westward, successively invading France, England, the New World and finally the whole of Christendom.

This tendency must be resisted, fought and destroyed. As to the means of doing it, Schleifmann had a very clear theory, which he claimed to have derived from the very sources of the purest Judaism. It was simple. All that was needed was for the wealthy Jews to return to the traditions of their race whose almost divine mission was to supply the nations with moral examples, their brains with ideas and their hearts with a religion.

To accomplish this purpose they were to repudiate their past errors, leave the worldly and clerical society where they grew soft at the expense of their dignity, return to the fold of democracy whence they had sprung, employ their rare abilities in the defense of the weak, the triumph of the right, and enforce victory against injustice. Finally, keeping back nothing but a personal income, in no case to exceed ten thousand francs, they were to give up all their acquired riches, the whole of which would be used in national, popular or colonizing schemes. Such, in brief, were the main practical means by which Schleifmann intended to secure the salvation and glory of the Lor chosen people.

After a few months in Paris, he thought the moment was favorable for him to lay his daring plan of regeneration before the parents of his pupils, the clergy and the notables of Jewry. His illusions of success were short-lived.

The Jews of high finance had recently fought the first round with the Catholics. Some said they had been helped by the Cabinet. Others, that they had enjoyed the secret approval of a government which had long been in sympathy with the Jewish cause. Others again, more conservative in their estimate, claimed that the Jews enjoyed the "non-official sympathy" of the Administration to which the revolt of the wealthy Catholic families caused much anxiety. In fine, whether supported or alone, the Jews had won and now they were blinded by the enthusiasm of their victory. Never had their conceited arrogance been more insane nor their trust in the efficacy of the law more dense.

Schleifmann was everywhere repulsed. The rabbis were afraid that he might place them in a difficult position with high finance, whose members were all powerful in the Consistory; they begged him not to persist in his dangerous utopias. The rich and the half-rich dismissed him with a few dry words or with scornful jesting.

Very few cared to enter into discussion with him. They would give a fatherly pat to the obstinate Galician and ask him whether it was really himself, M. Schleifmann, a wise and learned man, who prattled such nonsense. Anti-semitism! That was all very well in Germanic lands, or in Slavic countries where—they had to say it, but with no desire to offend him personally—the Jews were ... well, he knew well enough what! But in France, in the land of all the liberties, on the beautiful soil of France, the mother of Revolutions and of the sublime Declaration of the Rights of Man, never, never, never at all, he ought to know, would anti-semitism flourish. Thereupon they would burst out laughing and offer him a cigar.

These unfortunate rebuffs were not the only punishment met by Schleifmann. Many parents became alarmed at his theories and withdrew their children from his care. He was left with barely a third of his patrons, making just enough to live on, or rather enough not to perish of want.

The wreck was thorough, but he faced it with courage.

In order to prepare for such possible contingencies as sickness, he sold all his furniture, all his books but a hundred odd volumes which he termed indispensable. He kept his Bible, the *Imitation* of á Kempis, Goethe, Spinoza, Shakespeare, Mendelssohn, Renan, Taine, Victor Hug poetical works and the writings of socialist leaders.

Then he took a large, well-lighted room on the sixth floor of a house in the rue de Fleurus and waited, while reading, for fortune and humanity to change.

Three whole years passed by and he was beginning to doubt his own prophetic acumen when, suddenly, the events occurred that restored to him his faith.

Despite what he had been told, anti-semitism was beginning to germinate and blossom in the beautiful land of France. It had come through the fertilizing agency of the envy and resentments of some, of the clumsiness and the extortions of others. The ardent crop was growing daily in spite of regulations and legal fences, in spite of the laws and the proclaimed Rights of Man.

Johann Schleifmann was joyfully complacent at first, then deeply sorrowful. He followed the affair, always divided between these opposite feelings.

He deplored the cruel, partial attacks levelled at his co-religionists; but he could not free himself from a certain feeling of pride that he had predicted them. The more unfairly they were abused, the more his anger rose against them. Fools! Poor wretches! Had they but been willing! When the social columns told of their magnificent garden-parties, of their deer-and fox-hunting and of their *raouts*, he sneered wickedly, yet with sadness. He repeated the words aloud in a sarcastic tone or uttered them as so many curses: "Garden-parties! *Raouts!* Fox-hunting!..." Yes, they could "receive" and "dance" and "ride out." Those fellows were making the most of it! He was carried away, indignant, at the thought that so much money was stupidly thrown away, when, had they with a kind hand but given a portion of it to the people, it would have served a generous cause and settled and repaired everything.

It was about that time that he had become acquainted with M. Cyprien Raindal at the Brasserie Klapproth where they both took their meals.

They had liked each other from the first words they had exchanged. They were mutually attracted. Their nationalities were different, their religions antagonistic, their temperaments divergent but they found out that they shared the same grudges and detested the same castes. Curiosity also helped to foster their association. Schleifmann was to Uncle Cyprien a real mine of exceptional documents upon which he could feed his hatreds, and Schleifmann saw in him an unregarded specimen of the enemies of his race. Moreover, they cherished in secret their own plans concerning each other. The Galician wanted to convert his friend to the theories of Karl Marx; while the younger M. Raindal had sworn to himself that he would convert the exiled philosopher from his internationalistic views. Above all other motives, poverty united them, that poverty which kneads all the lowly into an identical paste, merges them into one family, transforms them into brothers and allies—age, origin or any other obstacle notwithstanding. Hence, they had hardly spent a day during the past ten years without meeting outside or visiting each other in their respective garrets.

Cyprien Raindal was ready and opened his door to go out. He fell back a step, surprised on seeing Johann Schleifmann himself, preparing to ring.

"You!"

"Surely, it is I!..." Schleifmann replied in a voice which the constant use of the Hebrew language had rendered somewhat nasal and slow. "I did not see you yesterday and so I came to ascertain whether you were not ill...."

"Oh, it is nothing at all; a mere touch of rheumatism, my wretched rheumatism.... Come in, come in, please," the younger M. Raindal added, removing his own hat. "It seems as if we had not chatted for ages!"

He closed the door and pulled his old friend Johann by the sleeve.

Schleifmann replied with a smile.

"Yes, let us talk! As a matter of fact, I have brought you the surprise which I mentioned the other day.... Here, enjoy yourself!..."

He threw on the table a book bound in reddish linen, on the back of which was printed in black letters: *Year Book of French Finance*.

While Cyprien examined the volume, Schleifmann half-stretched himself on the couch, following a sarcastic trend of ideas. His was the type of the eastern Jew, a Kalmuk face with a wax-like complexion, a flat nose, turned up at the tip and with broad nostrils and small, yellowish eyes that shone with malice. His gray hair and beard were crisp and curly like wool; to correct his shortsightedness, he wore large gold-rimmed spectacles, the supreme elegance of Teutonic university men.

Suddenly he exclaimed in his usual slow, dragging voice:

"There are enough names in there!... Jews, Moslems, Christians, yes, and goyim, too.... Names from all countries and all religions.... It is to these names that the whole wealth of the land belongs.... They are all the names of those who fleece and grind us; you understand, my dear Raindal?... One of these names at the bottom of a paper is better than a cartridge of dynamite under a house.... It makes the millions dance as oranges fly from the hands of a juggler.... But, God be praised! my friend, this will not last forever!..."

"Ah! you are clever, Schleifmann!" the younger M. Raindal murmured, throwing an inquisitive glance at the Galician over the book he held open in his hand. "We know your game!... You want to egg me on again to your socialism.... Well, no.... I not to be done! I stand for freedom ... and for property ... and for the whole system of our filthy society, provided, however, people are honest. Yes, to be sure! Otherwise, pan, pan! To the wall with the grafters!..."

Schleifmann protested mildly, asserting that his remarks were disinterested. Then he came closer to Cyprien, who had laid the book on the table, the better to consult it. He guided his frien search among the terrible complications of interdependent banks, boards of administration, committees, sub-committees and other mysterious groups bent upon conquest.

Gradually, the younger M. Raindal waxed excited as he read. When he saw the same name figure on two, three, four boards, he exclaimed in distress like a man who is being assaulted. His jocular anger was especially excited by the names that bore the signs of Hebraic descent.

"Another one!" he would throw at Schleifmann.

"So it seems! But is it my fault?" the Galician replied sadly.

Again they took up their reading. To see their backs, their elbows closely touching, one might have fancied that they were two good little boys greedily perusing some picture-book or a fascinating volume of adventures.

Suddenly Cyprien straightened up and struck his rounded forehead. "By the way, Schleifmann," he asked, "do you happen to know a certain Lemeunier de Saulvard?"

"Member of the Institute of France?"

"Yes, himself."

Did Schleifmann know him? Of course, he did. None better. As a matter of fact, Saulvard banked at the Stummerwitz Bank and the Galician had heard the Stummerwitzes mention him more than once. He was teaching German to their children, or rather he was perfecting them in the use of that tongue; for they had learned the rudiments of it from their maternal grandfather, born in Stuttgart, and their paternal grandfather, born in Cologne. Rapidly in a hundred lashing words, Saulvard was sized up.

A man, it might be said without injustice, who was not much of a Catholic, that Saulvard!... A third-rate savant, a most mediocre intellect, an anemic writer, moreover a sycophant and a greedy intriguer. He had made use of his relations with high finance to enter the Institute, and then of his title of Academician to join the boards of companies. One had but to consult the Year-book. (And Cyprien feverishly turned the pages again.) He was there in three different places, as member of three well-remunerated, although discredited, boards. As to his wife....

"Probably a bigot?" Raindal the younger asked.

No, she was not a bigot;—she was a shameless hussy. Schleifmann, usually better informed, did not know the names of her several lovers, but he could give him two at all events, asserting in a symbolic and summary sense, that she had sinned with gods and devils. She was vain, moreover, an inveterate snob, painted and powdered way down to her waist, a back-biter, whose stomach troubles had ruined her disposition....

Raindal could stand it no longer. He was choking.

"Excuse me, Schleifmann," he said, laying a friendly hand on the Galicia shoulder. "I forgot the time.... I am dining with my brother who is going to a dance to-night at the house of precisely this scoundrel.... I am very glad to be so thoroughly informed.... I assure you, yes, quite satisfied.... You do mind, do you? I have barely enough time! I must run away.... Are you coming?"

At the bottom of the stairs he parted hurriedly from his friend. A deep longing urged him to reach the flat in the rue Notre-Dame-des-Champs, there to unload on his indolent brother the mass of filth with which Schleifmann had liberally filled him.

Not without apprehension did M. Raindal watch the arrival of his brother, having earlier in the day found that it was one of his talkative days. He anticipated a fresh outbreak of hostilities and controversies and that ill-disposed him beforehand. He received his brother with marked coldness, and carelessly held out his hand in order to forestall any new attempt.

"Just a minute! I am finishing an urgent piece of work.... If yo like to wait for me in the drawing-room, the ladies are there...."

When Uncle Cyprien had gone he congratulated himself upon his firmness. As a matter of fact, he had always intensely disliked discussing any subject with his brother. It was as in the tourneys of old, which were open to none but Knights. Before he would oppose a man in a discussion, that man had to be his peer, a gallant champion of his own caste, of his own intellectual rank, and one who practiced without flinching the noble art of tilting with ideas. With other men, Eusèbe Raindal avoided the contest; he turned tail in courteous agreement or even, if necessary, shammed sudden deafness.

His self-satisfaction increased at the dinner-table. Never had Uncle Cyprien proved so gay, so affable or so little inclined to quarrel. He teased Thérèse about her "forthcoming marriage," repeatedly addressed her as "Mamzelle my nephew" or informed Brigitte, the young, ruddy-faced maid from Brittany, that, *sapristi!* it would soon be her turn.

Thérèse readily put up with his somewhat vulgar facetiousness. She tolerated much from her uncle, because she guessed at all the real tenderness hidden beneath his intolerance and his rabid abuse.

Mme. Raindal herself secretly admired her brother-in-law. She was grateful for the fact that he hated the Jews, whom she saw as the abhorred tormentors of the Saviour. She condoned his blasphemies concerning the priests because of his aversion towards the deicide race.

Her small, round face with its soft, pale cheeks reddened with a sudden flush of pride when he praised her pie. She laughed at all his remarks to the end of the meal, although she often missed his real point.

For politeness' sake, M. Raindal smiled with her. When they had drunk their coffee, he returned to his study with Cyprien while the two women retired to dress. Left alone, they remained for a while in silent meditation. The master of the house, his feet drawn towards the red glow of the fire, dozed with his eyes half-closed, in that perfect coil of peacefulness that one feels in the company of a trusted friend. Uncle Cyprien lighted his heavy cherry-wood pipe from the Vosges mountains and paced the room, blowing his smoke out in strong puffs. He was preparing to let out his exterminating ammunition, all those deadly revelations which he had been holding back for the last two hours in sheer refinement of pleasure.

Brutally, he sent forth the first volley.

"By the way! Your chap of this evening, he is a nice bird!"

The effect was that of the alarm gun calling forth the soldier asleep in his tent. M. Raindal shivered with emotion and asked angrily.

"What? Whom do you mean?"

"Your Saulvard, of course!... Yes, I have some fine lines on him.... That gentlemen may well boast of them!"

One after the other, all the munitions piled up by Schleifmann followed in rapid succession.

"You surprise me very much!" M. Raindal muttered. "I admit that I do not know Saulvard very much.... I never had any but professional relations with him.... Yet, I never heard it said.... Your friend Schleifmann must be exaggerating...."

His brother Cyprien smiled shyly at this evasion but did not reply at once. He emptied his pipe in an ash tray. After a while, he broke the silence.

"Tell me ... where does this Saulvard live?"

The query made M. Raindal restless in his chair. He foresaw how grave was the reply he would have to give and tried to equivocate:

"Why, really, I do know.... It is the first time we are going there.... Thérèse has the invitation; she will be able to tell you...."

"You do know!" Cyprien replied, aggressively sarcastic. "Go on! I am willing to grant you may not know the number of the house; but surely you know the name of the street; you must at least know in what district it is!"

M. Raindal hid his uneasiness and pretended deeply to search into his memory.

"It seems to me," he replied at length, "that he lives in the avenue Kléber.... Yes, tha it, avenue Kléber."

"Of course! I would have laid a bet on it!" Uncle Cyprien said victoriously.

Thereupon the dreaded storm burst upon the master in a tumult of abuse and imprecations.

Cyprien had effectively found the opportunity once more to air his theory of the "two banks" and he hurled it out with a crash.

As a matter of fact, it was not altogether his own. The Galician had supplied the idea and Cyprien had but added the eloquent developments and the vigor of his lungs. But they had so often recited it to each other, chiseled it together and together enlarged upon it that they no longer discerned their particular share in the collaboration, and each of them claimed the authorship, whenever the other happened to be absent.

According to them, Paris was composed of two cities, absolutely distinct in population, ways of life and customs. The river Seine divided these two enemy cities. On its two banks, Sion the venerable faced Gomorrah.

Sion, the left bank, that was, stood for the home of virtue, science and faith. Her people were chaste, modest and diligent; they had preserved, in poverty and toil, the honest and decent national traditions. There the men were pure and the women beyond reproach. The whole inheritance of the ancestors—loyalty, devotion and high-mindedness were transmitted from fathers to sons, sheltered from the corruption of money and the shameful example of the foreigners. In sooth, it was the holy city.

Gomorrah, the right bank, was the region of vice, license and dishonesty. It was the hunting-ground of all the cosmopolitan riff-raff, all the shifty hordes of exotics who had gradually foregathered and silently slipped into France after the war of 1870. They formed a nomadic, rascally and thievish multitude, without principles, country or morals and were united solely by their greed for gold or a thirst for coarse pleasures. Gambling in stocks had filled their coffers and criminal transactions paid for their fatuous homes. The women were no better than the men; the adultery of the former flourished by the side of the swindling of the latter. Whole districts, and some of the finest, had become their domicile. Chaillot, Monceau, Malesherbes and the Roule bowed at their orders and their money. There were long rows of hotels all filled with *rastaquouères*, and houses which the Jews had conquered from top to bottom, occupying every floor. Semites from Frankfort fraternized there with adventurers from the New World, shady Americans with dubious Orientals. And the whole country was sucked dry in the service of that impudent mob which gave its orders in doubtful French. The right bank—it was the cursed city!

Cyprien always drew great effects and lengthy orations from these descriptions and parallels; he used them also as a sort of touchstone by which to appreciate people. If one lived on the left bank of the river, he was at once entitled to Cyprie sympathies. But if one dwelt on the right bank, in a rich neighborhood, Cyprien was at once wary of him, and would only make amends later after his title to respect had been established.

M. Raindal had labored hard to point out how such a theory was psychologically doubtful and topographically inexact; but his brother persisted in it because it was simple, violent, and corroborated his passions.

Especially this evening when he had been rested by two days' silence and stimulated by Schleifman call, he was riding his hobby all around M. Raindal with an increasing air of challenge and daring.

"Yes," he shouted at his brother, stamping the carpet, "you are blind.... You know nothing, you see nothing.... You live in your corner, buried among your mummies and your old books.... You have never been further than the bridge of the Saints-Pères.... You are duped and exploited; you are a child—a kid, as Schleifmann says. Why do you go for a walk some day through those places I am telling you about?... Talk, ask, find out.... You will see.... In that world, in those houses, abominable deeds are performed and all manner of foulness!"

The voiceless patience of M. Raindal was worn out. He risked one of those defenses which he had used before in the course of that polemic when the returns had at length become regular and mechanical as in a stage duel:

"Yet you are not alleging that the whole virtue of Paris has found asylum in our district!... I shall never be tired of repeating it to you: on the other side of the water are to be found many people that belong to decent society, and even to the aristocracy, people who have left the Faubourg to go and live in the new sections, the Champs Elysées, for instance.... Well! those people—you are not going to tell me that they...."

Cyprien sneered with commiseration and took up the gauntlet.

"Ha! ha! I am not going to tell you?... Of course, I am going to tell you!..."

And tell he did. He jumped from digression to digression, slashing right and left, forward and back, twirling his ideas about and knocking heads down everywhere in the craze of a wholesale assault. One after the other, the degenerated aristocracy, the Jews, the grafters and the priests fell under his blows. He reinforced himself with quotations from his favorite masters and these excited him as a war cry.

M. Raindal kept his peace for a moment, but feeling that his silence was perhaps even more exasperating to his adversary than mild retorts, he turned on the tap of conciliatory generalities. They oozed from his lips in amorphous, unfinished sentences, in small, intermittent streams, similar to the colorless and limpid dribble that runs along the chin of a baby; or else they suddenly dried up under the wind of invective.

"The plague of democracies.... A necessary evil.... This M. Rochefort is truly clever.... Experience teaches us.... M. Drumont is not lacking in spirit.... One of the vices of the plutocratic régime.... It is not a new thing to see financiers and revenue farmers.... I do not deny that M. Schleifmann is a very distinguished thinker.... We have come to a turning point of history...."

Thérèse came in and interrupted him, for her Uncle Cyprien instinctively lowered his voice when he saw her. The shy evasions of M. Raindal increased his assurance; but he dreaded sarcastic remarks or the sharp retorts of "Mademoiselle his nephew."

"Well, what is happening?" Thérèse asked sweetly.... "Uncle, I bet you are teasing my poor father again?

"Hum! Not at all!" Uncle Cyprien replied shame-facedly.... "Not at all, we were merely talking.... You understand, one warms up, one gets excited...."

Thérèse pouted derisively.

"Yes, yes, I know, you warm up, you get excited.... I heard you from my room...."

She turned to M. Raindal.

"Come on, father, it is eleven.... Mother is ready.... Go and dress...."

Alone with her uncle, she walked to the fireplace to straighten in front of the mirror her hair which she had disarranged here and there when inserting her flowers. She wore white carnations—in memory of *Albârt*. Their spreading whiteness enlivened her face. Her neck seemed by reflection less sallow and more delicate in the pink muslin frame of her corsage.

Artlessly she smiled at herself, surprised to find herself thus dainty, attractive, almost pretty. As a matter of fact, she did have that ethereal iridescence of beauty which the unusual splendor of a party dress projects at once upon women. It is an ephemeral charm, light as a pastel, which fades away, evaporates in the heat and the jealousy of a ball; but at home it encourages the most homely. For one instant in the solitude of her own room, in front of her own mirror, a woman finds herself beautiful enough, too beautiful—and she is willing to go, and does, in fact, go.

Her Uncle Cyprien, in a friendly mood, observed her little coquettish ways:

"Well, my nephew? And so we are going to make merry in the merry world?"

"Oh, prodigiously," Thérèse replied with a sigh. "We must enjoy ourselves in this world.... There will always be people to enjoy themselves.... Always there will be a frivolous and depraved society.... If they did not make merry on the other side of the river, they would do it here.... It is the rule and you cannot alter it...."

Uncle Cyprien brushed back with his hand his hair which was so close-trimmed that is crackled with a ruffling noise under his fingers. He murmured disdainfully:

"Philosophy! Philosophy!... You know, my dear nephew, that we do not argue, you and I, ... you are too strong and too sure of yourself. There, I do mind admitting it, you make me feel ill at ease!"

M. Raindal returned, followed by his wife, her form hidden in her long cape. She wore in her hair an old mauve aigrette, the barbs of which were limp and spread out like a worn-out paint-brush.

"Well, are we ready?" the master of the house asked, looking at his brother.

"Yes, wl all go down together. Come along!"

A cab was waiting outside. Brigitte gave the drive number to M. Raindal.

The family sat closely huddled in the back seat. Uncle Cyprien closed the door on them and shouted as the carriage began to move:

"Good luck! A pleasant evening, nephew!"

He gave a friendly pinch to the chin of Brigitte, who stood stupidly smiling.

"Good night, my girl.... Go and dream of a fiancé!"

He turned up the collar of his coat and took the rue Vavin. In the fever of his triumph at every step he flourished his thick cornel stick as if it had been a gory mace.

CHAPTER IV

THE ball given by M. and Mme. Lemeunier de Saulvard (of the Institute) "in their apartment" in the avenue Kléber, on the occasion of the engagement of their niece, Mlle. Genevieve de Saulvard, to M. Brisset de Saffry de Lamorneraie, lieutenant of the 21st hussars, had attracted a large assembly of guests.

The army, the fine arts, literature, science, the upper bourgeoisie, men of learning, club-men, men of finance and men of the drawing-room—the full contingent of their acquaintances filled their apartment after 11 lock. All the guests, for lack of any other common ground, were at least agreed on the subject of the party and voted it a success.

As a matter of fact, the Saulvards deserved the praise, for they had shown themselves far from niggardly. The buffet was sumptuous, covered with silver plate, viands and piles of sandwiches, ices, sweet-smelling drinks and spread here and there with dishes of frozen fruit in large pale pink or green rings like dull-colored silk plaques. And everywhere there were flowers, in bushes, baskets and garlands. Rows of white chrysanthemums concealed the upper parts of the windows with their intricate strands, and chains of delicate winter roses climbed along the chandeliers, whence fell through the crystal the calm, intense glow of the electric lights.

The orchestra was made up of gypsies in red coats with heavy gold braidings. They formed a sort of barbaric guard of honor in front of the piano. In the interval between the dances people stopped to watch them cleaning their strange instruments as if they were wild men in a camp.

They began to play their sensuous airs. One couple rose, then two, then three. Then all at once the reflections made by the lights upon the empty shiny floor disappeared under the mixed crowd of dancers. Mothers smiled. Old savants dreamily beat the rhythm with their feet; the heads of young women were bent backwards and their eyes shone in enamored glances. The enervating beatitude of that music caused them all to tremble for an instant in spite of themselves with the same pleasure that drew them together. At those moments one might have imagined himself witnessing one of those gatherings where people of the same set are fused in joyous intimacy and with the feeling of being secure among themselves.

But the illusion disappeared with the last note. It was like refractory liquids which, as soon as one ceases to beat them together, separate and naturally resume their own color and their own place. The whirlwind of the dancers was broken up; close embraces ceased and steady glances turned away. Instinctively everyone fell back among his own set, returned to his caste.

Once more between hostile groups the floor in the center of the room stretched out under the lights a desert of frightening barrenness.

There were but a few daring young men from the great clubs who ventured on it; Gerald de Meuze, Tommy Barbier, Patrice de Vernaise, Saint-Pons and the little prince of Tavarande; they had committed themselves at the urgent entreaty of Mme. de Saulvard. There were also some brother officers of the fiancé, in sky-blue coats and red trousers with light bands, most of them titled or bearing those bourgeois names which, while not noble, announced at least an ancient worth and a duly established family.

They walked round the drawing-rooms alone, or by twos, seemingly meditative, supporting their bent elbows with one hand and curling their mustaches with the other. They examined the women, one by one, studiously, as if these had been cattle at a fair. With their heavy, disdainful eyelids, one could hardly tell whether they were purposely shrinking their eyes to the dimensions of that small world or whether they were perhaps tormented by a persistent and rebellious desire to sneeze.

Saulvard had vainly attempted at first to merge the other elements of the assembly. He had had to give it up in the face of resistance.

Thus high finance and great industry and their satellites formed a compact clan in the right-hand corner of the first drawing-room. They laughed, cackled and chattered, and were sufficient unto themselves; the minute a stranger dared to break in, seeking a chair or a little more elbow room, in short, the slightest opening, this group assumed dark countenances. They had a welcome for none but the representatives of the aristocracy. The latter, however, were massed a little away from them; they formed a small élite, had closed their ranks after the necessary greetings, and henceforth affected to ignore their jovial neighbors, reserving for each other their cordiality and their smiles. Apart from a few noblemen whom the smell of blood or the need for financial advice moved to approach the other clan, the aristocratic group remained effectively faithful to its principles of separatism and its arrogant virtuosity.

The Academicians also kept their distance. The five sections of the Institute kept to their circle but did not fraternize. They hardly even exchanged brief amenities or passed chairs to each other in order to avoid any promiscuity with the Academy of Medicine—intruders who were signaled to all by a volatile smell of iodoform or phenol brought in their clothing.

The literary men and their wives had constituted a close circle with the groups of painters and musicians. But even that brought forth constraint or reciprocal animosity.

The result was that Saulvard, who stood on duty near the door, assumed more and more the air of a guardian of a public dancing hall, or the controller of a casino who checked the entrance of the subscribers and jollied equally all his diverse classes of patrons.

He was short and bald; his yellow face was framed by two short white whiskers—the face of a Japanese turned butler; he smiled ceaselessly, bowed and straightened himself up again; he hopped on his high pointed heels as if waiting, or thanking for, a tip. He murmured, following them five or six steps, appropriate flatteries to all his invited guests, as soon as they reached the doorstep. His glances wandered round, discreet and confidential. From afar one might have thought that he was showing the newcomers the way to the cloakroom.

As soon as the Raindal family appeared, he nimbly rose to meet them.

"Ah, my dear colleague!... What joy!... I was almost despairing...."

His two hands caught that of M. Raindal and he went on:

"I have not seen you since your success!... What a triumph!... What a beautiful book!... Madame.... Mademoiselle...."

He bowed, then, standing on tiptoe so as to reach the ear of M. Raindal, he whispered:

"You know, our young man is here ... a charming fellow. He will attract your daughter very much.... No escape.... *Fata volunt*.... This way, please, come, my dear colleague, and I shall bring you that phenix...."

By an instinctive pressure on the shoulder he shunted Raindal towards a corner of the drawing-room where the section of the Inscriptions had disposed its trenches. A few chairs were left unoccupied in the first and second rows. M. and Mme. Raindal settled down behind and Thérèse sat in front of them between the two daughters of one of her fathe colleagues. They were thin and small, like the raw-boned hectic teams that draw the Paris public cabs. They conversed, but furtively inspected the gir dress. Thérèse looked up when she heard the voice of Saulvard who was making his reappearance, followed by a young man of very short stature.

"My dear friend, dear master," he called over the heads of the girls, "allow me to introduce one of our young confrères, whose name you surely know: M. Pierre Boerzell...." Each of the two savants mumbled courteous expressions which the other could not catch. Then Saulvard added:

"M. Pierre Boerzell ... Mlle. Raindal."

The young man bowed awkwardly. The orchestra was preluding with the slow harmonies of a waltz. He murmured:

"Mademoiselle, will you give me the pleasure of this waltz?"

Sympathetically Thérèse refused.

"No, Monsieur, thank you.... I do dance ... but if you wish ... we might, as one says, I believe, talk it...."

Boerzell stammered a grateful acceptance. The two "hackney horses" had started immediately for the waltz. He took one of the chairs they had left empty by the side of Thérèse. The conversation, which she had cleverly directed at once towards scientific matters, became cordial and almost familiar.

He was not handsome. His chest was narrow, his nose short; his cheeks were bloated and flabby, almost falling over a suspicion of a beard. His eyelids were heavy from night work. His eyes, however, behind the thick glasses of his pince-nez, shone with a kind and tender light. When he talked, his voice had those caressing and particular inflections of intellectual people who enjoy having their words sound like true coin; and while he spoke his gestures became more alert and vivacious; his arms relaxed as he grew less embarrassed.

M. Raindal out of curiosity soon brought his chair forward and took part in the discussion of the two young people. They were flirting over the interpretation of a tri-lingual inscription recently discovered in Mesopotamia. Thérèse was defending her interpretation with that professional assurance, that ma voice, which she always assumed in the course of scientific discussions.

"Ah, Monsieur!" Boerzell exclaimed in discouragement. "Mademoiselle is very strong; she knows much more than I.... She has beaten me...."

Smilingly M. Raindal agreed.

"Well, you are not the first!... Often I myself...."

The waltz had finished and the two cab horses were coming back to their stand which the young savant had to leave. He asked Thérèse:

"Would you allow me to take you to the buffet with Madame, your mother?"

"With pleasure, monsieur! Will you come, Mother?"

Mme. Raindal took Boerzel arm and Thérèse followed behind, going towards the buffet through the crowd of dancers who were returning to their seats.

M. Raindal watched them go. He was sitting in his favorite position: his elbows were pressed against his sides, his forearms up, and his hands hung limp at the end of his wrists like the paws of a "begging" dog. From his seat through the wide open door he could see without effort into the dining-room. He perceived the back of his wife; she was bent over the elaborate table hastily making her choice. Against the high chimney covered with white blossoms Thérèse stood with Boerzell; they were sipping out of their spoons a pink fruit-like ice; they stopped at times and looked at each other laughingly, chatting, their heads close together, like life-long friends.

If only she could make up her mind! If she would accept that young man!... No, that would be too fine!... And yet, who knew!... The ebb and flow of contradictory thoughts caused M. Rainda lips to stretch in softened smiles or to purse in bitter grimaces.

Then his colleagues approached and began to congratulate him upon his new book. More of them joined the first ones. A small, applauding group surrounded M. Raindal and hid his daughter from his sight. The last comers tipped their heads to one side, straining their ears to catch the maste replies. "You are very good...." "I am ashamed, really...." "Be sure that on my side...." The complimenters vied with each other in outbidding and protested their sincerity in extravagant praise.

At length the enthusiasm came to an end. They became silent and listened to M. Raindal, who was recalling memories of his youth and the misery of his early efforts.

Suddenly the purring voice of Saulvard caused the ranks of the audience to open.

"Pardon, Gentlemen! Pardon!"

With one hand bent like the prow of a boat, he was making a path for a dark-haired young woman who hung on his arm; he came to a stop near M. Raindal.

"My dear friend.... Will you help me satisfy the wishes of one of your lady admirers who is longing to make your acquaintance?... M. Eusèbe Raindal ... Mme. Georges Chambannes...."

M. Raindal rose and bowed, one hand resting on the back of his chair.

"Madame, I am delighted...."

Mme. Chambannes protested.

"It is I, on the contrary, Monsieur...."

They stood facing each other in distress as if, in spite of their mutual good will, they did not know what to say.

Shyly M. Raindal glanced at the young woman. Her little eagle face was softened by light brown eyes with a languorous expression; the waves of her black hair, brushed in classic style back towards her neck, concealed in its rich coils something savage and willful. At length she spoke again in halting sentences, the words often lacking the precision which she might have desired.

"Yes, Monsieur, I greatly admire your book.... It is a charming book, a great masterpiece.... I cannot say how much I was charmed with it, and how much amused.... Ah! it must be so interesting to write books like that.... And the style is so delightful, so pleasant to read!..."

"Well, I must leave you!" M. Saulvard interrupted, as he blinked his slanting eyes.... "My guests.... Excuse me!..."

He disappeared leaving them alone, as the members of the little group had discreetly vanished one by one.

After a glance of mutual agreement M. Raindal and the young woman sat down to continue their conversation.

But he noticed the pale blue satin dress of Mme. Chambannes so close to the black cloth of his trousers that instinctively he withdrew slightly to one side. Smilingly she piled up her compliments. Then the discomfort which the master habitually felt when conversing with people of inferior culture—ignorant people, men or women of society—was increased by the embarrassment he felt at being so close to the low-cut dress of his admirer. Despite himself his glances were fastened to it and followed her full and easy curves. It seemed to him that an invisible force compelled his eyes to look at that skin, dull and diaphanous like a piece of fine china, at those perfumed breasts that rose and fell quietly against the ruffles of the opening without needing its support for their young firmness. Distractedly, all out of place, with sudden flights of thought, he answered the exclamations and multiple queries of Mme. Chambannes. And while he tried to listen to her he was comparing her to one of Cleopatr attendants, one of those dainty Greek slaves whose saucy prettiness provided a setting for the Queen of Egypt, as nymphs around a goddess.

Nevertheless the lad flow of praise was ceasing. Her smooth little brow, framed by the two flat curls, was furrowed by a searching frown. She found no more chapters or passages in which to plant her "so charming" and her "so pretty" like equal good marks of alternate colors. Suddenly her graceful face smiled again and her wide nostrils palpitated with mischief. She teased M. Raindal with the challenge that he could not guess her last reason for liking his book so much.

The master pretended to search. Finally he declared with modesty:

"I do know."

"Well, think a moment," commanded Mme. Chambannes familiarly, rolling her .

M. Raindal was not trying to find the answer but thought to himself.

"She is very attractive but somewhat silly!"

What he said aloud, imitating her tone, was:

"No, I really ca think what it is."

Then she resigned herself and voiced her secret, her final surprise, and indeed her pretext for further acquaintanceship, her supreme bait. Well! precisely, next winter, she intended to travel with her husband, to go to Cairo, Alexandria and the Nile. M. Rainda book had come in most handy, at the precise moment when she was beginning to study the Egyptian antiquities in view of that expected trip and naturally....

"My dear lady," a guttural voice interrupted them. "Forgive me.... Would you be kind enough to introduce me to Monsieur....."

"Why, of course!"

Then she made the presentations.

"Monsieur le Marquis de Meuze ... one of our best friends ... and one who adores your book."

He was a powerful old man with a majestic waistband and an aristocratic carriage. His white whiskers and curled up white mustache gave him the air of an Austrian general, for his was one of those heads which one readily fancies wearing a gold-braided cocked hat ornamented with a panache of green feathers. At the time of the financial smash of 1882, he had suffered from an attack of facial paralysis which had deprived him of the use of his left eyelid. It hung gray and lifeless and hid three quarters of his eye—this infirmity completed, like a glorious wound, his resemblance to an old warrior.

He multiplied protests of admiration. Then, following the immutable rule which prompts most people to conclude their compliments with an apology, he broached the true cause that had brought him to the master. He had once possessed a collection of cameos, a quite remarkable and exceptional collection. (As to the quality of the different pieces of which it had been composed, M. Raindal could consult several of his colleagues: the Count de Lastreins, of the Academy of Inscriptions; Baron Grollet, unattached member of the Beaux Arts, or the Viscount de Sernhac, of the Académie Française, all good friends or old comrades of the Marquis.) Well, one of the gems of that collection had been a cameo of Cleopatra. Alas! M. de Meuze had had to part with it, following financial losses. But he knew where it had gone; into the hands of a Jewish stock broker, a M. Stralhaus, and, if M.

Raindal so desired, the Marquis fancied that he could obtain permission to examine that piece.

The master neither accepted nor refused. The conversation circled around the art of cameo-making, with a few comments on the closely-related subject of numismatics, of which the marquis was not altogether ignorant. Out of her element Mme. Chambannes piped softly at intervals her "very prettys" and "very charmings." M. Chambannes, a tall, fair-haired man, with a faded complexion, a weak eye and fine and scanty hair, had joined her in the meantime. His thick cylindrical mustache was like a hinged cover, so closely did it fit his lips. Taken as a whole, his tired appearance might have been either that of a flabby scoundrel or of a pleasant young man worn out by his excesses.

All three surrounded M. Raindal, who replied to their chatter with assenting but weary smiles. He would have reproached himself had he rebuffed ever so slightly strangers who were so courteous for all their stupidity. Nevertheless, after a while he grew impatient with this strained politeness, the end of which he could not foresee. He was now equally bored by that old marquis with his verbose chatter, which was worthy of a second-hand dealer, his stories about cameos, sales, and bargains, and his quotations from catalogues.

At last reinforcements arrived to rescue him. Mme. Raindal returned with Thérèse and Boerzell. Then began new introductions. Immediately Mme. Chambannes briefly repeated her compliments. Mme. Raindal, blushing continually, stammered replies that were like so many apologies. Thérèse observed in silence; her virile glance judged it all mercilessly. Then Mme. Chambannes asked what their receiving day was and if she might have permission to call. There came a period of quiet when they merely talked for the sake of talking, of the ball, the orchestra and the dances. Of a sudden Mme. Chambannes called the marquis.

"M. de Meuze...."

"Madame?"

"A little secret. Will you permit me, ladies?"

Behind her spread-out fan she whispered a few words to M. de Meuze, who listened, bent towards her, his eyebrows arched in deep attention.

"Do you think so?... I do know whether he will.... Well, I shall take a chance!"

He stepped uncertainly towards the next room, holding aloft his proud field-marsha head and searching the groups with his one small green eye. At the door of the buffet he promptly turned to one side, his hand stretched out like a hook to catch someone who was walking away from him.

Thérèse could distinguish nothing but the square shoulders and the brown neck above the shining white collar of the tall young man whom the marquis had caught. No doubt M. de Meuze must be asking something absurd and impracticable, for she could see that brown neck shaken in indignant denials; the young man was apparently asserting that they were mad or playing a trick upon him.... But suddenly she saw the neck assent and the tall man turned right about, shrugging his shoulders. The heart of Thérèse was suddenly twisted like a wounded serpent.

It was almost Albârt. An older Albârt, more refined, more fashionable, of a superior class, but himself: the same big eyes of the color of a dark agate, the same black mustache with its impertinent tips, the same swaying of the body over two straight legs. He was coming towards her preceded by the marquis, his eyes awake as if to reconnoitre from afar and see what enemy it was against whom he was led.

Thérèse bent her head down; her back was strained against her chair; she was gathered upon herself with fright. No longer did she see her parents nor the Chambannes, nor Boerzell, nor the couples that were beginning to dance, nor the people near her, nor those beyond. She saw nothing but the long patent leather shoes, the long narrow feet of the young man, and they were coming nearer, nearer still.

When they were quite close to her the marquis effaced himself and bowed.

"Mademoiselle, may I introduce my son, M. Gerald de Meuze...."

The young count was slightly swaying before her.

"Mademoiselle, will you please grant me the end of this dance?"

Unconsciously, in the tone of a schoolgirl, Thérèse replied:

"Monsieur, I cannot dance.... I do not know how."

"What does it matter? It all depends on your partner...."

He gave Mme. Chambannes a quick wink, either friendly or ironical, as if he were winning a bet.

"No danger, Mademoiselle, I guarantee the waltz...."

Sharply, in a sudden need to see him well, to take in all his features, Thérèse looked at him fixedly. She could not resist. Perspiration ran down her back. She was dominated by the desire to be in those arms, as once she had been in others so very much like them. She rose shortly, her voice almost harsh in spite of the smile with which she tried to correct it, and said:

"Very well, monsieur, let us try."

Gerald put one arm round her and they began to whirl. At the first steps she stumbled out of ignorance and fear of losing the rhythm. Then he lifted her as if she were a child and carried her off gently among the dancers. Her feet no longer touched the floor. Couples brushed lightly against her. She had the impression of sliding in rhythms upon clouds with a robust lover. She closed her eyes. Voluptuous sobs choked her throat. He thought she was out of breath and stopped.

"Well, mademoiselle.... What did I say?... It goes beautifully...."

Thérèse approved with a nod; her thin lips were pale with pleasure. The count went on paternally:

"Dancing is like swimming!... You must throw yourself blindly into it.... Music pushes you along like waves.... Then, after that, you have nothing to do but let yourself go...."

In order to avoid an impolite silence he continued his theory and his comparisons.

Thérèse gave him only half answers, in indistinct monosyllables. She was regaining control of herself as she did upon awaking from those guilty dreams when Albârt sometimes came in the night so gently to press her.

What! She, Thérèse Raindal, giving way as if she were a perverse child, a boarding-school girl, in the arms of this insipid male! She was disgusted with herself. In order to hide her chagrin she applied herself to watching the leader of the gypsies, a big, olive-skinned man who played with serious expression. The long movements of his bow tore from his violin these panting melodies and his fat scarlet-coated chest swayed with the effort; he had the listening eye and his eyelids trembled. Thérèse envied his bestiality and the unthinking joy which animated that ma dark face. Why was she not like that, a thoughtless brute, without subtlety, one who lived only by his senses, which supported him even in his art?... A movement from Gerald brought her back.

"Do we start again?..."

She was still hoping she might refuse and, constraining herself, murmured:

"But, monsieur, the dance is nearly over!"

"All the more reason.... One more round."

He had said this without enthusiasm and already his eyes turned to the place where he had to bring her back. A sudden fear seized her. She saw herself duly thanked, sitting down again, weaned for the rest of the evening from these rediscovered delights. In a surge of stronger desire she said resolutely:

"Well, yes, one more round."

He fell back with her among the dancing couples. His stretched arm gave the beat in an imperceptible palpitation; at each of these soft passes Thérèse felt the floor giving way under them. Unwittingly she fastened herself to Gerald, squeezed herself in his embrace. At this contact the whole past flew back to her in brutal jerks that maddened her.

She wanted to make a last appeal to her reasoning powers, to her dignity, to that Mlle. Raindal that she was. But she was dazed, ravished. She ceased to struggle and, her eyes once more closed, abandoned herself as a woman who gives in with dread and frenzy.

Gerald guessed nothing at all of this confusion. He smiled at his comrades. His scornful glances called upon them to witness what a "wall-flower," what a "package," what a "wood-basket" he had to steer around. Another great idea they had had, his father and Zozé!... Moreover that young child was pulling all the skin off his shoulder with her bony fingers that clung to him to save her from falling. Ah! Well! This was really too much! A feverish pinching gripped his shoulder. As he bent down to see if by chance the little one was not losing her head, he had to hold Thérèse back with his two arms. She had fainted, white and stiff as a corpse.

"This is the last drop! Just my luck!..."

He swung her rapidly towards the hall, jostling a little the people who were in his way. He set her upon a bench against a wall and ran out to warn the family.

In a twinkle the Raindals, the Chambannes, Boerzell and the marquis jumped to their feet and rushed with him to Thérèse.

Mme. Chambannes pulled out of her pocket a gold bottle of salts, the top of which was a shining ruby; almost on her knees she brought it to the young girl nostrils, but Thérèse made no movement. Only a faint sad moan escaped from her parted lips which showed her uneven teeth. They bathed her temples with fresh water but this brought no result either. As one goes to requisition the firemen on duty, Saulvard had marched straight to the corner where the Academy of Medicine was encamped in order to find a doctor. One came, put his ear to the moist skin of Thérèse and gave his diagnosis.

"The girl is choking.... You must loosen her dress!"

At last she opened her eyes in Mme. Saulvar room, where her mother and Mme. Chambannes had taken her.

At once her glance fell with stupefaction upon her opened dress. Then she recognized Mme. Chambannes bending over her in the pose of a guardian angel, and her mother praying beside her as if she were at the bedside of someone on the point of death.

She turned her head away. She saw again all the details of her accident, the unavoidable intoxication that had made her lose her head and her ridiculous fall in the middle of a dance. What a double insult to her pride! She wanted to plunge into nothingness, to destroy with her own body the memory of it all. Revolt caused her to choke and suddenly she burst into tears.

"Tha right! Tha right! Cry! Quiet your nerves!" Mme. Chambannes encouraged her.

This vulgar solicitude merely exasperated Thérèse. She mastered herself suddenly, stood up, and in a rage began to fasten her dress again.

In the mirror she shunned the eyes of her mother and of Mme. Chambannes. A growing anger put fresh speed into her fingers. Yes! They might well look at her! She had indeed the look of a woman who had just fainted. She could not have jumped up in worse disorder and less command of herself had a man seen her thus undressed and disheveled. Her eyes shone bigger; her eyelids showed a dark shadow as if she had spent a sleepless night. Perspiration had laid oily tints on the wings of her nostrils and marked her powdered cheeks with greasy lines. Her bunch of carnations had fallen down; there was a deep gap in her hair, just over her forehead, like a dark-edged wound. In her haste she had hooked her corsage awry and the gauze gaped over her breast, a loose, transparent cord.

"Poor girl!" Mme. Chambannes risked.... "Do you feel better?"

Thérèse coldly replied:

"Much better, madame, thank you."

She turned to her mother and asked in a tone of command:

"Well, mother, are we going?"

"Just as you say, dear," Mme. Raindal replied.

They went to the anteroom where the men were waiting.

As she came in sight, Gerald rushed forward to inquire and Boerzell imitated him. But Thérèse, with intentional oversight, hurried towards the cloakroom. When she came back, leaning on her fathe arm, they were gone. Stupefied, M. Raindal, his satin hat curled under his arm, supported her wearily. Mme. Raindal closed the cortège, her back bent under her cape as if she had been an aged servant. Saulvard escorted them to the top of the stairs.

"It is the heat, that damned heat!" he repeated petulantly.

Bending his little form over the ebony banisters, he shouted:

"To-morrow, I shall send for news.... It will be nothing, I hope, my dear colleague!"

In the cab that took them home M. Raindal had sat opposite them, leaving the back seat to his wife and daughter. For a long time they were silent. Dreamily they gazed through the windows dimmed by the steam, watching the black streets and the gas street-lamps with their yellow flames flattened in fanshape. Sitting sideways the master lost his balance at every jump of the wheels. He had to catch himself up with the help of the strap that hung in front of the windows; the hard leather cut his hands and the wooden door hurt his bones. A heavier jolt threw him against his daughter. Thérèse exclaimed impatiently:

"Father, you are very uncomfortable. Come and sit here between us."

"No," M. Raindal replied, "not at all.... Do you move.... Well, how are you getting on?"

"Very well, father, thank you."

Silence fell again and once more Thérèse sat motionless.

Through the semi-darkness M. Raindal contemplated her pouting profile behind which, no doubt, lurked sorrowful thoughts. He mustered all his energy and gently asked:

"Well, dear?"

She repeated, "Well, what, father?"

A pause. Then M. Raindal spoke.

"Well, this young man.... At the dance." Thérèse started; she looked at him fiercely and replied with bravado:

"What young man?"

"This M. Boerzell!"

A sigh of relief escaped her. Oh, only that one.... Poor fellow, she had forgotten him so! She smiled, and her voice firmly uttered:

"No, father, never!"

M. Raindal insisted.

"Why? You seemed to like him...."

"Yes, to talk to, perhaps ... but tha all."

"And so you do want him?... You have thought it over well? Let me know at least...."

"You know since I told you.... I do want him."

She grabbed her fathe hand and tenderly bent towards him, offering her cheek.

M. Raindal kissed her and grunted:

"As you like. I have no right to compel you."

Then cunningly, to make sure, he added, without releasing her hand:

"To be sure, he is not such a good-looking man as the other one."

He paused, feeling the contraction in his daughte hand.

"Yes, the other one.... Your dancer.... What was his name?... This M. de Meuze...."

Sharply Thérèse pulled her hand back and said with vexation:

"Oh, father, do make any comparison, please.... M. Boerzell does not appeal to me.... I refuse him.... Tha enough.... I think I am old enough, am I not?"

The master did not reply. There was no doubt about it. It was that tall man, that sort of worldly Dastarac, who had spoiled everything and ruined the prospects of little Boerzell owing to that advantageous height of his. A lost attempt! M. Raindal became absorbed in self-recriminations. Nothing more was heard but the noise of the wheels on the pavement and the vibrations of the carriage windows in their frames.

Thérèse, her head bent back, was apparently dozing, and so was Mme. Raindal in her corner. But she was not asleep. A remorseful torture, more atrocious than a nightmare, kept her eyes awake under their lids. With anguish she was estimating the number of hours that would stretch before the next morning, the blessed moment when she could confess her recent sins in the peace of the Church. Had she not, prompted by thirst, or led into temptation, helped herself three times to iced coffee and twice to *marquise au champagne*, without counting a number of *petits-fours* and other dainties?

CHAPTER V

IT was past eleven lock and Mme. Chambannes had almost finished dressing when someone knocked at her door. Her maid opened it just enough to allow one arm to pass in, holding a special delivery letter, while a voice proclaimed:

"Telegram for Madame."

"Give it to me ... quick!" Mme. Chambannes said.

Her maid was fastening her dress, but left it and hurried to take the message.

Mme. Chambannes tore it open with trembling fingers and read rapidly, glancing hurriedly at the lines:

Tuesday morning, 10 A. M.

My dear little Zozé: I am sure I do know what I could have been thinking of at the dance last night when I told you we would lunch together in our little nest. I pledged myself to the Mathays a week ago. Thank Heaven, I remembered it in time. We shall make up for this. Forgive my carelessness; till to-day at 4. In haste, all the kisses of your old

G.

Quietly she folded the note and laid it on the wash-stand. Then she selected two small pearl-headed pins and carefully pinned them on her broad-winged cravat. She found it growing too hard for her to repress her feelings, however, and there was a catch in her voice as she murmured:

"Leave these things, Anna! Bring me my pink negligé...."

"Madame, then, is not going out?" the maid protested, in feigned surprise.

Mme. Chambannes threw her corsage on a chair and feverishly began to unfasten her skirt.

"No! I am not going out."

"Will Madame lunch here? Shall I call the cook?" "Yes.... No...." Zozé stammered out. "Tell her to prepare lunch for me ... whatever she has...."

"Very well, Madame."

A moment later she returned holding on her arm a long soft gown with pink ribbons. Mme. Chambannes slipped into it; while she fastened the ribbons she ordered dryly:

"Go now!"

Anna disappeared. Mme. Chambannes dropped into a little cretonne-covered armchair.

They were not to lunch together. It was certain, definite, irrevocable. Between her and that Mathay woman Gerald had not even hesitated. Yet he must have foreseen how it would hurt her, and what poignant disappointment he would cause her by breaking his promise at the last moment.

Wretch! She conjured up a picture of him, sitting at the dining table beside the countess, that small fair-haired woman with her turned-up nose, her childish, impudent, saucy face. He was making himself pleasant, prattling pretty nonsense, fashioning his glances to hers and using his big eyes to offer himself. The lunch was perhaps ending, they were going into the hall to drink their coffee! Who knew? Mathay might be going out, leaving them alone, like the great fool of a husband he was! Well, then, what would happen? Did they not all know that young giddy countess? She had no name for being a stronghold, the Capitol!... Oh! what infamy! what an abject situation!

Mme. Chambannes would have liked to snatch out her own heart and hurl it through the window, far, far away. Her nails caught at her gown where it was beating against the armor of her corset. Her mind dwelt on reprisals, as it did whenever she saw Geral treason as an accomplished fact.

Yes! She would have revenge! She would do as he did; she would give herself to another, to anyone of the many who made love to her. Names of men began to surge in her mind, with proper settings. There was the studio of Mazuccio, the little sculptor, the flat of Burzig or that of Pums, the husband of her friend Flora. They were all eager to welcome her; all would receive her as a queen who condescended to offer herself. She would cry out from the door: "Here I am! Take me!" And they would fall on their knees, stammering their thanks with tears of happiness.

These flattering visions quieted her. She walked to her dressing-room, trying to fix upon her choice. To whom would she appeal? They were equally repugnant to her. As she imagined herself in the arms of any of them, a shiver of repulsion caused her to shake her head. Phew! She would require too much courage for her spite to make her lower herself to that extent! Moreover, it might be that none of them was free. She would then risk a polite refusal! No ... everything was against it ... and she admitted sadly to herself that, besides, she never could go through with it!

She fell back into her armchair. Her muscles pained her as if she had been walking all day.

She took up the note from the marble. As she read it again, every word in it seemed an insult or a lie. Tears rushed to her eyes. Sorrow took the place of rage. How nasty, how cold and pitiless Gerald was sometimes! She wished for the near presence of some mothering friend who could understand and pity her, in whom she could confide and who would weep with her. Yet she had none! Alas, neither Flora Pums, nor Rose Silberschmidt, nor Germaine de Marquesse, her friends with whom she had followed the lessons of Levannier, nor her kind Aunt Panhias had a soul that was lofty and charitable enough! Zoz pride revolted at the very idea of their concealed joy or their coarse comforting words.

She fell to sobbing again.

An impression rose in her that she was stranded on a desert island. She would have readily welcomed death. In such dramatic moments she felt forlorn, very much the "little Mouzarkhi girl," quite alone and alien, this unfortunate Mme. Chambannes, for all her French name and Parisian education! She was only a poor exotic flower, planted near the surface of an alien land and the short roots she had taken gave way at the slightest storm as if they were mere threads! There was no help for her in her distress! She had not even the solace of a trust in Heaven, of a refuge in God, since she had been brought up without any religion. When she wanted to pray, there came back to her nothing but a short, strange prayer, one that her kind Aunt Panhias used to make her repeat every night when she was a child, kneeling down in her nightdress by the side of her bed. Unconsciously she now repeated it.

"Be blessed, O my God!

"Help me to be good, to work well, to satisfy Father, Mother, my aunt and my uncle and not to let Father be ruined on the Stock Exchange to-morrow. Amen!"

The last words brought a smile to her lips. She remembered her father, dead these seven years, her good old father, at once so strangely kind and so dishonest.

He had been a type, that Mouzarkhi. His origin had remained obscure and inexplicable to his intimates, to his own countrymen as much as to the others.

He had, one day, landed in Paris from Aleppo, without knowing anyone, with no references, no patrons of any kind. In six months he had gained, on 'Change, one of the most powerful situations any broker could secure there. Of course, people said that he gambled and gained more by his coups than through his commissions. But he enjoyed the benefit of the respectful indulgence which, in such circles, is readily bestowed upon lucky gamblers. Nor did he hide his speculations. He had sworn to stop, to give up all work, as soon as he reached the million mark. He was on the eve of touching it when he met with his first smash. His liabilities amounted to twice his assets. He disappeared discreetly for a few weeks. Then he came back. He was active, cordial, and ingenuous and rapidly built himself up a new credit and a new clientele. His activities had now assumed a nobler aim, that of paying his debts. During the next two years he was most regular in paying sums on account. At the end of that time, there was left only an amount of 300,000 francs for him to pay. He lost patience, however, gambled once more to liberate himself faster, and thus he met his second "smash." Ill-luck did not break him. Once more he took up his traffic, leading a merry, easy-going life, working, paying off, speculating, being "hammered," springing up again like a light, strong balloon. He did not, however, survive his sixth smash. That time he had fallen from too high a flight, from a fictitious fortune of at least two millions down to nothing. He died of apoplexy, right on 'Change, insolvent, of course, but leaving the reputation of a very sympathetic fellow and of a highly gifted financier.

He had, nevertheless, as a good father should, assured beforehand the future of his family.

First of all, when Mme. Mouzarkhi had died a few years after their arrival in Paris, he had called his brother-in-law, M. Panhias, and his wife, and entrusted them with the bringing up of little Zozé. Where had they come from? From Aleppo, Ghazir or Stambul? Were they Greeks, Jews, Turks or Maronites? Nobody had been able to find out, since the Panhias had proved as reserved concerning their origin as M. Mouzarkhi himself. Both had an undefinable accent which suggested all in one the Spanish, the Hungarian and the Moldo-Vallach languages. Panhias, modest and reserved, acted as confidential clerk in his brother-in-la business house. Mme. Panhias watched with faithful care over the education of the little girl; she took her to her lessons during the day and sat up with her in the evenings, while the father went to the theater or elsewhere. She was large, pleasant and, by fits, communicative. Through her, people learned that the Panhias had not been seriously affected by the débâcle of their relation and that they still had, despite their losses, about 15,000 a year. Upon the other points, she had preserved the silence which was a traditional virtue of the family.

Again, M. Mouzarkhi had had the foresight to give his daughter a husband, a year before taking his final jump. The affair, which had been broached by one of his Bourse colleagues, had not been settled without difficulties. They were cautious on both sides. Inquiring agencies had been consulted and forwarded particulars that induced certain fears. They gave M. Mouzarkhi the character of a man personally popular among his colleagues but with a credit that was doubtful and often weak. As to George Chambannes, the son of a little doctor in the province of Berri, himself an ex-student of the École Centrale, they made him out to be an engineer of talent, industrious and daring, but one who had, so far, achieved nothing and who sought his way through dubious enterprises. They had, however, debated the matter on both sides, each side feeling that too much precaution would be out of place. A compromise was struck, on the ground of future expectations, of respective faith in better times to come. Finally the negotiations came to a successful issue.

Zozé, who had but one wish—marriage which would free her from the Panhias guardianship and assure her liberty, showed her willingness from her first meeting with young Chambannes. He was, moreover, good-looking and smart and had caressing, winning ways. He did not insist upon a Church wedding when M. Mouzarkhi, who was anxious to preserve neutrality—or was it his incognito?—in religious matters, declared it would be contrary to his principles, as an "Old Republican" and a positivist. In truth, Zozé would have had to exhibit a baptismal certificate; M. Mouzarkhi had neglected to provide her with one; the need to obtain one now would further delay the marriage. Thus they were married at the city hall. The whole of the Petite Bourse flocked to the place; there were even a few persons from the Haute Banque, among whose numbers M. Mouzarkhi counted, if no friends, at least some admirers. The evening came and the young couple settled down in a pretty mansion on the rue de Prony, a wedding present from the financier. To the house he had added a capital of 100,000 francs in order to help the engineer find that road to success which he was seeking.

George Chambannes found nothing at all, but he spent the whole amount in the course of the next two years and heavily mortgaged the mansion.

Nor did he cut down expenses. Quite the contrary. He kept them up and even increased them, by means of gambling, secret expedients and unsavory manipulations. Gossips said that he was in receipt of money from some generous old ladies, whose names were quoted. These rumors found few incredulous listeners, because Chambannes was handsome, a spendthrift, and with no visible profession or resources. Discredit is like glory; it has its own legends which everyone, out of spite or stupidity, wishes to credit. Zozé was not alarmed at his spending his nights in gambling houses, leaving his own bed untouched, or at his seeming peevish. She had never known what financial embarrassment meant, even during the unlucky periods of her fathe career. To pocket sums of money and, when these were squandered, to ask for, and receive more, seemed to her to be woma natural functions. Only a refusal, a reproach or a check upon her luxurious ways could have worried her. But George never was stingy.

It was only after she heard from a friend that George was running after women that she modified her existence. The change was hardly perceptible; it took place without scenes or noise. She took a lover.

The latter was a relation of hers whom she deemed her cousin. His name was Demetrius Vassipoulo. He had not been more than eighteen months in Paris, was quite young—just turned three and twenty—and sported a thin brown mustache that seemed drawn with a pencil; yet Demetrius was already racing up on the footsteps of his Uncle Mouzarkhi. His future was already being discounted "on 'Change," as if it had been a state loan; he would surely make a colossal fortune or suffer a far-echoing bankruptcy.

All day he ran through Paris, reclining in his carriage, which was hired by the month. His languid arm lay on the folded hood, like that of a rich capitalist stretching himself out. The brass on the harness and the hors bell signaled his arrival and sparkled in the sunshine, his ensigns of triumph.

Zozé loved him three months. He had the hot passion of an animal and the ingenuousness of a savage. He amused her and she told of his ardor to two or three intimate friends who drew comparisons with their own lovers. She initiated him into the attractions of social life, covering his candor with the web of established customs, just as his tailor dressed him according to fashion.

However, she was tired of Demetrius after three months. She kept him for another two, out of kindness, she thought, albeit it was really out of caution and, perhaps unwittingly, because she had not found a better.

The moment she fancied that she had discovered the matchless lover, she wasted no time in breaking with the youthful financier. She gave as a pretext that her husband had been warned and that she had to safeguard her honor. Demetrius wept bitterly and roared out his sorrow in words so harsh sounding that one might have thought it the cry of a stricken lion. Zozé felt remorseful during a whole week. At night she imagined herself hearing again his unintelligible cries. She dreamt of wild animals threatening her. Her new lover reproached her with being gloomy and sighing without cause.

Her grief was not really eased until she saw Demetrius one night at the *Noveau Cirque*. He was in evening dress, with a white bow and carnations in his buttonhole; leaning on the front seat of a private box, by the side of a fat blonde girl, he was blowing his smoke in the faces of the clowns.

Henceforth she felt no qualms; Lastours, her new lover, had no further cause to complain.

He dealt in paintings in a little house in the rue ffémont. He was dark and bald, with the beard of a minion, a brutal mouth and the hands of a street-porter. He held an advantageous place in the syndicate of those painter-dealers whom the Paris of the *parvenus* freely provides with both a living and notoriety. He frequented assiduously the fashionable drawing-rooms of the smart set, mixed with the élite of clubs and art circles, dressed like a sportsman, was as funny as a low comedian and carried about him a vague perfume of something beyond, an aristocratic vapor which seemed to float above his square shoulders. Listening to him, Zozé felt nearer the world of fashion. He was to her the higher step on the social ladder; merely to see that step was as good as believing she was on it and she clung to it with delight. She admired, as if they stood for the finest wit, his studio gossip, his prankish school ditties and the obscenity of his conversation. He had but to say a word and she laughed outright; she rushed to satisfy his slightest whim; in three months Chambannes took three paintings off his hands. Nevertheless Lastours soon abused his privilege. She dreamed of nothing else but the satisfaction of his desires and yet he treated her like a servant, ill-treated her when he was in bad humor; he even ordered the gentle Zozé, after their meetings, to fasten his boots for him.

Such insolence, daily renewed, exasperated the unhappy woman and acted upon her love as water upon flames.

She was fresh, loving and of a pleasant disposition; why should she be denied that happiness of the heart which fell to the lot of so many other women less beautiful than she was? In moments of passing intuition, Zozé gave herself the melancholy reply: They were often less beautiful, that was true, but they were Parisiennes; they were well read and resolute; they operated upon their native soil, while she was a little Mouzarkhi, blindly floating at the whim of her instincts, groping and stranded more than any girl lost on alien soil!... The next day, with renewed hope, she would go back to Lastours!

When she ceased to love him, she wanted to avenge the outrages he had piled upon her. Following a banal, instinctive strategy, she gave herself to one of his friends—also a painter and one of Lastours' competitors—by the name of Montiers, who lived two doors further down the street.

This man was fat and red-headed and concealed his nature even less than the other had done. He was more ambitious and greedy for money than Lastours and entertained not the least intention of wasting his time with women. It was business before anything else with him. For the sake of a prospective sale, a meeting with a client or a patro call, he would dismiss Zozé or put off her visit without hesitation. Once he had kept her, frozen and crazy with fear, shut up for a whole hour in the dark closet used by his models to disrobe in, because some rich American had chanced to turn up at the studio during her visit.

When the American had departed, Montiers walked about the room so elated by his successful transaction that he forgot to deliver his prisoner. He only opened the door when he heard her cries; and when he opened it he smiled, seeing only the humorous side of the affair, while Zozé wept for vexation and grief.

After six weeks such treatment she was thoroughly disgusted with Montiers, and with fashionable painters, and indeed—or so she thought—with adventurous *affaires* in general.

Who would have thought that these men, who were outwardly so courteous, so much made of and so much petted by the most beautiful women, could prove themselves so mean upon intimacy? Why should she keep up these casual liaisons, expose herself to such insults which lacked even the excuse of accompanying tenderness; why seek happiness in love instead of waiting for it?

What, moreover, did she lack in order to be the most envied young woman?

George was spending more nights at home: he showed himself more courteous and took her frequently to dances and plays. On her last birthday he had hired a carriage by the month for her. His affairs were at last taking a better turn. He was gradually paying off his bills and the interest due on the mortgage. Zozé had a vague idea that he was consulting engineer to a large mining company owning mines in Bosnia.

A sort of Indian summer of affection brought her suddenly nearer to her husband. She boasted of it to her friends and declared that the age of folly had passed for her. In order to fill the vacancy left by her lovers, she threw herself with ardor into the pleasures of the mind.

Mercilessly, without choice or respite, she read every new book her bookseller offered her. Memoirs, fiction, poetry and travel books merely whetted her appetite. "I am devouring them!" she would say. And in point of fact, that was precisely what she did; she swallowed and engulfed her readings; she digested nothing, retained nothing.

She became a subscriber to lectures, delighted in old songs and waxed enthusiastic over new ones. She went to concerts on Sundays and dreamt in music of her past liaisons. The only branch of intellectual pleasure she neglected was painting; she never went to the Salon, out of spite for the painters. However, no light of understanding pierced through this chaos of contrary studies. Mme. Chambannes was surprised that, having learned so much, she had not acquired more assurance. Her opinions ran away from her call, like so many flies. She stammered whenever she had to express a personal view. And, in the end, the joys of the intellect bored her....

Her memories of the next two years were misty....

What had she been doing during those two years? She remembered that George had received the Légion onneur on the 14th of July. But the rest, her furious hunt for the perfect lover whom her heart and her senses called for in spite of herself—what was there left of it? Was it not withered, pressed tight at the back of her brain by weightier and more urgent affairs? Two anemic shadows re-appeared at her conjuring, standing in a dim, gray light: herself invariably one of them; while the other was this one or that one, names and features forgotten, or confusedly mixed up under the stamp of time. There had been flirtations at dances, some mild drives in closed carriages, unfinished kisses, mere sketches of self-giving, several vain attempts to reach the ideal and many false hopes and shattered illusions. How could she have felt any affection for those men, those German bank clerks, those exotic, dumpy fellows, more elaborately dressed than gentlemen should be and more caddish than the worst bounders could be! Had she given herself to them? Perhaps she had. To one or two of them, or to none at all? In sooth, she was not at all positive about it. Later, when she gravely swore to Gerald that she had never had but one lover, her conscious fib put that bungling little Mouzarkhi girl only two out of reckoning!

Her search was not guided solely by mere animality.

She longed secretly for an ideal lover. Her day dreams accentuated one feature after the other of his exquisite portrait. But the imagination of many women acts as their body does. It can reproduce but not create. That of Mme. Chambannes, impregnated by the reading of fashionable novels, was acting on a given formula.

She imagined the expected hero with a large blonde beard, melancholy eyes wherein passed at times the moist shadow of an old sorrow; he would also have an income of 30,000 or 40,000 francs and a name which, if not a noble one, belonged at least to the smart and wealthy bourgeoisie.

He would have bitterly suffered at the hands of women, of one especially, a treacherous actress, in love with deceit, notoriety and money. Unwittingly, Mme. Chambannes allowed her mind to dwell on this last point.... The disillusioned lover to come would lift his upper lip in a contraction that showed what bitter experiences he had undergone. From his lips would surge blasphemies against the perfidious sex, ma enemy. Thereupon Mme. Chambannes would tenderly stop the anathemas with her kisses; she would lay that sorrowful head upon her breast and bring smiles back to those defiant lips. If necessary, and he wished it, she would go away with him. They would then become exiles on a small English island, far from the wicked world, and stay for hours together sitting alone on the sands of the seashore, hand in hand, indefinitely contemplating the changing play of the waves or the ships returning home.

Why did this hero fail to arrive? She had made everything ready to receive him, even to follow him; down to an imaginary list of dresses and things which she would hurriedly pile up in a wicker trunk held by yellow straps and covered on the outside with a shining piece of black cowhide!

He tarried on his way, but he did arrive.

He was of the stay-at-home variety, selfish, titled, a libertine, he wore no beard, he had no languorous airs and no spite against anyone. Nevertheless Mme. Chambannes adored him from the very first.

His name was Gerald de Meuze, son of the Marquis de Meuze, of the Poitou branch of the Meuzes. George had known him at college and later lost sight of him.

The introduction occurred at one of the Auteuil races. It was a quiet Thursday, almost an intimate spring meeting. It proved decisive.

George, out of pride or his passion for gambling, soon left them alone to look after his bets, and Gerald stuck close to Mme. Chambannes.

He walked her out before the reserved seats, escorted her to the paddock, lost his way with her behind the buildings on the broad green expanses which were deserted by the public whenever a new race began.

A strong odor of hay, damp and sharp as a sea air-laden breeze, entered their lungs. Mme. Chambannes could hardly speak for happiness. A new ecstasy caused her breasts to tremble under her light silk blouse. She walked with her head bent forward, her eyes aimlessly watching the tips of her shiny patent leather shoes sliding on the grass. At last the longed-for lover had come! She had got hold of him! No power could have dissuaded her! She laughed nervously at all the remarks of Gerald, thinking that, when she looked at him she was replying to him; she thought she was losing her mind; the handle of her saffron sunshade trembled against her shoulder.

The little Mouzarkhi girl would have felt even more intoxicated had she heard what was being said of her in the exclusive club members' tribune, among the friends of the young Count.

They were asking each other, with sly winks, who that pretty little woman was Gerald was keeping so close to. Not one of them knew. A professional? No, she could not be that. Probably a little woman from some sunny, hot land, whom that rascal de Meuze made feel warmer still, in order to tease the baroness.... Why, yes ... the Baroness Mussan ... from whom he had parted ... it was over ... did you know?... Oh, not more than a fortnight.... Just the same, this one was a jolly, good-looking creature!

And the success of Zozé was no less real in the ladies' tribune.

Of course, the good ladies did not spare her the contemptuous tone which they used indiscriminately when passing judgment upon all women who were not of their caste: demi-mondaines, actresses or plain bourgeoises. Yet, apart from that disdain, their verdict was a favorable one. They found the strange woman nice, her dress a good fit and Gerald a man of taste. Several maliciously inquired about Zoz name of the baroness who, to save her face, joined the others in praising her.

Yet, Mme. Chambannes perceived nothing of this exciting triumph. How could she discern it? She saw no one in the whole crowd but Gerald, her true mate, her lover to be. She walked on, with evasive glances, like a happy bride advancing to the altar on her wedding day.

She was almost there when the races were over. Gerald had begged her, had pressed her as if he were already her master. He wanted to see her again, to possess her, the very next day. She remembered his ardent voice when, on leaving her, he had dared to whisper in the midst of the crowd, within Georg own hearing:

"Why wo you to-morrow? Oh! please, do refuse me!"

Nevertheless, she had refused, with a slow movement of her head, while her eyes turned up as if plunging into despair.

She had to resist, to oppose this man with as much coldness and as much caution as he was deserving of her love; she had to make him gain her instead of abandoning herself to him. A voice within her dictated this unusual reserve to Mme. Chambannes; she heeded it like the voice of duty, being persuaded that her delays were safeguarding the future.

She gave in only after a siege of three weeks, at the moment when he had grown discouraged and was on the verge of renouncing his intentions.

During that period, she had thought deeply and found out what she wanted, with that superhuman cunning which women often show in order to arm and defend their threatened passion.

She now knew everything about Gerald. He had led an idle, discontented life since the time of the financial smash of 1882, when, in a fit of juvenile anger, he had resigned his commission in the *30th cuirassiers*. From the disaster his father had saved him a yearly income of about 40,000 francs. She learned also the names of the people of his set; heard of many of his liaisons, without names this time, all about the last one … with the baroness; she was told of his antipathy for a world wherein his reduced circumstances no longer allowed him to figure as he wished.

Upon this information, she had rapidly drawn her plans. Two methods were possible in order to keep Gerald a prisoner.

Either she could rise and enter, with his help, the haughty circles of his peers, where he would find no difficulty in introducing and imposing her. She could thus know of all his movements, easily keep an eve on him and fend off any possible danger.

Or else she could take advantage of his weariness, gently lead him away from this set of which he affected to be tired and afford him, in her own house, a home that would be brighter, easier and more novel.

In the first case, a thousand obstacles stood before her. There would be innumerable petty deeds to perpetrate in the midst of much uncertainty, delay and humiliation. A short while back, Georg candidacy had been "adjourned" in two sporting clubs. The committees of those clubs, more rigorous in their verdicts than a Council of Ministers, had successively denied the white balls of their assent to a man upon whom the Government had bestowed the guarantee of the Cross of Honor. She would therefore expose herself to a rebuff, on this hostile ground, where she would be on an inferior footing. Mme. Chambannes chose the second method.

A few months proved sufficient for her to transform her life, organize receptions and assume regular visiting days. She convened her most attractive friends, some of Geral comrades, men of letters, musicians and even artists, when she had conquered her own repugnance for them. Thus, gradually she established for his evenings, as a supplement to their afternoon meetings elsewhere, a composite but sympathetic salon, a place for simple enjoyment where both men and women could come, without putting on any airs and without afterthoughts, with the sole intention of meeting each other and the firm desire to have a pleasant time.

Mme. Chambannes was near her goal. Gerald was captivated, attracted and firmly held; he surrendered to his lady, swore fealty, faithfulness and lasting love—and made Zoz house his own. He reigned therein, an all-powerful despot, coaxed by the husband, flattered by the visitors, servilely obeyed by Mme. Chambannes who rejoiced in, and was thankful for, the love at last acquired and conquered, the love unique forever, and more than legitimate, since it was even romantic and glorious!... Then came one evening when the young Count brought in his father. The Marquis de Meuze was charmed with his "daughter-in-law," as he nicknamed Zozé to his own soul. He came again, of his own accord, having found the place attractive, the women pretty and the cooking excellent....

Yet, what struggles, what efforts she had made before she achieved victory! Every day she still had to use her craft and stratagems in order to keep her nobleman, to keep the thieves off and take care of the competition.

Mme. Chambannes thought of these things and gave a deep sigh. She stared aimlessly at the iridescent foam that the sugar sent up to the top of her coffee cup. Suddenly the sullen voice of Anna called her back to her reflections.

"Is Madame going out? May I get Madam clothes ready?"

Mme. Chambannes was stupefied.

"What is the time?" she asked.

"Almost two lock, Madame."

Two! Why, she had left her room, gone to lunch, eaten and drunk and sat there all that time, not knowing what she was doing, her mind wandering far away, on the obscure paths of the past!

Sleepily, she replied:

"Yes, I am going out.... Give me my blue dress.... My astrakhan coat...."

She went wearily to the window and lifted the curtains. A heavy white mist hung low between the houses. It seemed as if a smoke was rising from everything, from the trees in the park, at the end of her street, from the street pavement and from the asphalt on the sidewalks; even men and horses that passed by threw it out of their nostrils in thick, parallel clouds. Far, far above, the sun gave out a pale light, like a lamp in a room where men have smoked much.

Such a cold, funereal day was a good day for lovemaking, was it not? Mme. Chambannes dreamt. To love Gerald, all kinds of weather seemed propitious to her, as the lower classes think all days are good for drinking.

Where was her *Raldo* now, he of the great, wide, beloved eyes? How she detested the unworthy wretch!... What were they talking about at the Mathays', in the drawing-room darkened by the fog? Naïvely, she let the curtains down again, as if she feared to see. Once more sobs came to her throat! Well, she must forgot, get some distraction, take a walk until four! Where could she go?

She raked her mind for names; she thought of visits to pay, of dressmakers and modistes. Then all at once she skipped and beat her hands with a childish gesture.

Of course! She had decided on the previous day to invite M. Raindal to her house, to make of him a super, if not a star, at her receptions, a noted and venerable pillar of her salon; why should she waste time, why not seize the opportunity? Tuesday was Mme. Rainda day. Again, there was their daughter accident; to go there and inquire about her—why, these were all pretexts that no one could suspect. She must not lose an instant!

She ran to her room. Ten minutes later, her muff under her arm, she was fastening her gloves outside the house, waiting for the cab she had sent for.

CHAPTER VI

THE cab passed slowly through the parc Monceau, and proceeded faster through the Champs Elysées towards the boulevard Saint Germain.

Mme. Chambannes sat huddled up in the left-hand corner; her feet pressed on the hot water bottle, scorching her soles on the white metal; rocked by the motions of the carriage, she all but closed her eyes.

She opened them for an instant on entering the boulevard Saint Germain, looking out to peep at the rue de Bourgogne where Gerald lived with the Marquis; then she dozed off again.

She preferred not to think, to let herself remain benumbed with sleepiness. Yet, when the cab left the rue de Rennes and turned into the rue Notre-Dame-des-Champs, Mme. Chambannes instinctively straightened herself up, as does a traveler at a change of scenery.

The street was deserted and lined with long, austere buildings. Were they colleges, seminaries or convents? Mme. Chambannes did not know. Most of them had black iron bars that stretched their dark stems against daylight and the noise from outside. Here and there she noticed a few houses that had none and were not quite so high as the others. Beyond them, the bare heads of the trees spread their leafless branches. She could guess at courtyards behind, immense gardens and discreet paths where people walked and meditated.

In her own district of the plaine Monceau, there were streets that Mme. Chambannes had thought no less mournful. On some afternoons, even during the week, they gave an impression of Sunday calm and the houses seemed empty of people, as if all had gone to the center, to the gayety of the boulevards. Yet here the aspect was a different one; the quietness was less idle and seemed to vibrate with thought. She felt that there were crowds behind these strong walls, all busy with pious or cherished occupations: a silent activity, zeal, ambition and faith, and disciplined passions. At moments a hidden bell sent a deep note into the air.

Without much understanding, Mme. Chambannes felt a little shiver of surprise. She imagined a multitude of monks and nuns dwelling in these buildings. They knelt down and prayed, in long black or gray rows. The dark sanctuaries softened their silhouettes and the smoke of incense twisted its curls above their heads. She had a sudden curiosity to be among them, to learn their prayers and share their ecstasies. Especially she wished to go in and see.

Her driver had to knock at the window to warn her that they had reached the house. The concierge was an old woman with catarrh. She told her where M.

Rainda apartment was: at the end of the path, on the fifth floor, and the door on the right.

She paused a little while before pulling the cord of the bell. She wanted to look about her. Opposite stood the wall of the next house on the other side of the path. But to her right, she saw gardens, uneven houses, a whole panorama of strange roofs, separated by streets or a purple mixture of trees. A perfume of *pot-au-feu* escaped from the door of the Raindal family.

She rang at last and was ushered into the drawing-room by Brigitte.

Mme. Raindal, dressed in black silk, was chatting with two elderly ladies whose dresses showed no care for the fashions of the day. She hesitated on seeing Zozé, then recognized her and went to her.

"I came to inquire about the young patient," Mme. Chambannes said, as she sat in the dark-red plush arm-chair which Mme. Raindal offered her.

"Thérèse! She is quite well again.... She is working with her father.... You shall see her very shortly.... How kind of you to...."

Mme. Chambannes thanked her with a smile.

Mme. Boudois, one of the two visitors, the wife of a professor at the Sorbonne, exclaimed:

"Poor child!... Has she been ill?"

"Not much, thank Heaven!" Mme. Raindal replied. "A mere indisposition while she was dancing at the Saulvards last night...."

The other lady, Mme. Lebercq, the wife of the famous mathematician, inquired:

"Dizziness, was it?"

"Yes, I suppose so," Mme. Raindal replied.

Mme. Boudois confirmed these presumptions. There was her husband, for instance; God knew he had his sea-legs and sailed up and down the seas every summer, at Langrune, in a fisherma boat. Well, her husband never could waltz; he felt giddy at once.

On the other hand, Mme. Lebercq was no sailor but had been able to bear dancing without inconvenience when she was young.

A silence followed and Mme. Chambannes began again:

"The party was charming, was it not?"

"Delightful!" Mme. Raindal admitted.

Mme. Boudois and Mme. Lebercq asked for details, and received them. But at the turning point of a sentence, the conversation was directed toward another subject. Mme. Boudois spoke of the forthcoming festivities of Advent. She advised Mme. Raindal to attend some of the Benedictions of the Host at Saint-Jacques-du-Haut-Pas, where the Noël O would be sung with rare brilliancy. Mme. Raindal rather preferred those of Saint-Étienne-du-Mont. The discussion grew quite heated. Mme. Lebercq, who was not devout, remained silent. Mme. Chambannes, ill at ease at this talk of things that were mysteries to her, examined the pattern of the red and black carpet around which the arm-chairs were disposed.

She took advantage of a pause for breath and asked:

"Would it be indiscreet to disturb the master and your daughter?... I would be so glad to say how do you do to them!"

"Of course not! Quite the contrary.... They will be delighted."

She knocked at a side door.

"What is it?" the voice of M. Raindal grunted.

"A visitor!"

She made way for the younger woman. Thérèse lifted her head at the sound and rose from the table at the same time as her father.

"It is Mme. Chambannes who comes to inquire after you, dear," Mme. Raindal explained.

Thérèse, whose lips were already pursed with vexation, attempted a smile.

"Oh, you are too kind, dear Madame.... It was not worth it...."

M. Raindal joined his grateful protestations to those of his daughter. Mme. Raindal excused herself and returned to her visitors. As on the previous day, at the ball, when he had been introduced to Zozé, the master stood still, embarrassed. At length he said:

"Wo you sit down, please?"

She took a chair and said:

"How gay your study is!... How light!"

"Oh, we do lack daylight here!" M. Raindal replied. "The room has quite a good light."

Mme. Chambannes continued:

"You were working?... I interrupted you...."

"With the most agreeable of possible surprises," M. Raindal answered, with a wave of his hand.

The conversation dragged on. Thérèse wore a persistent frown, said little and was absorbed in drawing lines on a sheet of paper. Mme. Chambannes' visit roused her indignation. Why had that woman come? What more did she want? What right had she to disturb them with her prattling, her childish queries and her very presence which brought back the memories of the previous evening, the shame of that accursed party?

"Your windows look out on gardens, do they not?" Mme. Chambannes asked.

"Upon gardens and our whole Paris! We have a marvelous view from here!" he replied.

She walked with him to the window. At last the sun had burst through the clouds and scattered the fog. Below them was all M. Rainda Paris, the whole of the religious, studious and simple-minded Paris, stretching out its stiff endless stone buildings in a milky light. The tops of certain edifices rose high above the level of the others. To the right was the square tower of Saint-Jacques-du-Haut-Pas, then the immense dome of the Pantheon, then a thin, fine point—the spire of the Sorbonne. Further to the left rose the shining sphere of the cupola of the Missions and at the end a truncated pyramid upon which floated a tiny, discolored flag: the palace of the Louvre. Between these, the houses sketched in the air the irregular lines of their roofs. The thin-hooded chimneys bristled in compact ranks, like reversed bayonets. At the back was a deep hollow space, indicating avenues and a park; it was the Luxemburg, but it could not be seen.

M. Raindal complacently commented upon this panorama. Mme. Chambannes gushed over it all, finding everything either charming or pretty. When he had finished, he pointed out the garden next to their house.

"It is the garden of the *Visitandine* Sisters of Notre-Dame-du-Saint-Rosaire.... See, there are two of our neighbors out for a walk!"

Mme. Chambannes bent forward to look at them. They walked one behind the other around the enclosure of brown earth. They held chaplets in their hands that were red with cold, and let the beads slip one by one. Their bonnets were bent down and hid their faces. One of them, thin and light, seemed young; the other was stouter and appeared old. Both had the square, unshapely waist which the bands of their aprons mark on the corsetless flesh of nuns. Mme. Chambannes examined them in silence for a few seconds, but thought it wiser not to ask what it was these holy sisters were doing with their rosaries. She turned round and, perceiving a glass case set up against the wall, near the window, exclaimed.

"Oh, the pretty things! what charming little mummies!... They seem to be asleep standing up...."

She pointed out the middle shelf where peacock blue, pale green and white china statuettes stood in rows. All wore the Egyptian headdress that fell down on their shoulders like manes. Their eyes were black lines above squat noses which were in several cases worn out at the tip. There were inscriptions all down their bodies even to the feet, which were swollen like those of gouty people. Some had their arms crossed in front. Others showed only their hands as if they had bathing gowns on. The sand of the desert had stuck to many of them, leaving upon them the mark of its centuries-old atoms.

M. Raindal explained the use of those statues. They had been placed in the tombs in order to help the dead in their labors in the other life. He then gave Mme. Chambannes the names of the divinities on the shelf above: Hathor the cow-headed, jackal-headed Anubis, hawk-headed Horus, Osiris, the god of the netherworld, with his huge tiara; Thueris, a frightful idol with the head of a hippopotamus and a woma breast, who was, it was thought, consecrated to motherhood or to preserving people from ill-luck. The master spoke of them all tenderly and volubly as if he had imagined them and made them himself with his own hands. Well, had he not created them? Had he not given them life when he tore them one by one from the Nothingness of the sands or the depths of the tombs? The scarabs of colored stones were also, every one of them, his own discoveries. He had put a pin through them and laid them side by side on white grooves as one does with a collection of real insects. Near these scarabs there was a case in which had been thrown three heavy gold rings, their bezels engraved with hieroglyphics, which had doubtless been worn on the dry, yellow fingers of imperious Pharaohs.

"All these things are terribly old, are they not?" Mme. Chambannes asked.

"It depends," M. Raindal replied. "On an average, they date back 3000, perhaps 4000 or 5000 years!"

"Really!... And if I went to Egypt, next year ... I could find some like these?..."

"It is possible ... if one digs deep enough.... The desert is chock full of them!"

"How interesting!" the young woman murmured dreamily.

Behind her, Thérèse stamped the floor with impatience. She started when she heard Mme. Chambannes proceed:

"And now, my dear master, I have a small favor to ask of you.... Are you free in a fortnight, on December 12th?"

"Well, Madame!..." M. Raindal stammered, trying hard to guess, in spite of his poor eyesight, the meaning of the grimaces Thérèse was making at him.

"Because, if you were free, you would do me great honor and give me much pleasure if you would dine with me at my house."

M. Raindal bowed.

"Hm! Hm!... Certainly, Madame.... I can ask Mme. Raindal.... At least, I do not think she is engaged for that evening...."

He turned to his daughter.

"Is it not so, dear? Your mother has not, so far as I know...."

Thérèse cut his sentence short with the brutal admission:

"No, father, we are free!"

She felt her hand tremble on the glass case where it lay. Anything, anything, just so she could get rid of that woman! So that she would go away, back to her tall coxcomb, that Gerald whose mistress she must surely be! Later they could get out of the engagement. Let her only go! Not to see her any more in the room, not to hear her voice any more, no longer to breathe in her perfume, like that of Gerald, heavy!

They returned to the drawing-room. Mme. Raindal, surprised, accepted at once. The whole family saw Zozé off at the door. Even Thérèse followed them. When Mme. Chambannes reached the stairs and looked up for a last parting word, it was the girl challenging glance that met her last one.

"A peculiar look!" Mme. Chambannes thought in the cab that took her away. It was a look that held both admiration and a little envy, such as the poor give when they watch the beautiful women going into the opera.... Well, this little Raindal girl was strange!

Her cab passed the bridge of La Concorde and entered the Champs Élysées.

Zozé could not refrain from making eyes at the first well-dressed young man she passed. At last she was back in her own element, on her own soil, in her own district.

Once before, she had had a similar impression; it was when she had returned from abroad and saw, on crossing the frontier, the first French customs inspector. As she returned now to the right bank of the river, she found everything different from the place she had just left. Clothes, faces and gait—it was all different. The cold seemed less bitter, less cruel to her cheeks. Men walked down the avenue, comfortable, peaceful, covered with soft fur coats.

Women passed in rapid victorias, their faces a smile in the midst of furs; children played and ran among the trees. Everywhere the pleasures of summer were carried on in spite of the hostile winter. Rich people met rich people, all well dressed, quite *au courant* of the latest thing, among connoisseurs, in their own sets. Zozé shut her eyes tight in an attempt to visualize again the rue Notre-Dame-des-Champs, so far away, in the provinces as it were, gray and flat as a stereopticon view....

Her mental comparisons were cut short when she heard the Élysée clock strike four. What! already! She would be late! What would Gerald say? Fortunately she was almost there. Yet it was not fast enough for Zozé who, with her feet propped up against the back seat of the cab, pushed the hot water can with her two feet, as if to help the horse along.

At length, the cab came to a stop in rue guesseau, before a quiet-looking house. Carelessly, she settled her fare, ran madly up one flight and entered the apartment, all out of breath. Gerald was there. He was dozing on the divan of the dressing room. His arms were folded around his head, making a dark setting for it. The obscurity of the corner where he lay further heightened his peaceful expression.

Mme. Chambannes contemplated him tenderly. Poor little Raldo! How beautiful he was in his sleep!

Emboldened, she whispered:

"Are you asleep? Are you asleep, darling?"

Without opening his eyes, Gerald replied:

"No, I am not asleep but I am affecting a deep sleep!..."

"Why?" Zozé asked smilingly.

"Because," he replied in the same way, "you are late, Madame, and I detest that kind of joke."

He rose to kiss her. She returned his caress with effusion and asked saucily:

"Guess where I have been!"

"I take orders from no one!" Gerald replied.

"Well, I have been to see père Raindal!"

"The Kangaroo!"

Surprised, Zozé opened her eyes wide.

"The Kangaroo!"

"Why, of course!" Gerald said. "Did you notice the way he held his arms and his hands? A regular kangaroo! All he lacks is the pocket in front, and little ones inside."

Zozé laughed. Then she gave him a humorous account of her visit, described the furniture, the carpet, the hangings; she told of the smelling pot-au-feu; she gave an imitation of Mme. Raindal, of Mme. Boudois and of Mme. Lebercq, all in the hope of amusing Gerald.

The young man had a certain amount of natural acrobatic talent, although he had not appeared in amateur circus performances. While he listened to Zozé he stretched his limbs by walking round the room on his hands, his legs bent back and his feet hanging over his neck. When she had finished her story, he turned a somersault, slipped his arms behind his knees and, in that uncomfortable position, took a few frog-like jumps. Then he straightened himself up smartly and asked:

"Well then, are you going to engage this mummy merchant?"

"Why not; do you mind?" Zozé ventured, somewhat frightened.

"I!" Gerald replied. "No, not at all!... All tastes exist in nature!... You already have a novelist, three artists, two musicians and an *abbé*.... The kangaroo will complete your collection.... I congratulate you!"

He bowed with an affected grand manner and declared, as he pointed to the next room.

"You are at home here, dear Madame."

Zozé obeyed him, throwing him as she passed a passionate look. Gerald joined her after a few minutes. While he lit the candles on the mantelpiece, Mme. Chambannes lay silent, looking up to the ceiling, with a sudden serious expression.

She had a fleeting vision of the two nuns who were walking in the cold, in the grassless garden, with their chaplets in their hands.

That brought her a sensation of shame. Confusedly, an idea came to her mind, showing her another life, as good and even probably better than her own, a life devoted to other aims than to go to bed every afternoon, with candles lit.

But Gerald approached and asked imperiously.

"What are we thinking about?"

Suddenly, like a child caught doing a forbidden thing, Zozé assumed again her happy, lover-like expression.

"We are thinking.... We are thinking that we adore you, wicked Raldo, who made me feel so miserable this morning."

She stretched out her arms in a gesture of surrender and appeal.

Gerald slipped into her embrace, coaxing her in naughty whispers.

CHAPTER VII

THÉRÈSE had never worked so hard as she did during the following days. It was her own way to cure herself, her one infallible medicine whenever her "crises of remembrances" as she termed them, returned to haunt her. She punished her brain with a surfeit of study, as devout people tame their rebellious flesh by means of pious exercises.

For weeks at a stretch, she only left her fathe study to go to one of the libraries. The moment she came back, she fell to work again. She started once more immediately after dinner and worked until she felt too sleepy to continue. And the next morning she started again.

The remedy had seldom failed to bring prompt relief. Her effervescence calmed down gradually under the icy blast of accumulated knowledge. She was so tired that her desires weakened; the immense drama of the history of humanity helped her to hold as futile her little sentimental regrets. These lofty thoughts brought forth a supreme breath of pride and dried the inner tears which her heart persisted in distilling. Caught up once more by discipline, like a refractory horse brought back to the shafts, she assumed once more her customary existence; her soul was quieted and joyless but also too weary to attempt another revolt.

An excess of scruples even caused her this time to make no attempt whatsoever to avoid the Chambannes dinner. Her relapse had been so serious, so sudden and so childish that she stood in need of punishment. She wanted to meet again, face to face, that handsome M. de Meuze, in order to prove to herself by a defiance of the danger how foolish she had been.

Her bravery, however, much resembled the confidence inspired by an underestimated adversary. She no longer stood in dread of Gerald because she thought him the lover of Mme. Chambannes and he shared in her mind the contempt she felt towards the young woman.

But was it really contempt? Thérèse was too proud to admit a feeling of jealousy towards this little brainless creature. The only feeling she avowed was one of pity.

She delighted in remembering the ill-chosen expressions and the bad grammar which characterized the conversation of dainty Mme. Chambannes. And Gerald himself, how futile his words were! His voice was that of a debauchee, an oily drawl, with accents that were imperious but carried no authority; he seemed to be in the habit of giving orders to no one but maîtres ôtel and loose women. The two of them made a pretty pair, a nicely matched couple!

The day of the dinner party seemed to her a long time coming, so much did she long at once to challenge them both, to hold them under the hostile coldness of her gray eyes....

Several times, M. Raindal had to drag her away from her work at night. She always grumbled before she allowed herself to be persuaded. He chided her gently and took her arm to lead her to her bedroom. They walked together along the dark passage. Everything was quiet in the house. Sometimes they paused, smilingly listening to Mme. Raindal, whose snores reached them through the closed doors. Then M. Raindal kissed his daughter and retired, feeling his way about in the dark.

"Poor girl!" he thought in mingled admiration and tenderness.

Had he but known! Had he but guessed at the struggles and the anguish of her masculine soul! Had he but heard the "Poor Father!" with which his daughter expressed to herself pity for his lack of understanding!...

The weeks passed rapidly and the day came at last when they were going to dine with the Chambannes.

Shortly after seven, Thérèse was putting on the heavy dark coat she wore when she went out in evening dress, when she heard a sudden outburst of discussion in the hall and someone knocked at her door.

"Come in!" she said.

Her father entered in his shirt sleeves. His white tie hung unfastened over his waistcoat.

"Do you know what is happening?" he exclaimed. "Your mother now thinks we have been too ready to accept this invitation of Mme. Chambannes; she says that we should have tried to find out more about her.... Find out!... Find out what, I ask you, and where?... All this because of a dinner that has no importance!... She wants us to put it off now, five minutes before we are due to leave the house. What can one do? I ask you! especially I fancy that you yourself did not take greatly to the lady?..."

"Phew!" Thérèse said doubtfully.

"You can guess where she gets such ideas," M. Raindal went on, as he paced the room. "She gets them from those fellows! From the vestry!... Oh, she did deny it long.... And I have warned her that the next time they have the audacity to...."

He did not finish his sentence. Mme. Raindal entered the room, her corsage unfastened:

"Hush!" she whispered. "Someone has rung the bell. Thérèse, go and open the door, dear! Brigitte has run down to get a cab."

"Very well, mother."

Thérèse went to open the door and was surprised to find her Uncle Cyprien, who was wiping his shoes on the yellow mat in the dark hall.

"Good evening, nephew!" he exclaimed merrily. Then he noticed that Thérèse had her cloak on and wore white gloves.

"Oh! you are going out! And I came to share your dinner.... What bad luck!"

He walked in. Thérèse replied with constraint. They had said nothing to him about the Chambannes dinner party, for fear of his criticism.

"Yes, uncle, we are dining out."

Hearing his brothe voice, the master came out of the room. He exchanged the customary greetings and said, to fend off any query:

"You are unlucky.... We are not dining here.... Can you come to-morrow?"

"Of course!" replied Uncle Cyprien. After a pause he added:

"Hm! Is it indiscreet to ask where you are dining?"

Thérèse dared no longer to deny.

"We are going to the rue de Prony, to Mme. Chambannes', a lady whom we met at the dance at the Saulvar."

"Chambannes! How do you spell it?" Cyprien asked, with a suspicious grimace.

Thérèse spelled it out for him. The younger M. Raindal frowned.

"Chambannes, Chambannes!" he repeated, as if he were testing the sound of a name with which his ear was not familiar.

Finally he gave it up.

"Well, au revoir!" he said, "till to-morrow!"

He shook hands with them and walked down the stairs, still muttering to himself, "Chambannes, Chambannes!"

In spite of its general aspect, the name sounded vaguely Jewish to him. Then, he reflected, everybody knew how cunning Jews were in disguising their original names and changing them into French names. They called themselves Duval, Durand or Dubourg and hid under those Gallic, Roman or Frankish syllables, names bestowed on the mount of Sinai, and Uncle Cyprien boasted of an exceptionally good scent when it came to unearthing such deceptions. He had not even admitted the purity of his own family name until after a thorough search in the libraries. The moment he reached the street, therefore, he hurried towards the Brasserie Klapproth where Schleifmann could, he felt sure, throw some light on his suspicions.

"How late you are!" the Galician exclaimed, as he started to enjoy a plateful of roast veal and jelly.

Uncle Cyprien sat beside him and studied the bill of fare.

"Yes!" he said. "I am late; I wanted to dine with my brother ... but they are dining out, at Mme. Chambannes'."

"Rue de Prony?" Schleifmann asked.

"Then you know the lady?" Cyprien inquired.

"Oh! very little.... She is charming.... I meet her sometimes at the house of one of my pupils' parents, young Pums, the son of M. Pums, assistant manager of the Bank of Galicia."

"Well, I never ..." Cyprien exclaimed.

"I even knew that your brother was to dine there.... Mme. Chambannes invited Mme. Pums and gave her the names of the other guests.... She seems to think a great deal of your brother."

"You knew it and you said nothing of it to me?" said Raindal, with a reproachful glance.

Schleifmann repressed a smile.

"Well, no! *You* said nothing about it.... I assumed that your brother had not told you ... out of discretion, you understand?"

Cyprien became thoughtful.

"Listen, Schleifmann.... Tell me the truth!... What kind of people are these Chambannes?... Are they all right?"

Schleifmann pretended to have some trouble in swallowing the last mouthful, in order to gain time for thinking. Of course, he could not tell a falsehood to his friend. But why, on the other hand, should he further excite this savage ill-will, ever ready to spring up; why should he help to stir up family troubles? He chose to answer with harmless fibs and did it with studied indifference.

"Well!... I could say.... The husband seemed to me a somewhat colorless person.... He is an engineer and specializes in mining affairs, I believe.... The woman is pretty, smart and pleasant.... Besides, as I told you, I hardly know them."

Cyprien was not eating. He bit his mustache; then suddenly he burst out, as if a spring had been released:

"They are Jews, are they not?"

"I am not sure!" Schleifmann replied. "The husband comes from the Berri, where Jews have not, as a rule, colonized very much.... His wife appears rather of the Semitic type ... but so refined, so very mixed, that I dare not affirm...."

"Yet, their name!" Cyprien insisted.

"Their name!" the Galician replied, feeling his philologis pride provoked. "Actually, there is nothing to prevent it from being a Frenchified Jewish name.... Chambannes might well be derived from Rhâm-Bâhal, or from the corrupted Rhâm-Bâhan, which means, if my recollections are correct, something like *high-idol*, a *lofty idol....*"

"Rhâm-Bâhan!" Uncle Cyprien repeated complacently.... "Rhâm-Bâhan!... Of course ... tha what it is.... I thought to myself...."

The admissions made by Schleifmann had whetted his appetite and, his mouth full of food, he insinuated:

"It seems to me you spoke a little while ago of a list of guests who would be there...."

"Yes, yes," Schleifmann said evasively.

"Well, who are they?" Cyprien insisted.

The Galician shifted uneasily.

"I have not a very clear recollection of them.... I assure you.... I have forgotten."

"I do believe it, Schleifmann! Try to remember; there is no hurry."

The temptation proved too strong for his friend. He could not miss such an occasion to air his rancor; he could not refrain from flaying the whole dubious clique of men who had in the past refused him a hearing. He began to feel that he lacked the strength to resist his inclination. He began, mildly at first, a few points at a time, throwing his venom upon those he hated least.

"Very well," he said. "Le see!... To-night there will be M. Givonne, an artist who paints fans and dancing tambourines for society balls and sells anything he likes to the Americans.... Hm!... M. Mazuccio, a little Italian sculptor who spends his time telling how the women whose busts he has made are fashioned below the waist...."

"A pretty lot!" Cyprien encouraged him.

"M. Herschstein," Schleifmann went on, more vigorously, "that excellent Herschstein.... Ho, ho! here is one I recommend to your notice.... A patriarc gray beard, fat cheeks, the head of a pleasant grandfather, as good as gold.... This does not prevent him from being one of the heads of the black band.... You know, the clan of German financiers who daily speculate against the French bonds.... Ah! many legends, many lies are told concerning the Jews.... But, alas, this is not an invention; the foul black band does exist! And it is on the cards that your comrade Schleifmann will be one of those, when the people take a fancy, on the first day of the riots, to go and find out, under their very noses, what they are brewing in that corner!"

"Good man!" M. Raindal said with emotion.

"M. Herschstein, then ... and Madame ... a tall, lanky woman with a narrow mind, who thinks she can wipe out these crimes by throwing money to all the poor people and contributing to charitable works...."

Schleifmann hit the table with his fist.

"Charity! The damned fool. I charity shl get on the day when her rascally husband has had us all expelled from here!"

"Hush, hush! Calm yourself, Schleifmann!" Uncle Cyprien whispered. He knew now he could rely on the Galician, as one could trust a roaring, flaming fire. "Calm yourself, my friend!... Who else, did you say?"

"M. de Marquesse!..." Schleifmann continued. "Another pretty fellow!... A consulting engineer.... Adviser! Ha, ha! Legal adviser, I have no doubt!... Already two societies which he "advised" have ended before a magistrate.... But he gets on just the same!... People say that his wife helps him.... Not that she is good-looking ... a head like a horse.... But men are so stupid in that set.... For the sake of an aristocratic name, my dear friend, they would entertain a mare."

"How delightful!" Cyprien remarked, his lips twisted in a disgusted pout.

"Then there is my countryman Pums, a dark little man with a black mustache, the face of a gypsy, and his wife, a small red-headed woman.... But she is pretty, this one! plump, with a turned-up nose ... regular painte meat!"

"Wha that?" Cyprien asked.

"Yes, it is my name for these ladies, because of their inclination towards artists.... Any painter has but to stoop down to pick them up, like a 'rag and bones' man in a heap of rubbish."

"And so you think that Mme. Chambannes herself...."

Schleifmann stopped him quickly.

"No, no! not at all.... Quite the contrary!"

He added maliciously:

"Mme. Chambannes leads a regular life, absolutely regular...."

Thereupon he took up the normal thread of his ideas:

"Let us go back to our people.... The Marquis de Meuze and his son, the Comte de Meuze."

"Ah!" said M. Raindal with irony. "Sham nobility, are they?"

"No, true.... They are very friendly with the Chambannes.... By the way, you would like the old Marquis very much.... I have been assured that he shared your horror for the Jews, who nearly ruined him at the time of the panic...."

The flame of his anger was abating. He gave a few more names, but without commenting upon them: Jean Bunel, the novelist; M. Burzig, a young broker; M. Silberschmidt and his wife.

He became silent and Cyprien asked:

"Is that all?"

"Yes, absolutely," Schleifmann replied, as he took off his gold-rimmed spectacles to wipe the glasses, tarnished by the perspiration caused by his excitement.

M. Raindal the younger assumed a jocular expression.

"One more question, please!"

"I am listening," Schleifmann said.

Cyprien came closer to him and asked engagingly:

"Of course, they are all Prussians?"

"No, my dear Raindal," the Galician replied. "They are all French, or—and it is all one—naturalized Frenchmen.... Since the war.... The little Pums is their veteran.... He has been French since 1878, this little Pums.... Well I remember how proud he was of it when he came back to Lemberg, at his next annual visit.... He ran from house to house, to his friends, to his relations, showing everywhere his naturalization papers.... Anyone might have thought he was showing the diploma of a degree...."

"It is one!" remarked Cyprien.

"Yes, yes, all are naturalized French citizens," Schleifmann continued, "with the exception of Burzig whom I was forgetting.... It is not his fault, however.... He owes that to his father.... They have the mania for change in that family. The grandfather was born in Mayence and became an American. Good! The father came to Paris and turned into a Frenchman.... Pouf! It was not enough!... He made an Englishman of his son to save him from military service.... I tell you, these damned Burzigs are never satisfied!"

He laughed, a sneer on his lips.

"If the Jews of France had red blood in their veins, I can assure you that they would have thrown out all these tourists! You, the true Frenchmen, should have made life so unbearable, so hard for them that...."

"What about yourself, Schleifmann?" Raindal asked. "Are you not going to be naturalized also?"

The Galician gave a melancholy smile.

"I, my good friend?... At my age!... What is the use? Fate made me a man without a country and a man without a country I must remain.... I am plain M. Schleifmann, a citizen of humanity, as someone said...."

"That is all very well!" Cyprien objected. "But what would happen to you if war broke out?"

"War!" Schleifmann murmured dreamily.... "First of all, shall I see it?... Then I am very old, my dear Raindal; I would make a poor kind of a soldier.... I am sorry.... However much I do detest war and the imbecile reasons for which nations massacre each other, I would have liked nevertheless to serve France, the least stupid of all nations, after all, and the most generous I have ever known...."

"Phew! You could make yourself useful in other ways," M. Raindal said.

"True!..." Schleifmann said in a low voice, as if he were addressing his own soul. "In 1871, the Commune came!"

But Cyprien missed the tragic retort. He was already lost in joyful thoughts of the morrow. He imagined with glee how stupefied his brother would be when he heard: "Well! How is old Herschstein! And that charming Mme. Pums?... and the honorable M. Burzig!..." He laughed so loudly that he apologized to Schleifmann.

"Forgive me, I was thinking of something so funny.... Ha, ha! It is wonderful!"

He felt moved to show his gratitude:

"Here, Schleifmann, you will not refuse a glass of kirchenwasser?... Garçon, kirchenwasser and two glasses, two big ones, customers' glasses, you know!..."

The waiter returned with a bottle protected by a cover of twisted straw. Cyprien poured two big drinks and lifted his glass to touch that of his friend.

"To humanity, Schleifmann!" he said courteously.

"To France!" the Galician replied, and they toasted.

At the same time, the Raindal family were making their entry into the salon of Mme. Chambannes.

Zozé stepped out rapidly to meet them. She wore a loose dress of pink silk with subdued flowered-work. It gave her the silhouette of a Spanish princess. Chambannes followed her; he was perhaps smiling under the mystery of his huge blonde mustache. Then began the series of introductions.

Ladies first: little Mme. Pums, in a tight-fitting black robe with gold spangles, which made her plump face appear even fresher, whiter by contrast and gave added zest to her red hair; Mme. de Marquesse, a tall blonde with a horsy jaw, whose mauve crêpe dress showed, revealed about the hips, the massive bones of a Republic or a Liberty; Mme. Silberschmidt, a thin dark woman with the face of a sick hen; Mme. Herschstein, more angular and haughty in her white satin corsage than a lady of ancient lineage. Then came the men, one by one, as they happened. They bowed low; all gave deferential yet curious looks; all shook hands eagerly and yet with shyness; they spoke in respectful but unfinished sentences, as one does in the presence of a foreign potentate with whose etiquette and language one is not very well acquainted.

Pums, the dean of the naturalized ones, was introduced last. Small, neat, yellow-faced, dressed with sober correctness—what struck one most in his physiognomy was not his Viennese stockbroker type, nor his thick black mustache, nor the gray about his temples; it was the projection of his two big light chocolate eyes, so keen in seeing things, so ingenuous and so languorous that, but for a flicker of sly archness at the bottom of them, one might have thought them the eyes of a good little boy surprised at seeing so many people. He spoke a decent French, with not more than the suspicion of a Teutonic accent: a French that was, like himself, naturalized. He was the only one who succeeded in reaching the end of his compliment.

M. Raindal had no time to thank him; they were passing into the dining-room.

Mme. Chambannes sat between the master and the Marquis de Meuze. Her husband faced her, with Mme. Raindal to his right and Mme. de Marquesse on the left. The neighbors of Thérèse were Gerald and Mazuccio; the latter a sort of brown faun, who droned his with the fury of a Venetian mosquito. The rest of the company sat round the table, at seats marked by cards bearing their names. The soup was served in attentive silence.

They were obviously waiting for the master to say something important and unusual; the ladies were especially anxious to hear M. Raindal whom they imagined, after his *Life of Cleopatra*, to be a famous raconteur who would surely deliver some "stiff ones" during the dinner.

They were soon undeceived. He was really not very amusing, this M. Raindal, nor very original, with his fat, flabby neck, his hands that hung loose, his manners of an ill at ease ex-prefect—and his almost inaudible voice. Moreover, they were not missing much. Details on the climate of Egypt, the means of transportation, the favorable time of the year for traveling in that region—I ask you, would Baedeker or the Joanne guide give one as much?

Soon, M. Raindal had but two left to listen to him, the Marquis and Mme. Chambannes who was never tired of asking questions.

To tell the truth, he did not feel in the mood. It was not that he felt intimidated by Mme. Chambannes' fervent glances, or the caressing roll of her *r*'s which made her voice softly imperious. On the contrary, he was grateful to her for not wearing a lower dress; he found her most graceful in that corsage which barely showed a modest opening and exposed a small square of skin with her fine neck free from jewelry. The surrounding sumptuousness embarrassed him much more than the tender glances of the young woman. He had written a whole chapter on the Pomp of Cleopatra; he had not winced at the gems, the gold, the incense and all the sumptuousness of the Inimitable Life; but he now remained as one dazed before the reality of a magnificence that was much inferior to it. The profusion of flowers running in garlands all over the table, the light shining in the cut glass, the dainty silver, the shining elegance of the guests were to him as so many sharp points of brilliancy that caught his eye and his thoughts. He was, moreover, further distracted by a noise that resembled the purring of an engine, the *schh*, the *harrh*, the *horrh* and the *pff* which were now fusing from the group of the Silberschmidts, the Herschsteins and the Pums, who were massed on one side of the table.

They had evidently made themselves at home; their tongues wagged, they used their native language, which sounded like a gargle. The French language? Why, that was a dialect for official use, good enough when one had to be polite, for social life.... But why should they place such a check upon themselves when they talked business, when it came to serious or intimate matters? How could they do it, anyhow? Was not this native language of theirs which sprang to their lips with a naïve instinctive vigor stronger than anything else, stronger than any decree or any oath of allegiance? You should have seen the jeering wink that accompanied Pums' inquiries concerning the *krankheit* (illness) of the Sultan and the no less knowing look in the eyes of Herschstein when he replied. That indisposition of the Sultan had proved devilishly successful; it was Herschstei idea, had been sent from Paris to Vienna, re-telegraphed from Vienna to Paris, and had upset the Bourse throughout the afternoon. Turkish stocks had tumbled down, 3 francs, 6 francs, 10 francs at a time and the panic had spread to the French rent! Result: about 100,000 francs for each of the active members of the black band and a paltry 25,000 for Pums, who was only an ally, a sort of honorary accomplice. However, he was not dissatisfied with his share and even wished to pay back Herschstein who explained to him the new plans of the Bank of Galicia concerning certain gold mines. That scheme consisted in forming a syndicate which would be named an Investigating Society and would glean from the market the least suspicious mining bonds. Moreover, it was an easy operation; they had first only to depreciate these values by means of alarming news and then send them soaring up to the highest point by means of optimistic news. The art of the market at its infancy! The infallible process. Young Burzig who, being a British subject, had been ceaselessly flirting in English with pretty Mme. Pums, brusquely returned to the German of his family in order to take part in the discussion and the projects of the group. They were discussing with de Marquesse what bonds they could choose, what mines would be drained in the course of the operation. English or Dutch names, more blazing than tiaras, were quoted: the Pink Star of South Africa, the Transvaal Sun, the Source of the Carbuncles....

Suddenly there were signs of restlessness in the one little green eye of the Marquis de Meuze. It rolled, turned and trembled in its orbit like a fishing cork. He tried hard to take in what was being said. What! There was no mistake about it this time! They were talking about gold mines at the end of the table. Quite so.... Gold mines! *Nom n bon homme! Nom n chien!* How could he listen to these gentlemen without being discourteous to the other one, that M. Raindal with his damned stories about mummies and Mariette Bey?... The marquis tried vainly to follow both conversations and his face became purple in the attempt. He could only hear a few words of the one that was carried on further from him: *fontein ... rand ... chartered ... Cecil Rhodes ... de Beers ... claim* ... and their technical syllables further pricked his curiosity. Well, it was no small matter to him! 120,000 francs engaged on the mining market. "120,000" the marquis repeated to himself; did it not give him a right to a certain amount of anxiety? And it seemed that it was in answer to him that he heard the voice of Pums in a half silence.

"*Ya! Gewiss.... Ich glaube das die Red-Diamond....*"

The Red-Diamond—Fontein!... Why, that was the favorite mine of the marquis, his most beloved stock, "his little Red Diamond," as he called it victoriously! This time M. de Meuze could no longer contain himself. Brutally he turned right about and addressed the financiers:

"Excuse me, M. Pums, you have just mentioned the *Red Diamond*, I believe? Would it be indiscreet to ask what you were saying about it?"

"Not at all, marquis," Pums replied, for he always felt honored when M. de Meuze consulted him.

And out of regard for the aged nobleman, the sizing up of the different mining stocks was carried on in French.

However, M. Raindal had not noticed this desertion. It was some time already since he had been speaking for Zoz benefit alone; he felt that a gradual mist of sympathy isolated them together from the rest of the party. He thought to himself, charmed and perhaps also emboldened by the mixture of wines he had been drinking:

"I was right.... One of Cleopatr followers!... A little Greek girl.... A true little Greek!"

Then he went on:

"One day the fellahs refused to carry our luggage on board; Mariette Bey rushed upon them, revolver in hand...."

Zozé exclaimed, amazed by his tales. She was not lacking in good will or respect for philosophical maxims; she only relaxed her zeal when she could not understand. At such time her eyes wandered, innocently settling in turn upon each of the guests, in an impersonal and almost mechanical need for tenderness which she still preserved from her past quests.

The little Pums rushed forward; his eyelids quivered; he was like a gymnast anxious to catch his trapeze. Poor fellow, he was so much in love! Geral reply was a cordial grimace, made with his nose or his mouth or his cheeks, and Zozé understood him: "Yes, of course, it is quite understood, we two are lovers!" But Mlle. Raindal, alas, seemed less satisfied. Poor girl! Gerald and Mazuccio—they were leaving her shamelessly alone. One inclined his face towards the flat chest of Germaine de Marquesse and almost touched her; the othe face was aflame; he had turned entirely to one side, close to that lascivious hen, Mme. Silberschmidt! What a gap there was on each side of the poor girl! No, it was really not nice for them to treat her in this fashion as if she were a governess.

Thereupon Mme. Chambannes would look again into M. Rainda eyes. That had the same effect upon him as if someone had poured something hot inside him, and he became quite red. His eyes blinked with pleasure. He coughed to gather himself together again and lifted his head, unconsciously awaiting the next soulful look, or else he admired Zoz profile; it was so neat, so delicate under her gathered hair which was caught behind by a tiny bow of pearls. And as he went on with his anecdotes, he repeated to himself:

"A true little Greek!... A little Greek girl from the Islands."

Suddenly the true little Greek became restless on her chair; her face showed suspicion; she looked hard towards Mlle. Raindal who was half-hidden from her behind a bunch of mauve orchids set up in the middle of the table.

Well! What was amusing the girl so? What was it that brought to the corners of her mouth this set, oldish smile like a wrinkle? What was the meaning of the contemptuous glances and the commiserating attitude with which she scrutinized all the guests one after the other!

"Upon my word," Mme. Chambannes thought, "one might think she was looking at savages or niggers!"

But a new thought came to her.

"Oh, well! The poor girl is annoyed!... I can well understand it!..."

Mme. Chambannes called Gerald in friendly words, to bring him back to his duties. They were serving the finger bowls. It was too late, after all! She would see to it next time! She pressed her nails into the translucent slice of lemon which floated on the surface of the water. She pushed back her chair with slow discretion and everybody rose.

"Mademoiselle!" Gerald said, offering his arm to Thérèse.

The young girl laid her hand on it but avoided his eyes, disdainfully turning her head away. They walked to the drawing-room without a word. Gerald multiplied his courteous, deferential attitudes; he drew in his chest and gave all the signs of a well-bred man of the world who knew that he was at fault and exonerated himself silently. He escorted her to Mme. Raindal and softly withdrew his arm.

"Mademoiselle!"

He bowed with much ceremony and directed his steps towards the smoking-room. Thérèse could not prevent herself from watching him.

The balancing of his tall frame on his bent legs gave him the relieved, weary gait of a man who has just come down from his horse, or of one who has accomplished an imposed task. Outside the smoking-room he took Mazuccio familiarly by the shoulders to make him pass in front; she heard them still laughing behind the old tapestry portière—a mysterious throaty laugh which even at a distance had an obscene sound.

"Well, dear?" M. Raindal murmured, as he approached in short and somewhat heavy steps. "How was the dinner?"

"Excellent," Thérèse replied coldly, and sat down to the right of her mother. "I am delighted that we came...."

"That is what I thought," M. Raindal continued softly, mistaking his daughter tone. "This Mme. Chambannes entertains people in the most perfect fashion.... Now ... you agree that I was right not to let myself be stopped by certain prejudices, certain preconceived ideas!..."

This allusion caused Mme. Raindal to blush suddenly, but Thérèse, a sneer on her lips, whispered:

"Why, surely, father, I told you.... These people improve very much on closer acquaintance...."

M. Raindal turned round. Mme. Chambannes was calling him away to offer him some coffee.

At the other end of the drawing-room little Mme. Pums and tall Mme. de Marquesse were holding each other by the waist and exchanged joyful secrets concerning the use they had made of their afternoon. Their outward contrast brought out all the more the best points of each. One guessed that they shared the same tastes and the same aptitudes, everything they needed to take part in full agreement in some party of four, especially with two pleasant men of corresponding height.

Still linked together they marched through the room. Mme. de Marquesse pulled aside the curtain of the smoking-room; joyful exclamations greeted the graceful pair. They went in altogether and the shouts increased. These gentlemen were not ungrateful.

The conversation dragged until their return. Mme. Chambannes tried to make small talk with Thérèse and Mme. Raindal, while Mme. Herschstein paid compliments to the master. But the subjects of conversation were getting scarce. She remarked on the late hours of modern dinners and gave out some prognostications concerning the forthcoming winter; and then Zozé began to feel ill at ease. Great Heavens! What could she talk about? Dresses! She must not think of it! Poor women, they were rather "trussed up!" Theaters? They had admitted that they had not been to one for two years. Zozé tried; she groped for ideas; the gray eyes of Thérèse looked sternly into hers and put her further out of countenance. She was very intelligent perhaps, this Mlle. Raindal, but she was not easy to get on with.... "No go in her," as Gerald would declare. Zozé was on the verge of forgiving him his brutal silence during the dinner.

At last the men returned, with the exception of the marquis, whose apologies George Chambannes offered to M. Raindal. As a rule, that was the hour for smutty stories. They would go by twos to whisper in the dark corners; the old people usually remained in sight in the center of the room, peacefully discussing aloud their money matters or their infirmities.

The presence of the Raindal family probably made the guests feel ill at ease, for they did not attempt their usual customary maneuver. Two of them only, Givonne the painter of tambourines, and little Mme. Pums, who had been last in leaving the smoking-room, dared to maintain the tradition. They settled down in a window corner. With the exact expression of an English commercial traveler it seemed, at a distance, as if Givonne was praising to Mme. Pums some article which, he promised, would give her complete satisfaction.

M. Raindal examined them for a moment with a mechanical benevolence. But he felt his eyelids becoming heavy. The abundant meal or the efforts to recall his memories which he had made during the dinner made him feel very tired. To avoid speaking he made free use of affable smiles.

The entrance of Jean Bunel, whom Mme. Chambannes brought towards him, gave him a pretext to rise.

"M. Jean Bunel, whose beautiful novels sure you have read," Zozé said in presenting him.

"To be sure…. Delighted, my dear confrère!" said M. Raindal warmly, as he pressed the hand of Bunel, whose name he was nevertheless hearing for the first time.

He was a young man with a fine brown beard; rapidly he turned out an admiring sentence, as pointed and pretty as a candy cone.

M. Raindal thanked him with a bow, and made a sign to Mme. Raindal and Thérèse, who rose at the same time.

"You are not going already?" Mme. Chambannes asked, exaggerating her regret.

M. Raindal mumbled some excuse and they all walked together towards the hall.

A wave of relief passed over the guests. It was not one old maid but three who were disappearing through that door! A feeling of frolic was in the air; they all felt a need to let out foolish remarks and to fall back into their habits. Yet they still held themselves in hand, out of the respect which notoriety inspires in the minds of uncultured people.

When Mme. Chambannes returned, she found them all silent.

"Well, you are not very gay here," she exclaimed, and added after a pause:

"What do you think of him?"

"Oh, your little friend is charming!" said Gerald, in the midst of an explosion of laughter.

Pums encouraged by this success tried also to say something very funny, but Jean Bunel declared in commanding tones:

"His is nothing less than one of the most remarkable minds of the day!"

"*st-ce pas?*" Zozé murmured.

"Yes," Bunel went on, moved as much by a generous impulse of solidarity as by a malicious delight in contradicting a clubman.... "Yes, without comparing him to Taine or Renan, I think that within the last few years the science of history has produced no more vigorous brain nor a purer stylist...."

"Really?" Pums exclaimed, suddenly brought round to another view.

As a matter of fact, the only reproach which he had for M. Raindal was that he spoke too low. Silberschmidt agreed with him. Mme. Herschstein, to whom the master had listened, affirmed that M. Raindal was one of the most interesting of men. Mme. Pums thought he had a very expressive face. Givonne was called down for voicing a criticism of Mme. Rainda dress. Did such things count?

The change was so decisive and so general that Zozé felt much pity for her little Raldo. Poor darling! What a snubbing!

She walked to the fireplace where he stood, his elbows resting on the marble of the mantelpiece. When she came quite close to him she murmured in a passionate whisper the query which had kept her throat dry for the last three hours:

"Do you love me?"

Free from spite, the count instantly affirmed that he did.

CHAPTER VIII

THE clock of the Collège de France sharply struck three. A little door hidden in the gray wall was opened and M. Raindal entered.

He sat behind his large white table, facing his usual audience of eight who waited, pen in hands, ready to take notes.

He took a few manuscript sheets from his portfolio and began simply:

"We concluded, in our last lesson before the new year, the study of the oblatory paintings which have been found in the mastabas of Abu-Roash. From the same point of view we shall begin to-day the study of the mastabas of Dahshour. The paintings contained in this necropolis afford to the historian perhaps more interesting insights than those of Abu-Roash. We find there particulars concerning the private and industrial life of the Egyptians, which may well be considered unique. I, therefore, call your particular attention to this lecture and those that will follow...."

M. Raindal paused and consulted his notes:

"The chief painting in the mastabas of Dahshour is that which was preserved in the tomb of a rich trader of that period, one of those important merchants whose caravans carried on the traffic with Lybia and the Syrian coast. It was first brought to public notice by Brugsch; then it formed the subject of two detailed communications from my young and eminent confrère, M. Maspero; these appeared in the *Annales du Musée de Boulack*; and the *Revue gyptologie*. The name of this trader was Rhanofirnotpou...."

M. Raindal rose from his seat and quickly rubbed the blackboard behind him. A little cloud of white chalk, light as smoke, floated about his sleeve.

"Rha-no-fir-not-pou!..." he spelled out, as he wrote the hieroglyphics of the word upon the board.

He had scarcely finished when the padded door was pushed forward and fell back again noisily. Insidious emanations of iris perfume sharply passed through the room. A lady entered, and with a rustle of silk, sat down behind the students. In spite of himself, and as if compelled by the odor, M. Raindal turned round anxiously. Yes, it was she, it was the pretty little Mme. Chambannes!

He was so upset that on coming back to his place he could do nothing but repeat his first sentence concerning the defunct Rhanofirnotpou.

" ...One of those important merchants, as I said, one of those rich traders whose caravans...."

Mme. Chambannes! Mme. Chambannes at his lecture, in a blue skirt, a white veil and her otter fur coat! Who could have expected such foolishness, such a childish caprice? And now she was making little signs at him as one does to friends in a theater from box to box: "How do you do, M. Raindal. How do you do, how do you do," the head of Mme. Chambannes kept on saying.

She desisted, at last, when she noticed that the maste face remained impassive despite her politeness.

Moreover, the coldness of M. Raindal was not her only cause for disappointment. To begin with, she did not understand anything of this story about the paintings of the late Rhanofirnotpou. What! Paintings in a tomb! The great trader must have been an original character! And then she was astonished by the setting.

She had thought that she would enter a grandiose amphitheater, with the audience crowding on the tiers built of oak and varnished by age. Below she had imagined a huge chair as high as that of a judge, and flanked by two ushers with silver chains. In the chair, M. Raindal in a crimson red velvet robe bordered with ermine.... M. Raindal discoursing, playing with his braided bonnet, drinking sugar and water and interrupted at every word by his enthusiastic audience....

What a disillusion! What a contrast to the realities! Who could have imagined this narrow hall with dirty gray walls, those two imitation bronze busts—Plato and Epictetus—perching like Chinese pottery upon two pedestals of imitation stone, this coarse white wood bench that resembled a kitchen table, and rush-bottom chairs piled up on one side near the washed-out Plato as in an old furniture storeroom.

Zozé felt almost the same imperceptible melancholy which the spectacle of misery inspires in worthy people. She sought distraction in a successive inspection of the backs and of the necks of the eight students. Two were already bald. Three showed between the shoulders the shining line which the hard back of the omnibus pressed into the cloth. The coat of another was faded. Towards the end of the table, to the left was one with a brown mane—oh, what a wol head!—he surely did not squander his money at the hairdresse!...

She was full of pity for these brave young men. She wished she could give them advice about their clothes, and if necessary help them with her purse.

A scraping of chairs brought her back from her charitable dreams. The lecture was finished. M. Raindal had disappeared. But where? Through the wall, no doubt. And not even a sign of applause! Zozé was dumfounded.

She stood up, cramped from having sat so long, and followed the students who were passing out. Some made way for her. None of them stared at her. And those who walked ahead did not turn round to look. She found them discreet and well-bred but somewhat shy.

She paced the huge vestibule, sounding her heels on the tiles for the sake of hearing the echo. Ten minutes passed; she was freezing with cold. She was going to ask Pageot when M. Raindal came forth from the shadows, his portfolio under his arm.

He repressed an angry gesture and assumed a smile as he advanced towards her.

"What! you here, dear madame!" he exclaimed hypocritically.

"Did you not recognize me? I heard your lecture.... I did not understand everything, but it was very interesting!"

M. Raindal sought an excuse in his poor eyesight and asked more anxiously:

"Well, my dear lady, what can I do for you? What is it you wish? To what fortunate hazard do I owe your presence here?"

Fortunate hazard! No, not at all fortunate. Yet, she could not reply: "Gerald has once more played me one of his tricks and put me and my caresses off for two hours.... That is why, having nothing to do, and out of sheer boredom, I came here to see what one of your lectures was like, and perhaps, also, to arrange a little dinner party!" What she said was this, accompanied by a child-like smile:

"No hazard at all, dear master!... I wanted to hear you, that is all.... When it was over, I waited for you, so as to shake your hand...."

"You are too kind, a thousand times ... really!..." M. Raindal murmured distractedly.

He darted frightened glances to right and left as they walked out. When they reached the street, and he saw Mme. Chambannes' own carriage waiting, he was unable to dominate a desire to run away. He took off his hat.

"Good-by, dear madame.... I hope soon to meet you again.... Please give my compliments to M. Chambannes."

Zozé protested.

"What, master! Do you want me to drive you home?... In such weather!"

With a quizzical frown she showed him the sidewalk which the thawing temperature had apparently coated with syrupy iced coffee. The master declined. From outside her coupé, Zozé insisted, beating the leather of the cushions as if she were calling a little dog. M. Raindal lost all his composure. If the students, or some of his colleagues were to see him in this ludicrous position! Fear carried the day. He sat beside Mme. Chambannes.

"Tha better. It would have been silly to refuse," Zozé said, and she lowered the front window to give the address to her coachman.

When she closed it again, M. Raindal noticed with relief that all the panes were covered with steam. Protected from sight by the opaque glass, he began to feel more at ease. He smiled at Mme. Chambannes, who was smiling at him.

The carriage rolled rapidly over the carpet of yellow snow. A soft warmth came from the hot water can; the pleasant scent of morocco leather blended with that of violets. M. Raindal sighed with comfort and, waking up, said paternally, to try to blot out the rudeness of his attempted leave-taking:

"It appears then, dear madame, that the lecture did not bore you too much?"

"Quite the contrary! Moreover, I firmly hope that, next time...."

"What next time?"

"I mean the next lecture I attend," Zozé corrected, "and those after...."

M. Raindal darkened.

"Are you thinking of coming again?"

"Perhaps!... Why not?... Are you angry?..."

"Not at all, dear madame, not at all!"

He could say no more. He was paralyzed with stupefaction. So! She wanted to come every Monday, to attend all his lectures, publicly to compromise him, turn him into a laughing-stock for the whole Collège, the scientific world and perhaps the whole press! He fancied that he heard the voice of Cyprien: "Ah ha!... it appears that Mme. Rhâm-Bâhan"—the younger Raindal never used any other name for Mme. Chambannes—"it appears that Mme. Rhâm-Bâhan takes to Egyptology.... Bravo! Charming! Delightful!" Then would follow the sly irony of his colleagues, the jealous jests, the allusions, the scandal! No, no! M. Raindal was not going to risk such a misadventure as had often wrecked the careers of many of his illustrious colleagues, because of the fancies of a lady who was, he did not deny it, graceful, attractive and sympathetic, but nevertheless frivolous and devoid of reflective power. He declared firmly:

"Listen, my dear lady.... I have enough esteem for you to tell you the truth.... Well, it seems to me that you are not in a position to derive any benefit from my teaching.... The Collège de France is a sort of seminary ... a seed-plot as it were, destined to form young savants ... you understand? The essential aim of the Collège de France is to...."

"Yes, yes!" Zozé interrupted sadly.... "Yes, my dear master, I can see that my presence is not welcome to you.... But how can I learn for my trip to Egypt, next winter?... What can I do?... What can I do?"

She hung on to her old project of "preparing for her trip"; she clung to it with an alluring obstinacy which was gradually getting on M. Rainda nerves. Phew! Let her "prepare" as best she could! He moved away from her and, in his impatience, let fall his portfolio.

Mme. Chambannes caught it deftly. "Poor M. Raindal!" she said, giving him one of the sidelong looks that were her natural way of looking at people. "I am boring you, am I not?"

He blushed for his brusqueness. "Not at all! I am trying to think of some way in which I can help you with your studies, with your preparatory reading...."

Zozé frowned with attention. Suddenly, a joyful flicker swiftly passed over her caressing eyes.

"I ... I have an idea," she insinuated; "an idea which has just occurred to me."

"What is it?"

"But it is so indiscreet!"

"Never mind!... Tell me!" M. Raindal urged, feeling that his indulgence was once more wearing out.

"No, I shall never dare!"

She still hesitated, her eyes plunged into his. She decided to speak at last, when the carriage stopped at the door of his house.

There it was: she wished, if it were not too much trouble, that the master would agree to come to the rue de Prony, once a week, on Thursdays, or at least twice a month, not to give her lessons—no, Zozé would never bring herself to risk so impudent a request—but to talk to her, simply, as a friend, to guide her in her studies, to indicate to her what she should read....

"You understand.... I know that it is very indiscreet.... Yet, if you would ... it would make me so happy!... Wo you, dear master?"

Gently she laid her white-gloved hand on the maste knee, in a familiar gesture that had no touch of second-thought coquetry, as she had touched the knee of a kind grandfather—of her Uncle Panhias, for instance, when she was asking a favor. M. Raindal was intimidated and dared not move away. On seeing this slight, elegant creature bent before him in such an ingenuous and humbly craving attitude, he felt pleasantly troubled and mistook that feeling for regret, for tenderness.

"Hm!... Madame!" he murmured, assuming again a pleasant voice.... "It would grieve me very much to displease you.... Nevertheless, you must realize that my obligations ... my work...."

"Oh! I know, I know!" Zozé said with feigned resignation.

Time passed. Raindal looked through the steam, at the soft silhouettes of the passers-by, unable to make up his mind to bid her good-night.

Suddenly he started, as if a shooting pain had passed through him.

"What is it, dear master?" Zozé asked in a solicitous tone.

"Nothing, nothing, my dear lady!" Oh! almost nothing—he had merely recognized at the end of the street certain swaggering shoulders, a certain martial gait, merely Uncle Cyprien who was walking straight to the carriage, flourishing his thick reddish cornel stick.

M. Raindal envied for a minute the distant shelter of the late Rhanofirnotpou. Why was he not in the deepest part of the *hypogee*, in the dark serdab, in the cement-sealed partition, instead of finding himself in a cage that seemed suddenly all windows, with a young and pretty woman who harassed him with her prayers!

"Do you really want to, dear master?... Nothing like set dates.... I promise you.... You could fix the hours, the days...."

"I am trying to find, I am trying!" he replied mechanically, while attentively watching the rapid march of the enemy.

Uncle Cyprien was coming nearer; his features became more distinct; he reached the carriage. As he passed, he gave the turn-out a contemptuous and yet mistrustful glance and walked up the alley. Unconsciously M. Raindal heaved a sigh of relief. He put his hand out to Mme. Chambannes.

"Good-by, dear madame.... I shall think about it; l let you know."

Zozé pouted with disappointment.

"And I was in hopes you would give me your answer now!"

M. Raindal passed a hand over his eyes, to sweep a painful vision away—that of his brother who might be coming down again, meeting him as he came out of the carriage and thereby acquiring a pretext for interminable sarcasm.... The savant murmured hurriedly:

"Very well then, madame, very well.... I shall come this week...."

"How kind of you.... How about Thursday? Next Thursday at 5...."

"Yes, Thursday at 5 lock."

"You do know how sweet you are." She grasped his hand and looked at him with an expression of radiant gratefulness. But M. Rainda fingers were slipping out.

"Oh! excuse me!" she exclaimed.... "You are in a hurry.... Till Thursday, then, 5 lock!... I am counting on you, dear master...."

M. Raindal closed her door and saluted awkwardly. The carriage started. A "Good night! Good-by!" caused him to turn round again. He saw Zoz little white glove making a parting friendly signal from the window of her coupé.

M. Raindal put off confiding the tale of this meeting to Thérèse from day to day, until Thursday arrived; it was as if he dreaded to bear her criticism. Phew! he knew well enough the objections she would make: his position among European savants, his academic standing, the ridiculous situation he risked finding himself in when engaged in so vague a task of popular instruction. He was even less anxious to hear the not unfair remarks of his daughter since the idea of going again to Mme. Chambannes was not repugnant to him, although he did not go so far as to admit it to himself. Once out of the hallowed atmosphere of the Collège, and saved from his brother Cyprien, he had begun to reproach himself for having so sharply rebuked his attractive admirer. Poor child! Should he not, on the contrary, find it touching, the case of this futile young person who was seized with a sudden passion for knowledge? Did it not afford him matter for observation, a subject most highly fascinating for a man of thought? Why, here was a chance for a thorough study of a personality! His mind recalled the picturesque attitude of her profile—a little suppliant—the tiny hand on his knee: "Do you want to come, dear-r master-r!" To be sure, he wanted to go! Certainly, he was going! If for no other reason, he would go for sheer selfishness, out of a savan curiosity. And Mlle. Thérèse—he thought, almost snappishly—well, it would be quite soon enough if he informed her after the lessons had begun!

Thus came the Thursday morning, and M. Raindal had not betrayed the mystery of his appointment.

He felt, therefore, somewhat ill at ease when Thérèse entered the study about 9. How unfortunate! Precisely at that hour he was busy packing books for Mme. Chambannes! However, he did not lose countenance, but exclaimed gaily:

"Hello! here you are, dear!"

She submitted to his kiss, then touched two of the large volumes he had piled up on the table.

"What is it, father?... Maspero.... Ebers!... Are you beginning to lend books?...."

"No!" M. Raindal declared, stiffening against his uneasiness. "These are books I am going to send to Mme. Chambannes."

"To Mme. Chambannes!" Thérèse replied, dumfounded.

"Well, yes...."

He then related all the episodes of the previous Monday, with the exception, however, of the decisive appearance of Uncle Cyprien.

Thérèse listened quietly. When he had finished, she looked up. Her thin lips met in sarcastic contraction. Anger was gathering under her heavy frown. She asked him:

"Are you going?"

"Well, since I promised her!... I shall go two or three Thursdays.... The most elementary courtesy requires it.... Later, I shall see whether I should continue or not."

"Very good, father!" she replied, disguising with difficulty the trembling she felt in her voice. "Just as you say.... You may be sure I would not presume to give you my advice...."

"But if I were to ask you for it?" M. Raindal said pluckily.

She burst out.

"If you were to ask me, I would tell you that this Mme. Chambannes is a little fool, that her set is extremely frivolous, that those you are taking up with will bring you nothing but unpleasantness and affronts.... I would tell you.... But, no, father, my respect commands me to be silent."

The tips of her fingers rose and fell on her crossed arms, like two palpitating wings.

"Oh, ho! We are getting excited!" M. Raindal replied, as if he felt jocular. "Phew! If I remember rightly, little girl, you were not so severe on the evening of the ball.... Do you recollect, after dinner?..."

Thérèse could not repress a shrug.

"What, father! Did you understand that I meant it to be sarcastic, that those people were hateful to me, that they were revolting to me?... Have you sized them up yourself?... All that Uncle Cyprien tells us is mere childishness in presence of the truth.... Race, blood, nationality—there is much more than these! They are people of a species different from ours, do you hear me, father? All of them, Germans, Prussians, French, English, Italians or what not, they belong to one and the same band, to one tribe, and one that will never be ours.... To think that you, a man in your position.... because this little fool flattered you, coaxed you!"

These last words caused a sharp contraction of his mouth.

"Allow me," he said. "No, no, you must allow me, child.... You are wandering.... You forget somewhat whom you are addressing.... And you must admit that I have the right, with my ripe experience, to tell you that I am perhaps quite as good a judge of people as you are.... You must admit also that, up to the present, I have led my life in a way that gives neither you nor me any cause for blushing. Am I not right?"

Instead of replying, Thérèse affected to glance through the pages of a book. He went on, more softly:

"Believe me, my dear!... You should leave these and other theories to your excellent Uncle Cyprien.... Tell me that you do not like Mme. Chambannes; that her company inspires you with repulsion and mistrust.... Have no fear! If your impressions are justified, I shall be the first to notice it and to regulate my attitude accordingly.... But give up at least this attempt to delude yourself or me; do not transform your personal animosities into social views.... This would be unworthy of you, of your culture, of your intellectual position.... And when all is said, you know it yourself!"

He smiled and gave her a look of appeal.

"Come, give me a kiss!"

The girl approached and offered her forehead. M. Raindal laid a long kiss upon it and pressed her firmly in his arms.

"Huh lah! le laugh!" the master exhorted her, for the face of Thérèse, although now calm, remained inert and dreamy.

Her lips parted in an oblique smile.

"Very good! Perfect!" M. Raindal said, exaggerating the satisfaction he derived from her incomplete grin.

Lunch was a silent affair. M. Raindal avoided his daughter eyes. He was secretly relieved when he heard that she was going to the Library after lunch. He did not ask what she was going for; he preferred her to be away when he left.

Towards 4 lock, he donned a smooth frock-coat and took up a pair of new gloves, whose gray skin stuck to his flesh. He hurried, for fear of missing the omnibus. But he noticed, on reaching the street, that the sidewalk was muddy. He called a cab.

CHAPTER IX

MME. Chambannes was waiting for him in the smoking-room, which had been arranged as a study.

In the center stood a large table, on a dark red carpet. There was an English crystal inkstand, bought for the occasion, Oriental cigarettes in a cup, a notebook bound in morocco and gold, and on each side of the table, an Empire armchair. To the Iris perfume emanating from Zozé was added an aroma of incense which pervaded the house, even to the hall.

Mme. Chambannes took M. Rainda hat and gloves, which he hesitated to deposit on the table.

They sat facing each other and the lesson began.

First of all, M. Raindal dictated a list of books which Zozé was to get.

Mme. Chambannes wrote rapidly, her lips moving a little. The pale rose of the electric lamp left the top of her hair in the shadow; but her clear-cut oval face remained in full light. Powder, spread with a light hand, covered her flesh so artfully that it seemed a natural velvet. Rays of light skimmed it without being reflected, and they touched likewise the soft, thin silk of her afternoon dress. The shades were pale, its pattern indistinct, being covered with a quantity of creamy lace. The white tone of it gave to her face a revived brilliancy of early morning purity. She seemed hardly dressed at all under the ample folds of her robe and as fresh as if she had just emerged from her bath.

She looked up whenever M. Raindal paused. Her watching eyes spread an overflowing tenderness around the master. M. Raindal coughed to cover his discomfort; he brought his forearms and hanging hands closer to his frame and seemed anxious to withdraw further back.

When he had dictated his list, Zozé asked him:

"And now?"

"Now, well, you will have to work, dear lady, and to learn to work alone! In spite of my eagerness to help you, you must realize that there will be weeks when...."

Zozé interrupted him. "I know, my dear master, I know.... They will not be lessons; ... we shall have our little talks ... friendly advice, when you can, when you are free...."

M. Raindal nodded his approval and drew towards himself one of the large volumes of Eber work on Egypt. He turned the pages and pushed the volume towards Zozé whenever he found an illustration or when he had to give an explanation. She bent over the table. The soft curls of her hair sometimes lightly tickled the forehead of M. Raindal. Quickly, he would fall back; and his anxiety amused her. She soon felt ashamed of herself for teasing him and said abruptly:

"Oh! we are very uncomfortable!... Will you allow me, dear master, to sit beside you?"

"Of course, dear lady!"

Nevertheless, they had barely taken up again the study of the engravings when M. Raindal deplored his ready willingness.

Zoz perfume, now so close to him, made him feel dizzy with its effluvia. Whenever she bent down, the light texture of her floating dress released a stronger whiff. But it was no longer iris or violet; it was a sweet, warm odor like the scent of fruit, the live perfume of her flesh, married to that of the scent. And M. Rainda comments became muddled.

Of course, he knew that a chosen few possessed the gift of radiating a delightful fragrance through their epidermis. Several personages of antiquity were thus favored; there was, notably Cleopatra, according to a papyrus found at Boulaq, and quoted by M. Raindal in his book; Plutarch was no less precise concerning the skin of Alexander.

But, in recollecting these facts, and other similar instances, the master was but increasing the confusion of his ideas. He vainly groped for words. Each time that the perfume struck his nostrils, he pinched them shyly, as if they were threatened with a poisonous gas. He often remained speechless before a picture, unable to complete his interpretation of it. Absentmindedly, he dreamed of Alexande skin and the flesh of Cleopatra; he wished also that Zozé would not keep her gilded armchair so close to his.

"One word, may I say one tiny word, if I am not disturbing you?"

Mme. de Marquesse it was who made this appeal; she merely slipped between the hanging portières her profile with its powerful chin and the one white-gloved hand that held the curtain back.

"Come in, dear!" Mme. Chambannes said.

The two women kissed each other. M. Raindal saluted Mme. de Marquesse, and casually noticed that she wore a blue coat and skirt, black-braided and with a girth about the hips like a riding-habit. They begged his permission and retired to the next drawing-room. M. Raindal sighed deeply. Now that he found himself in calm solitude he suddenly lost all his anxiety. His impression was one of hidden pleasure, danger overcome and flattering mystery. In this new mood, he would even have thought it not unpleasant if his colleagues of the Academy had seen him in this luxurious room and near two such charming persons who treated him with so much respect. He was standing before the mirror, smoothing down his beard, his lower jaw brought forward, when the ladies returned.

Mme. de Marquesse wished to go. Zozé gracefully stood in her way, her arms stretched across the portière in a Sarah Bernhardt attitude.

"No! not yet!... Am I not right, dear master? Mme. de Marquesse cannot go like this?"

M. Raindal agreed silently. Zozé rang the bell and had port wine and biscuits brought in. The latter had a taste of vanilla for which M. Raindal showed great partiality. Mme. Chambannes wrote down for him the address of the confectioner who sold them. Mme. de Marquesse pretended to know a better brand. Each of the two praised her own dealer. The port wine had enlivened them—and, laughingly, forefingers stretched out, they taxed each other with appalling cases of *gourmandise*. They called upon the master to act as referee but he gallantly declined. The argument made him laugh—and also the port wine, for he had drunk two glasses in quick succession, and his temples were warming up.

"Well, we are forgetting our work!" Zozé exclaimed suddenly.

Before M. Raindal had time to word a reply, the curtain was once more drawn aside. A bald, corpulent ecclesiastic, who seemed to be in his fifties and wore a broad smile under his broad spectacles, advanced slowly into the room.

"Ah! it is you, my dear abbé!" Zozé exclaimed in a tone which showed so much sincere surprise that it was hard to guess whether the pries visit had been planned beforehand or brought about by mere hazard.

She introduced the men to each other:

"M. bbé Touronde, director of the Villedouillet orphanage, our neighbor in the country and one of our best friends ... M. Raindal...."

The master bowed with the ceremonious affectation he always showed in order to dissimulate his aversion towards those of the cloth.

Respectfully, the abbé asked, with a slight Southern accent:

"M. Raindal, the author of the *Life of Cleopatra*?"

"Quite so!" Zozé confirmed.

The abbé Touronde congratulated him profusely. He was not acquainted with the book itself, but had read enough accounts of it in the newspapers, to speak of it freely. He praised the master upon some particular chapters. M. Raindal thanked him with modest gestures of his hand as if he were fending off the compliments.

But the abbé went on, in a slightly droning voice. The book appealed to him all the more because he was no stranger to its subject matter. He had once studied Egyptian history thoroughly for a brochure he was preparing concerning the sect of the United Coptic Church. He had, moreover, published in the *Annals of Christian Archeology*, two articles dealing with the Hagiographs of the Thebaid. M. Raindal confessed he had not read them; and the abbé volunteered "if it were not too indiscreet" to send the issues of the periodical that contained them.

His head was oval yet chubby, all flesh, as it were, but for a crown of brown hair around his baldness. M. Raindal thought he had a good-natured smile. Gradually the master thawed out. He imparted to the abbé some picturesque details concerning the Thebaid which, from professional instinct, he had explored. The priest listened studiously, showed him deference and solemnly nodded from the back of his head. Zozé took advantage of a pause to ask:

"You will stay for dinner, M. bbé?"

"Well, yes, madame," he replied without hesitation, his round cheeks distended in a cordial smile. "Yes, surely, if you will have me!"

"And you, dear master?" Zozé pursued. "Will you join the party?"

"Oh, it is impossible, dear lady," M. Raindal sighed. "I am expected.... Believe me, I am very sorry...."

He ceased abruptly as Chambannes entered, wearily caressing his thick hinge-like mustache. Everyone stood up. He shook hands with M. Raindal and asked, patting Zoz neck, as one might do to a school-girl:

"Well, how did the lesson go, my dear sir?... Are you satisfied with your pupil?"

"Very much gratified, monsieur ... an excellent beginning."

"Oh, we have not accomplished very much!" Zozé said. "But you are coming next Thursday!... Thursday, I shall forbid the door.... I shall be at home to no one.... You promise to come, do you, dear master?"

M. Raindal promised. Zozé and Germaine went with him into the drawing-room and the latter left with him. They shook hands as they parted, Mme. de Marquesse pulling his arm so sharply that he felt a cramp in the shoulder. He looked at his watch under a lamp-post. It was a quarter to seven.

"Sapristi!" he murmured, horrified.

And once more he hailed a cab.

The boldness of fear moved him to anticipate irony or unwelcome queries by an affectation of jovial talkativeness.

In a light vein, he told of his visit as if it had been a séance at the Institute or a lecture at the Collège de France. He multiplied the details, described the dresses and even gave an imitation of the abb southern accent.

Thérèse affected to be interested and replied with good humor; she seemed to have forgotten the mornin quarrel.

Mme. Raindal was silent. Why should she protest? Why should she wish to dissuade her husband from this fatal intercourse with people devoid of religion? Did she not know that he was irrevocably damned, marked beforehand, because of his own atheism, for eternal torments? She remembered, moreover, the maste anger at the occasion of the Chambannes' dinner party: it was still alive in her mind and closed her mouth with wise caution.

She only allowed herself a frown when M. Raindal gave a parody of the abbé; her pained expression made Thérèse laugh so much that her father began to have his suspicions concerning her good-natured remarks.

This gayety of hers, this sweetness—were they truly frank? Was not Thérèse laughing at him? M. Raindal examined her furtively; then, waxing cautious, brusquely cut short his narrative.

He was more reserved the next Thursday. He barely mentioned his visit to the rue de Prony more than to transmit Zoz compliments to the ladies; and the following Thursday, he said nothing at all.

On the fourth Thursday, towards half past six, a telegram-card from M. Raindal was received in the rue Notre-Dame-des-Champs. He asked his family not to expect him, as he was detained by the gracious entreaties of Mme. Chambannes. Under his signature, Zozé had written in her large handwriting: *Approved*.

To be quite frank, when M. Raindal had left home that day, he was not altogether unaware that he would not return for dinner, since he had, on his last visit, almost promised to be the guest of his pupil for the following Thursday. Nevertheless, he had done his best beforehand to consider this escapade as if it were to be an impromptu, which he had no cause to expect.

It was Thérèse who opened the message. She read it, shrugged her shoulders and threw it into the fire.

"What is it?" Mme. Raindal asked, coming in at that moment.

Thérèse replied sarcastically.

"A telegram from father who is staying over there to dinner!"

Over there! At these words the two women instinctively exchanged glances. Then, at once, seeing her mothe alarmed expression, Thérèse bent down over her notes. What was the use of saying more? They had never had any possible communion of the spirit; they had never formed against M. Raindal one of those little jocular alliances of the kind that amused the master and his daughter at the expense of Mme. Raindal! Bah! she must needs perforce resign herself to a solitary enjoyment—alone as usual, alone as she was everywhere—of the humorous side of this adventure!

"So, he is dining there?" the old lady repeated disconsolately.

"Yes, mother; as I told you!" Thérèse replied impatiently.

"And you think he will go there every Thursday?"

"I do know."

In the same vexed tone, Mme. Raindal went on:

"Oh! mon Dieu, mon Dieu!... I do hope these Chambannes will bring him into no danger!... Tell me, you ... do you think you could say something to him?..."

"Say *what* to him?"

"Tell him ... tell him ... to take care, for instance, not to entangle himself too deeply.... Dear, you know better than I do how to speak to him.... You are ... you are better friends!"

With this veiled reproach the old lady complained unwittingly of her isolation, of her life-long relegation with her God, and her fears moved the heart of Thérèse.

"Listen!" she said more affectionately.... "Listen to me, mother! I assure you that there is as yet no danger.... Therefore, do worry before there is any need to.... And if yol believe me, let us meet father with pleasant faces; we must tease him.... I know him; we would only succeed in pushing him still deeper into the intimacy of those people."

"And later?..."

"Later?... we shall see. We shall discuss it together and find out what is best under the circumstances."

"Then you are willing that I should talk with you now and then about...."

She hesitated.

"Well ... of this ... of this affair?"

Thérèse rose to kiss her mother and held her tightly.

"Of course, dear mother!... You are so funny!... Why not?"

A tear rolled down the cheek of Mme. Raindal.

"I do know.... You have such a wicked air, you and your father ... sometimes, each at your desk, with never a word for me when I come in.... Upon my word I am afraid of you both!"

And she left, taking short, weary steps, to warn Brigitte in time.

At the same time, Mme. Chambannes, to please M. Raindal, was giving him the names of her guests.

"I assure you, dear master; it will be absolutely among ourselves.... My Uncle and Aunt Panhias, our friend, young M. de Meuze, and perhaps the abbé Touronde...."

She had hardly said his name when the latter entered the smoking-room.

He evinced great pleasure at meeting M. Raindal. Behind his spectacles, his eyes shone with joy. Zozé started them in conversation and ran out to dress.

"Yes," M. Raindal said politely, "your articles seemed to me excellent, well thought out, replete with learning.... I am surprised—should I admit it?—that with this obvious gift for science, you have not made a, what shall I say? a more voluminous, more considerable literary output...."

"Oh, dear master, you are too indulgent, too ... too kind!..." the abbé stammered, his voice quivering with satisfaction.

He then justified himself eloquently for his lack of literary production. Could anyone rightly charge him with being lazy? No, his sterility was due to other causes. First of all, there was the orphanage which required his assiduous, daily care, care of all sorts, financial as well as moral, literary as much as administrative. Then, there were his enemies, his numberless enemies who, had he published more works, would not have failed to discover in that fact a new motive for calumny, as they found some in every act of his, even the most virtuous, even the most innocent!

For there was no doubt about it, the abbé was, alas, the most calumniated priest of Seine-et-Oise. All the parties hated him! They all rivaled in ill-using him, in bringing him into discredit. Under the pretext that he was sought for at the neighboring châteaux—that of Mme. Chambannes, for instance, the Château des Frettes—the radicals of the region accused him before the prefect of carrying on a reactionary propaganda. On the other hand, anonymous denunciations poured in at the bisho palace, and they bore the clerical hall-mark. They asserted that the abbé Touronde compromised daily—here the abb voice was lowered and became confidential—the supereminent dignity of his cloth in worldly frivolity and association with heretics.

"Heretics!" the priest repeated with indignation. "Hah! can I pick and choose? Can I ask the donors for their regular baptism certificate? Should I decline the money of the Israelites who help me bring up my children?... Poor little things! Were it not for them, Heaven knows that the world, mundane frivolities, would not see much of me...."

He paused suddenly, as if he had heard the voice of his own conscience:

"Yes, yes, Bastien Touronde, you would still go there, because you enjoy good dinners, the sight of pretty women, luxury and comfort, and also because in the midst of this society, which knows little of dogmas, you are aware that your presence among the temptations causes much less scandal than it would elsewhere...."

And the abb lips whispered softly, as they did on his visits to the bishop, when Monseigneur blamed him for his worldly behavior:

"Non culpabiliter! non culpabiliter!"

"I beg your pardon?" said M. Raindal, who had listened only with half an ear to these long complaints.

The abbé Touronde started.

"I was thinking of these bad men, dear master. In my own mind I was abusing them.... You know, we of the South, we are warm-blooded and our tongue is not always sufficiently Christian!..."

The return of Mme. Chambannes, followed by her Uncle and Aunt Panhias, brought the dialogue to an end. The introductions were made. Panhias was in evening clothes with a black tie. His head hung down, like that of a thinker, but the expression was that of a gray-headed bookkeeper. His gait, the way he stood and the folds of his bearded face showed the fatigue of one of those office clerks to whom money has come too late. Mme. Panhias, on the other hand, seemed optimistic and jovial. She wore a brown silk dress tightly stretched around her ample shape. She rolled her *r*'s more than Mme. Chambannes did, and only a connoisseur could have perceived the Oriental in her, through her semi-Spanish, semi-South-American accent.

A few minutes later Gerald and, behind him, George Chambannes entered the smoking-room. Both were in evening dress. Instinctively M. Raindal lowered his eyes to examine his own frock coat. The butler announced that Madame was served and the party went into the dining-room.

The dinner was cordial and merry. M. Raindal felt no longer the shyness and the self-consciousness of an unwelcome stranger which had made him stiff at first. From so much intercourse with the Chambannes, he had become familiar with the names of their relations, the ways of the house and the tastes of the guests. In consequence, there were very few conversations in which he now hesitated to take his share owing to discretion, fear of a faux-pas or ignorance of the subject. Nothing seemed to trouble him any more. The ogling and the perfume of Mme. Chambannes now proved to be nothing more than stimulants to his ready tongue. They addressed each other as comrades, with a slight touch of fatherly superiority on the part of M. Raindal and of willing submissiveness on that of Mme. Chambannes. Even Chambannes made use, when he spoke to the master, of such turns of speech as were reserved as a rule for old friends. How different from the first dinner, when M. Raindal had felt himself so awkward and slow in recovering his heartiness. When Uncle Panhias admitted, absent-mindedly or under the effect of the wines, that Smyrna was his native town, the master almost congratulated him! Smyrna, the pearl of Tonia, was an exquisite city; its Greek name meant myrrh or incense, the perfume beloved of the gods. He never stopped until dessert was served, praising the city, supporting his theory with anecdotes and historical reminiscences. Aunt Panhias thanked him with enthusiastic replies that were to each of his sentences as the rolling of a drum.

When they went to the smoking-room, Zozé asked M. Rainda leave to light a cigarette. Then, by slow degrees, she went over to Gerald. He had let himself fall down on the divan and was sending spirals of smoke to the ceiling through his pouting lips. She sat beside him and asked coaxingly:

"What are you making a face for?"

He did not reply at first but, after a while, he grunted. "Is this kangaroo going to be here often?"

Zozé suppressed a smile.

"I do know! I hope you are not jealous."

Gerald sneered contemptuously.

"Jealous!... Well.... No!... But he does bore me somewhat!... Your little friend is too fond of hearing himself talk."

He rose and joined Chambannes, who was pouring himself a glass of brandy in front of the liqueur cabinet.

M. Raindal was unconsciously gratified when he saw their conversation ended. He was taking careful stock of "young M. de Meuze," as Zozé had termed him; young Gerald was in the light of a lamp over which he bent in order to relight his cigar. Well, he was not so very young, in spite of appearances! The light now revealed at the corners of his eyes, of his lips and of his nostrils, through his still firm, youthful face, undefined lineaments, the colorless signs of forthcoming lines; and the veins were beginning to stand out on his temples.

This put M. Raindal in good humor, a feeling that confused him, since he had pretentions to generosity and magnanimity. Was it any reason, because M. de Meuze did not bestow admiring glances upon him, because the ma face had worn a constant expression of bored peevishness, to rejoice in these signs of the fatal decrepitude which advancing years....

Mme. Chambannes interrupted him in the midst of this return to fairness.

"Tell me, dear master!... What about our great visit to the Louvre?"

Alas, they must give up the idea of it for this week, as they had had to the previous weeks for a month, the "great" visit had been put off from week to week. Zoz every day was taken up. They finally decided to wait and settle upon the date at the next lesson. The conversation turned to less serious subjects. Aunt Panhias, as if she were relieved from a professional secret, let herself go on the subject of Smyrna. Fearing to fall asleep, M. Raindal withdrew at eleven. Downstairs, Mme. Chambannes asked him to invite the ladies on her behalf; would they join him and come to dinner on the forthcoming Thursday? He thanked her profusely but, once he was in the street, he could not repress the annoyance which this difficult mission caused him.

"What an idea!" he said to himself.... "Ah, yes, how easy *that* will be!"

He delayed risking the attack for three days; and as soon as he ventured to broach it, the two sharp refusals cut his words short. A rush of blood colored his brow. Of course they agreed; their joint refusal was only a concerted maneuver, a deceitful manifestation of disapproval.

He retorted scornfully:

"Very well! As you please!... Nevertheless, I have no intention of being a party to your fancies!... I give you warning; I shall go alone...."

Neither of them took up his challenge. He renewed it on the Thursday morning but obtained no further reply. His anger prompted him to leave the house at three, an hour earlier than usual. He had donned his evening clothes and, because his dress tie showed in the opening of his overcoat, a few gazers turned round to look at him. This increased his displeasure. He hurried on and arrived half-an-hour too soon. Conversely, and quite against her custom, Mme. Chambannes was half-an-hour late. He waited a whole hour in the smoking-room while daylight gradually faded. The servants had forgotten to turn on the lights. M. Raindal, daring neither to ring for them, nor to tamper with the electric lamps, remained in darkness. Bitter and violent ideas harassed him. Why were Thérèse and Mme. Raindal embittered against the Chambannes? What was it they had on their minds against these people? What did they say of him when he was away? His fury was exasperated by the venomous sting of these queries.

"You here, in the dark, dear master!... Is it possible? I am late, am I not?... Do you forgive me?"

At the same time that he heard her affectionate voice, the room was flooded with light. Mme. Chambannes came in, muff in hand, her veil drawn up above her eyebrows. Her dainty little nose was pink at the tip, owing to the cold weather outside—or perhaps to the recent caresses. She renewed her apologies and threw on a chair her sable coat and her flowery hat, in which two hatpins vibrated an instant. Then she declared:

"Do you know, master.... I have an idea, a new combination.... Let me tell it quickly!... At five lock, we are forever being disturbed.... First it is one; then it is another who drops in and, between you and me, we do nothing of any value...."

M. Rainda face was serene once more; he nodded his benevolent approval.

"Well, then, here is my idea.... We could fix the hour of the lesson for six.... W work from six to seven ... and yo stay to dinner every Thursday.... Are you willing?"

M. Raindal had a rapid vision of Thérèse, with the sarcastic smile, and the contemptuous tightening of her thin lips with which she would receive the news of this new arrangement. A longing came over him to defy her, to have his revenge on her and to reduce her silent irony with an audacious coup. He coughed, seemed to debate with himself, and finally said in a clear voice:

"Well, yes, that suits me.... It is agreed, dear Madame!"

But a remnant of caution made him add:

"Unless, of course, anything unforeseen occurs, unless there is some major impediment."

Mme. Chambannes pouted reproachfully.

"Oh, dear master, it is very wrong to lay down conditions!... Are you not free, absolutely free?... Do you think that your little pupil would wish to encroach upon your occupations?"

"Your little pupil!"... How sweetly she had said that! M. Raindal was moved and apologized for himself; then he apologized equally for the ladies. Zozé did not seem offended by their defection. Had she not gained something that would console her? She was saving one hour for her dressmakers, for social calls and for Gerald, and this without losing the maste friendship. Only within herself, she thought:

"Oh! this Mlle. Raindal is getting on my nerves."

From that day, M. Raindal was the guest of the Chambannes every Thursday.

Towards five lock he slipped on his evening clothes or a frock-coat, according to his inclination, since Zozé had left him free to dress as he pleased. He then hailed a cab and arrived in the rue de Prony at six. He stopped on his way usually at a florist and bought two or three large roses, some orchids, a very large bunch of violets or early lilac and offered them to Mme. Chambannes, whom he knew to be very fond of rare flowers. She thanked him chidingly, placed the flowers in a vase or, if they were short, kept them in her hand. Then the lesson would begin.

It was usually regulated according to certain points raised haphazard by Mme. Chambannes. The master replied with ingenuity, illustrating the past with facts from contemporary life, smoothing it over, thinning it down to the precise dimensions of his little pupi brains. Zozé smelled the flowers as she listened to him, or arched her eyebrows in order to accentuate her zeal.

Gradually, however, the teaching turned into a chat. Egypt, its chronology, mysteries and hieroglyphics were put aside. Mme. Chambannes confided to the master her amusements of the past few days or bits of social gossip, or she sketched for his benefit the character of some of her chief women friends. M. Raindal had no curious details to give of his own daily life and went back to the hard times of his youth. Zozé expressed much pity for him because he had greatly suffered from want and opened her tender eyes wide when he told her of certain privations he had undergone.

Sometimes—and this with a persistence which was only worn out one day to reappear the next—she begged M. Raindal to translate the footnotes of his *Life of Cleopatra* for her. Invariably the master refused, alleging that if he did, Mme. Chambannes would be the first to regret his compliance. Moreover, the greater number of the words belonged to what was termed low Latin and were untranslatable.

He felt strangely oppressed when, one night, after dinner, the abbé Touronde called him aside and informed him that Mme. Chambannes had almost succeeded in becoming acquainted with the meaning of the forbidden annotations.

"Would you believe it? The day before yesterday, she asked me if there existed a dictionary of low-Latin! I replied, 'Yes, Madame; there is the

Dictionary of Du Cange.' ... 'Well, my dear abbé, please be so kind as to buy it for me!'... I smelled an evil temptation and replied, with some readiness of wit, I may well say: 'Alas, Madame! it is no longer on sale.... It has been out of print these forty years.' Later she admitted that she wanted it to translate your notes. You will agree that but for me...."

M. Raindal warmly pressed the hand of the cautious ecclesiastic.

Apart from the abbé Touronde, and in accordance with the particular desire of the master, Mme. Chambannes invited only her near relatives on Thursdays, such as her Uncle and Aunt Panhias or the Marquis de Meuze, who had solicited the favor of being a guest at those select dinners.

Gerald was afraid of being bored and scarcely ever attended them. Zozé took pride in this constant abstention, taking it for a symptom of a jealousy she had never hoped to arouse.

Who could have foretold that these conversations, sprung from an idle caprice, a fortuitous inspiration, were to serve, one day, as reprisals against the perpetual coquetry of the young Count! Moreover, these were harmless reprisals and allowed Gerald, at the most, to take lessons from an old lady!... Is there no equality in love, and are not the rights of the one an exact replica of the rights of the other? Zozé, at least, firmly held to this view.

It made her more attached to M. Raindal. He was an ally, as it were, a show accomplice; when her friends asked her, in Geral presence, if her flirtation with her "old savant" still endured, she defended herself with malicious smiles, with a "how silly you are!" or a "leave me alone!" which revealed her joy at the coincidence. How M. Raldo must rage, how much more he must now love her!... Had not caution held her back, she would, at those moments, have kissed him for sheer gratefulness.

Again, the exclusive intimacy with which M. Raindal honored her brought her daily flattering comments. The rumor of it spread among her guests. People talked about it. They questioned Mme. Chambannes touching the maste habits, as if they had been those of a savage she had miraculously tamed. Many women thought this friendship a suspicious one, this craze for learning incomprehensible, this preference on the part of the master unaccountable, and they protested that "there must surely be something behind all this." Others said of Zozé that she was mad, and disparaged M. Rainda personal appearance. The most faithful pleaded and recalled the irreproachable tenderness of the young woman for Gerald. But these arguments left Marquesse shrugging his shoulders and Herschstein humming a hunting air, with this much to add to their skepticism, that the master had twice already declined the pleasure of appearing at their tables. These stories were good enough for women! Facts were still facts. Let the Chambannes pride themselves upon monopolizing père Raindal; nothing was more natural. But to come and tell them that the old man came there for the sake of science, for the love of art, oh! dear no, not to Herschstein or Marquesse! This much, and no more, did they concede to the defense, that they did not specify what the nature of the flirtation was, or its limits.... And yet, one does see such strange things in life! It seemed therefore best to these equitable men to remain on the ground of suppositions and to render no decision.

Zozé was made acquainted with this gossip by Mme. Pums. She replied proudly that she was "above such horrid things." She now neglected the abbé Touronde, who was still the cherished hostage of her set, every member of which vied with the others in pampering him, as if his black robe had been a flag of guaranty and safeguard. She bestowed upon M. Raindal all the delicate attentions and the kind deference she had once shown to the conciliating ecclesiastic. She presented the master, on his birthday, with a gorgeous scarf-pin made up of a turquoise scarab mounted in pale gold. She had thought of this gift as much to please him as in the hope of getting him to give up the narrow black ribbands which he wore as a rule. Her attempt met with success. On the following Thursday M. Raindal wore a wide, dark blue satin scarf enriched in its center with the pale blue turquoise pin.

"You are wearing a very pretty tie!" Zozé remarked during the dinner.

M. Rainda features assumed a modest expression.

"Do you think so?..." he asked.

However, he cared nothing for fashion. He dressed according to the ideas of his tailor—a little tailor of the rue de Vaugirard, whose client he had been for thirty years.

"You are wrong!" Zozé remarked. "Good tailors are not more expensive than bad ones.... Why do you go to Blacks, my husban tailor?"

Chambannes agreed with her. M. Panhias joined them; the master gave in and made an appointment with George to go and order a suit from Blacks.

The tailor was obsequious at first, when Chambannes mentioned the name of M. Raindal of the Institute; he became peremptory and sharp when it came to selecting the material. The master was dashed and dared not oppose him. It was even worse when it came to trying on. M. Raindal did not want any silk facings to his frock-coat. Blacks wished to force him. M. Raindal lost his patience and rebelled. He did not want any facings and he was not going to have any. Blacks bowed with a hypocritical grimace, admitting that every client had his own taste. When, however, the suit was delivered and M. Raindal opened the folds of his new frock-coat, the silk facings struck his eyes with their shining triangles.

The master softly complained of this impudence to his friends the Chambannes. Both laughed exceedingly and said that Blacks was right. M. Raindal was softened by their gayety and fell in with their opinion. Henceforth, Zozé did not hesitate to advise him in the matter of his wardrobe. He obeyed readily, owing alike to his desire to please her and to a craving for refinement which secretly tormented him.

But these accumulated expenses had made a hole in his budget. He increased his deficit every week with such things as cabs, flowers and gloves, and, of course, with such heavier expenses as the order to Blacks. The Académie had finally given him the Vital-Gerbert prize, and this helped him out just on time. He invested only 8000 francs of the 10,000 he received and reserved the balance for unforeseen expenses and pocket money.

At any other time of his life, he would have blushed thus to frustrate his family. But duty is a burden that is best borne by all the parties together. And M. Raindal certainly found a pretext for his egotism in the attitude of his family.

It was not that a state of warfare had been openly declared. Far from it; faithful to their compact, the two women multiplied their concessions in order to preserve the old harmony. Thanks to their efforts, the household had never seemed freer from discord. They vied with each other as to who should most skillfully avoid any allusion, contradiction or motive for disagreement. The master, on his side, fearful of their sarcastic comments, preserved silence concerning his weekly dinners. It had come to this, that the name of Chambannes was never uttered, unless it became necessary; even then, the women wrapped up its syllables with a light intonation, as one rolls explosives in cotton-wool. Whenever M. Raindal formulated unexpected theories upon the public usefulness of luxury, the dangers of puritanism, or the social advantages of pleasure, Thérèse discussed them with him without the slightest bitterness, as if they were matters of economics which bore no relation whatsoever to their daily life. As an additional precaution, she had persuaded Cyprien to renounce his usual jesting comments concerning Mme. Rhâm-Bâhan. The younger Raindal now kept his sallies for his usual audience of one, Schleifmann.

Nevertheless, in spite of this outward appearance of calm and good entente, the master had no longer the feeling of peace and confidence he had felt in his home. He guessed every action and word of his to be spied upon, jeered at and censured either aloud or in low voices. He could hardly contain his anger against this secret, impalpable, yet ever awake, hostility which continuously dogged his movements.

While dreading its outbreak, there were nevertheless days when he could not help wishing for an open dispute, a straightforward attack, a solid and clear-cut family altercation, when each one could cry out his grievances and defend his own cause.

Let them attack him; let them but ask a question and he would know how to exonerate himself! What harm was he doing, anyhow? Was he running from salon to salon, as did so many of his colleagues? Had he taken advantage of his triumph to break into the little literary Bastilles which were the final goal of so many paltry ambitions? Had he not, on the contrary, declined, one after another, all the invitations given him, by Mme. Pums, by Mme. Herschstein, by Mme. de Marquesse, even by ladies of higher social status whom he could name if called upon? Had he not a score of times discreetly urged his wife and daughter to pay the call they owed the Chambannes? Was he not ready to take them to the rue de Prony as often as they could wish? Did he manifest any spite, as so many others might do, for all the deceptions and for the bitterness which Mme. Rainda uneasy religiosity had scattered between them? Did he play the part of a bad husband, a bad father, a frivolous and dissipated man?... Well then, what was it they reproached him with? Why was he compelled to suspect his own family as he had to suspect his own sworn enemies? There was that wretch of a Saulvard, for instance, who carried the rancor of his defeat to the point of declining three successive invitations of Mme. Chambannes.... The entanglement of his worries, added to the silence he imposed upon himself, made him feel disgusted with his own house, his home and everything that he had until then considered as happiness and quiet.

He proved his own innocence to himself so often that doubts came to him at times. He asked himself whether his friendship with young Mme. Chambannes was not such as might cause him some prejudice in the scientific world, whether it might not be more seemly for him to allow more time to pass between his visits, and whether his regularity might not be affording the evil-minded an opening. At once a rebellion which he attributed to pride moved him to smile at such scruples. He derived from his reflections a new energy for the indulgence of his inclination. Throughout the week, he lost no opportunity, whether at the dining-table or elsewhere, to flay the ridicule of pedantry, the hypocrisy of austere people, a whole mass of foibles and of anonymous characters, upon whom, with no less good grounds, Mme. Raindal, Thérèse and Uncle Cyprien might have bestowed their own names as well. Thus came the Thursday, and he made his exit with a provocative, almost bellicose, banging of all the doors in succession.

He reached the Chambannes' house, from the very hall a warm smell of incense caressed him as a first greeting of welcome, and his resentment vanished. Here everyone smiled at him and showed an eagerness to please him, from Firmin, the butler, who took his overcoat and affectionately inquired about his health, to the abbé Touronde, to Aunt Panhias and even the indolent Chambannes himself! Upstairs, Zozé came out to meet him and gave him her hand to kiss. And, during four good hours, M. Raindal forgot his vexations, his family troubles, his little pangs of the past week. Only when it was time for him to go did he remember them. When eleven lock came, he had an impression of melancholy, of an ended happiness, like a boy who must return to college.

Zozé always accompanied him to the hall, saw to it that he covered himself well, told him not to catch cold. As the end of the winter was in sight, she murmured to her husband, once the door was closed:

"Poor old fellow!... All the same, it is a long way to go for a man of his age.... I am glad that spring is coming back."

Whenever the weather permitted it, M. Raindal returned on foot, for the sake of the exercise. The road seemed a long one to him but, as he neared the rue Notre-Dame-des-Champs, he slackened his pace and his steps became less regular. It was as if he wished to delay the moment of regaining his home.

At last he climbed the waxed steps of his staircase; they slipped from under his feet. The walls were as cold as a cellar; they were painted to imitate marble, and the candle threw a gigantic shadow on them. M. Raindal opened the door. Smells of cooking and washing soda caught him at the throat. He crossed the little apartment on tiptoe; the silk lining of his frock-coat rustled against his legs as a last echo of the elegances he had left behind. The mediocrity of his lodging was all the more apparent to him. What poor furniture, what a lack of comfort after the luxury, the ease and all the delicate things which abounded in the rue de Prony! M. Raindal gave a deep sigh and slipped between the sheets, near Mme. Raindal, who snored imperturbably in a twin bed.... Often he left the light on and lay there dreaming, retracing the evening; and his nostalgia vanished as his memories revived.

It returned the next day at the sight of Thérèse in her coarse morning garb, that common, dark dressing-gown which was so different from the soft gowns of Mme. Chambannes.

Ah! M. Raindal understood the severity of the girl towards his little pupil. Envy, alas; of course, it was envy! A jealousy that was incapable of discerning anything in Mme. Chambannes beyond the gaps in her learning and her intellectual poverty—as if erudition meant everything in a woman; as if beauty, elegance, the art of attracting did not also rank among the precious gifts and the powerful faculties. His discovery exalted him to such a point that he felt himself caught in a sudden rush of compassion, instead of mentally reproaching her for the physical disgrace she had suffered which had for some time unwittingly ill-disposed him toward her. He ran to Thérèse and ardently kissed her forehead. She kissed him in return on the cheek, in an attempt at tenderness. But her body was bent back and gave the instant lie to the smile on her lips. There had passed between them an intangible sorcery which prevented their hearts from opening as of old, forbade confidence and precluded the solidarity which had united them as co-workers for so many years....

They went back to their work, resenting their powerlessness to commune with one another again, mutually embittered by the failure of their attempt, cursing each other inwardly for the wrongs which each laid at the othe door. The week started anew in this state of apparent harmony that was heavy with discord.

One night in early March, as mild as a summer night, M. Raindal, returning home from the Chambannes', saw a light in his daughter room.

This made him anxious, for the hour was late; he knocked at the door and entered almost at the same time.

Thérèse was sobbing in her pillow; she had not undressed but lay on her uncovered bed.

M. Raindal rushed forward to help her up, but she did not wait for him. She looked up and rubbed the tears from her eyes. He inquired, still holding her in his arms:

"What is the matter, dearest?... Were you crying? What is the trouble?"

She released herself with a brusque movement of her shoulders:

"Nothing, father! Thanks.... It is nothing.... Leave me alone, please!"

"Then you do not need me?" M. Raindal murmured in surprise.

"No, no, I assure you.... Go away.... I tell you it is nothing at all.... Just my nerves!..."

He dared not insist, for fear of exasperating her; he retired and shut the door behind him with particular care, as if he had left a sick-room.

Nerves!... Hm!... A woma excuse, a veil of sickness with which they cover up the secret of their anger. What could be the matter with Thérèse? What was it that caused her such great pain? Remorse insinuated: "If it were you! Suppose your Thursday visits, your obstinacy were the cause of it!" M. Raindal resolved to probe this to the very bottom, to question Thérèse the very next morning.

But the next day passed without his following up his intention. She was not thinking about it any more. Why should he torment the poor child with questions? Again, it was possible that she had told him the truth. It might have been nerves, after all.

CHAPTER X

NERVES, that sort of "nerves" had been the trouble with Mlle. Raindal for a whole week, as they were each year at the coming of the new season.

When, one evening, a gust of warm breeze swept through the icy air, the breath of advancing spring, her customary seriousness turned to melancholy; and she waited for the inevitable trial of which this perverse breath was the herald.

The universal magic which at that time threw all human beings into confusion always struck her with special vigor. Neither her learning, her reason nor her virile will-power could protect her. She fell a languid prey to aimless fancies, which because of this very confusion, allowed full play to the dreams of a chastity suddenly in revolt. She passed from the most childish transports of tenderness to the most fanciful flights of imagination. Tears of emotion came to her eyes; sometimes she burst into sobs; the perfume of a flower, the tunes of the street-organ below, or a beggar singing an old-fashioned romance in the street caused her heart to be overfilled with sadness and gave her an instinctive desire to lean her head on some robust shoulder.

The times of her weakness were precisely those when her hatred for Mme. Chambannes was strongest and when she was most intolerant towards her father. Their behavior seemed to her more revolting, more absurd, more ludicrous than at other times. She found her consolation in mistaking for contempt the jealousy which their happiness at being together roused in her.

The acute consciousness of her own lack of attractiveness and of her isolation led her to formulating wishes all of which were impossible.

Ah! were she but beautiful; were she simply one of those seductive women over whom a few men disputed among one another and who could choose! That she could be a woman, in short, excite desires, repulse assaults, lead the warring life of her sex instead of turning white in an unnatural existence, busy with mental work and the distractions of the learned!...

Yet, lacking the needed charms, how could she change her life? How could she try to please with her bony hands, discolored eyes and thin lips which had pleased but once and then not more than for eight days?

In her discouragement, she reached a point when she felt jealous of the street girls she met passing the Boulevard Saint Michel, the grisettes. There were times when she would have readily given up everything, her knowledge, her honor and that of her family. She remembered also that there had been women, famous for their wit but too ugly to be loved, who had indulged in clandestine debauchery; and she secretly read over again with a sensual shivering the historians of scandals who related such facts. Sometimes, when she returned home at dusk, she heard a ma footsteps following her. What would he do? Was he going to address her? Although she was sure she would defend herself, yet she felt almost a vain hope that he would.... One evening, in the rue de Rennes, she was emboldened to turn round: she saw an old gentleman of M. Rainda age who smiled at her with knowing grimaces. She hurried away, stumbling, full of rage, deception and disgust with herself.

She found no peace until the day was ended and she slipped into her bedsheets after blowing out her candle. There was to her no more delicious moment than this one. She lay on her back and let the tide of sleep gently come up to her. Her limbs became paralyzed; her thoughts ran into each other; she had a feeling that her body was leaving her and the darkness of night favored this reassuring mirage. Because she no longer saw her own homeliness, Mlle. Raindal gained more audacity. Her soul at last freed and naked, as it were, bravely soared away on the wings of love. Whom, then, did she invoke in her adorations? Albârt? Another man? Sleep carried her away before she could be definite, and during the hours that followed, she stretched herself out, panting in the midst of strange dreams which were forgotten the next morning.

But she measured the nothingness of her days according to the feverish fullness of her nights. She was tortured throughout the mornings with the anxieties that affect old age. When would it all end? Had the valor of her heart, of her reason and of her mind forever vanished? Or would her sorrow gradually wear itself out, as it had done before, for lack of remedies and relief?... These queries filled her with anguish. She held her pillow tight against herself and crushed her lips in it, for fear they might hear her through the door, as on the occasion when M. Raindal had found her sobbing.

One afternoon, at the Bibliothèque Nationale, she was standing before an oak desk, examining the huge folio of the *Corpus inscriptionum aegyptiacarum*, when a shadow suddenly passed over the pages. She looked up and recognized Boerzell, the dismissed suitor, the young Assyriologist of the Saulvard party. Facing her, leaning on the other slope of the desk, he greeted her smilingly.

"How do you do, mademoiselle!" he asked. His affectionate eyes blinked behind the crystal of his glasses. "Hm! It seems to me that you indulge in very frivolous reading!"

"Do I?" Thérèse said, and returned his smile.... "This is nothing to what I have been asking for?"

"What was it?"

She gave him the titles of the books she was awaiting. Boerzell pretended to be indignant and exclaimed that it was sheer robbery and usurpation. Were women now going to meddle with such studies! They talked for a few minutes, in their idyllic attitude, over the desk which was to them as a flowery gate.

At length, Thérèse exclaimed:

"Well, au revoir, monsieur.... They are bringing me my books.... The time for gossiping is past.... I must return to my seat...."

Boerzell had a huge volume under his arm. He bowed and said:

"I hope that we shall soon meet again, mademoiselle!"

"So do I, monsieur!"

Instinctively she watched him walk away, between the rows of readers bent over their tasks.

Without knowing why, she found him less awkward than at the ball, less unpleasant and like one transfigured.

He walked calmly, dropping "a good-day" here and there, pausing for a handshake, delayed an instant for a quick exchange of words; in this favorable atmosphere, he was served by his very disadvantages, by his tousled hair, his ill-cut beard, the shiny cloth of his coat and his careless silhouette which showed that he was a champion of ideas. He benefited from the temporary beauty which comes from ease and authority enjoyed in appropriate surroundings. He was handsome like a high official in his office at the Ministry, handsome like an adjutant at the gate of a military barracks.

"Well! the poor fellow is not so bad!" Thérèse murmured as she returned to her seat.

Then she fell to work and completely forgot him. When she came out, however, going to the checkroom, she heard the voice of Boerzell behind her.

"Yes, it is I, mademoiselle!... Will you allow me to accompany you?... I believe we are neighbors.... I live at the end of the rue de Rennes."

Mlle. Raindal hesitated. It was not that she questioned the propriety of his offer. She had long since disdained petty prejudices that affected such cases; for old maids are as deposed sovereigns who free themselves from etiquette once they have lost their power. On the other hand, she was weighing the point whether Boerzel company would not bore her before they reached the rue de Rennes.

Finally she gave her reply:

"Yes, surely!... I shall be very pleased.... Le go together...."

It was drizzling outside. The streets were shiny; in the narrow rue Richelieu, horses were slipping; they all trotted sidewise as if a strong wind were arching their croups. A few passers-by opened their umbrellas. Boerzell imitated them in order to protect Thérèse. He was bumped into at every step; the ends of the whalebones made lines against the grain of his silk hat. At times they were parted by a pressure from those who walked in opposite direction. Thérèse turned round, looking for the young savant; and she distinguished him, as he smiled over the heads of people, holding his umbrella as high as he could and shaking it to signal to her.

They began to converse with some sequence only after they had passed the door of the Carrousel.

As on the first evening, at the ball, the talk assumed at once a professional turn. But Boerzell it was who now directed the game. He led the conversation towards the notorieties of science; and he gave out his opinion of each of them, in insidious terms. Most of the time, it proved to be sarcastic and disrespectful. He withdrew in one word the commendation he had given in another, mingled restrictions and praise, stinging comments and soft words; even his voice, at once coaxing and clever, the smile of his lips or his eyes with which he softened every expression that was too bitter, his choice of expressions, the turn of his sentences—all these seemed to suggest a proud old master, but had the added zest of youth.

Every now and then, Thérèse could not refrain from glancing at him. What! had he, then, out of calculation, concealed his strength on the evening of the dance; had he affected shyness in order to attract without scaring her? Had he wished to flatter her pride as a savante by allowing himself to be defeated and conquered by her? Or had he been troubled by the surroundings?

Be that as it may, she was enjoying herself. This young man was not a fool, nor was he mediocre, nor yet servile. She listened so attentively that she did not notice that they had passed over the Seine.

They climbed the rue des Saints Pères, where drivers of entangled carriages abused each other. At times an omnibus rocked noisily, and hit the stone curb with its trembling wheels. Mlle. Raindal and Boerzell huddled close to the shops. Then the terrible machine having passed them, they went on again. Now it was Boerzell who asked questions, inquiring of the gir studies, and Mlle. Raindal readily answered, gave him the time-table of her work and the rules of her studies.

When they turned the corner of the Boulevard St. Germain, Boerzell suddenly sighed:

"What a pity!" he murmured.

"What?" Thérèse asked.

The drizzle had ceased and he closed his umbrella.

"Nothing, mademoiselle.... Or rather, yes.... It is a pity that I do not please you more.... Oh! I had guessed that much at the Saulvard ball, even without the help of the silence you preserved afterwards.... I could see it in your eyes when you left.... And yet, believe me if you like, the more I talk to you, mademoiselle, the more I am convinced that we would have made an excellent couple."

This declaration was so unexpected that Thérèse could not repress a sudden laughing exclamation.

"We?" she said.

"Yes, we, quite so, we!..." Boerzell went on, with a pouting movement of his lips which gave a touch of puerility to his bearded childlike face.... "It is useless, is it not, between people of our type, to play a comedy?... They introduced us to each other in order to have us marry. Well, suppose, mademoiselle, that I had pleased you, at that ball...."

He paused to look at her.

"You must understand what this word 'please' means. Of course, I did not hope that you would fall in love with me on the spot.... No.... Thus, you ... you pleased me; that is to say, you inspired me with a deep sympathy.... I thought to myself: 'Here is a worthy lady, one of strong intelligence, a wife such as I would like mine to be, a companion and a friend in whom I could confide, whose advice I could seek, without any fear of meeting with silliness or indifference....' Well, let us suppose that you had thought likewise about it, that would have been enough.... We would have been married and I should be happy."

Thérèse remained silent.

"But, there we are!" Boerzell went on, in a grumbling tone.... "You did not think this way.... I do not please you enough.... Or, to be more exact, I displease you too much.... Yet, allow me to say it without any fatuousness, I am surprised.... If I may judge from our two conversations, we would, intellectually speaking, hit it off very well.... Upon people, and upon things, we almost share the same opinions.... Our lives are cut along the same lines, and occupied with similar studies.... Our tastes and aptitudes agree.... There remains my physical appearance! It is obviously on this ground that you dislike me, and it is precisely such weakness of judgment which surprises me, coming from you.... Ah! if you were one of those little coquettes ... a brainless little woman, one of those worldly dolls...."

"But, monsieur!..." Thérèse protested smilingly.

Boerzell interrupted her, gradually more excited.

"If you please, mademoiselle, allow me to finish.... If, as I say, you were one of those fashionable women without culture, without nobility of character, and as choke-full of prejudices as a stuffed goose is with chestnuts, I would not be surprised.... I know well what my faults are, and all that I lack in order to attract a little woman of this class.... But you, a person of your quality, that you should look upon marriage as these others do, that marriage should be in your estimation a sudden stroke of lightning, a confused heart, an irresistible passion, a handsome man with a mustache and the whole claptrap of romance, I assure you, I cannot get over it! And when I think that we very likely are made for each other, when I think that we met, by an extraordinary chance, that we could form an intelligent sensible, clear-sighted union, and that we are not doing it, see, that almost rouses me to anger!"

He struck the pavement with his umbrella.

"Are you through?" Thérèse asked anxiously.

"Yes, mademoiselle!" he replied distractedly.

But he recanted at once.

"There is but one case in which your repugnance would appear to me logical and justified, worthy of you, in a word!... That would be if, by chance, you loved another man...."

Mlle. Raindal suddenly darkened. The lord of her existence surged again before her; Albârt, with his impudent smartness, his big, horse-like eyes and his ironical lips. Thérèse took in the young savant with a disdainful look and replied, her voice lowered by a sudden sadness:

"I love no one, monsieur!... Or, if you prefer, I am in love with a memory...."

"A memory!" Boerzell stuttered, all out of countenance.... "Ah, very good!... That is another thing.... I crave your pardon, mademoiselle."

The silk of his hat was turned back; his thick lips, like those of a sea-god, were rounded into a ball and he wore such a disappointed, baffled and childish look that, despite the gravity of the circumstance, Thérèse found it difficult not to smile.

"You see, monsieur!" she said heartily, "you were mistaken, if not as to my intentions, at least concerning the root of my feelings.... To prove to you that I find pleasure in your society, I ask you, if you care to, to come every now and then to see us on Sundays, as a colleague, as a friend; and I should be delighted...."

"Thank you, mademoiselle," Boerzell said without enthusiasm. "Certainly, I shall come on Sundays.... Now it is unfortunate, however, that you have such ... do not take offense ... such accepted ideas, the ideas of everybody on the subject of marriage!... The dictates of the heart and love count, I admit, for much ... but they are not the only feelings in life!... Besides love, there exist sentiments of affinity, of sympathy and mutual consideration which can establish very strong links between two human beings who are all independent and superior."

He noticed the darkening brow of Thérèse.

"Well, I do not intend to importune you any further, mademoiselle.... That would be poor return for your kind invitation.... If, then, you will permit it, I say, 'until next Sunday.'"

"Until next Sunday!"

Thérèse turned into the rue Notre-Dame-des-Champs. Halting words called her back.

"It is I again, mademoiselle!" Boerzell said, running up to her.... "There was one last word I forgot to say.... It is possible that you have suspected an interested motive...."

With a gesture of the hand, Thérèse denied that she had.

"It does not matter!" Boerzell retorted. "I would not, for anything in the world, be mistaken for one of the young gentlemen who seek a fine marriage, a useful marriage.... Moreover, you should consult M. Raindal.... He will tell you himself that my scientific life is, to use the current expression, all marked out.... My professors like me and help me.... My competitors are few and are, most of them, but second-rate men.... From the École des Hautes Études, I am therefore bound to enter the Sorbonne or the Collège de France, and thence, I hope, the Institute.... A marriage with you would certainly not have been unhelpful.... Nevertheless, without this marriage my career, happiness apart, will be the same.... This was what I wished to say.... You will agree with me that, for the sake of our future friendship, these details have their importance!"

"They might have perhaps, if I had doubted you...."

"Phew!" the young savant said with skepticism. "You say this.... You are polite.... It remains a fact that one cannot be too cautious in such matters.... But I am delaying you, excuse me.... Until Sunday, mademoiselle...."

"That is agreed!" said Thérèse, in a tone that already showed comradeship.

When she entered the study where M. Raindal sat talking with her Uncle Cyprien, the latter welcomed her with a volley of compliments:

"Pristi! My nephew!... How well we are looking! And such shining eyes! Gayety all over your face! I could swear that you have not spent an altogether boring afternoon!"

"So it looks!" M. Raindal approved shyly.

"Well, it may be so ..." Thérèse replied.... "Guess whom I met? Little Boerzell. You remember him, father? The would-be fiancé at the Saulvard party.... A very strange young man; he has a whole series of theories and systems which amused me.... I am still laughing now.... Well, I asked him to visit us and he will probably come next Sunday!"

"You did quite right, dear!" M. Raindal asserted, as much in order to conciliate Thérèse as because of a mania he had to praise his inferiors.... "M. Boerzell is a young man with a rare future.... Everybody at the Académie holds him in high esteem.... It was only yesterday that someone was telling me...."

"What about you, uncle?" Thérèse interrupted. "It is my turn to ask you questions! Can you tell me what you are doing here, on a week day, a Wednesday, and at the sacred hour of the apéritif!"

"To begin with," the younger M. Raindal objected ... "it is not more than half past five.... The apéritif lasts normally until half past seven.... I have therefore, mademoiselle, two good solid hours, if you please.... Now, you want to know why I am here. Hah, nephew, this rouses your curiosity! Well, I came to ask your father to take me to Mme. Chambannes."

Thérèse bit her lips to repress a smile.

"Yes," Uncle Cyprien continued, rubbing his close-cropped hair. "It was an idea that occurred to me ... a matter of curiosity!..."

"And I was telling your uncle," M. Raindal put in rapidly, and without looking at Thérèse, "that I was quite ready to take him there, whenever he wished...."

"Why not to-morrow, Thursday?" Uncle Cyprien inquired.

M. Raindal hid under a short laugh a sigh that came to his lips.

"Hm! Hm! To-morrow, that is rather sudden.... I must have time to inform Mme. Chambannes.... Especially since her husband left last night on a journey."

"Ah! on a journey!... Where to?..." Cyprien asked.

"To Bosnia, I believe."

"Bosnia!... Ah, really, to Bosnia!" the younger Raindal repeated, in order to memorize this particularity or to discover therein a piece of probable evidence.

He said resolutely:

"Well, write at once to Mme. Chambannes.... Two lines, two simple lines.... I shall drop your letter in the box when I go.... She will have it the first thing to-morrow morning ... and if she does not want me...."

"Oh! very well!" M. Raindal said coldly, as he took up his pen.

But he added, before writing a word: "Nevertheless, I give you fair warning.... You may perhaps meet at Mme. Chambannes' house some people who are not to your taste...."

"Who may they be?"

"I do know for certain.... Let me see, there may be the abbé Touronde, a friend of the family...."

This revelation caused Uncle Cyprien to forget himself. What! Madame Rhâm-Bâhan had an abbé, a curé, a black-robed one! Ah! that was really pretty good! What morals! What a century! What a muddle! And Uncle Cyprien laughed outright.

He only calmed down when Thérèse gave him a severe look to remind him of his promises.

"I am laughing," he declared, "I am laughing, because ... you understand...."

He gave up the explanation.

"I laughed without malice.... You may rest assured that if I meet the abbé Tour... Tour what?—well, never mind!—I shall make myself agreeable ... most agreeable.... Go on, write, my dear fellow!"

Thérèse was exhausted. A mad impulse to laugh was overcoming her. Under the pretext of going to look for a pamphlet, she went to her room and ran to her armchair, bursting out in guffaws.

"Poor father!... What a woeful face! And my uncle wants to join the band now!... Ah! life is really funny!"

She was in a jocular mood, ready to find everything amusing and grotesque; at heart, she had an impression of being at last cured and delivered from the crisis. She had a spontaneous feeling of gratitude for Boerzell. Was it not to a certain extent to this worthy young man that she owed this miracle? Had he not consoled her, distracted her, as if she had been a weeping child, with the sparkle of his conjugal thesis, the unusualness of his speeches and the insistent warmth of his voice? But for him, for that blend of comic and sound reason which emanated from his person and which now survived their conversation, she would probably still be desperately fighting the fever of evil, and exhausting herself in the dangerous nightmares of her unsatisfied desires. Could she have been, but for Boerzell, even amused by the worldly ambitions of her uncle, or by his sly waggery, or by anything at all? Poor Boerzell! She could never bring herself to accept him, to overcome the repulsion which his bearded old schoolbo face inspired in her. Nevertheless, who knew but that he might help her in the hours of her distress, might become a friend, a faithful comrade who would render her solitude less mournful, less forsaken?

She walked up and down her room, working herself up with such hopes. Brigitte had to knock twice at the door before she could inform her that dinner was served.

CHAPTER XI

"HIS brother ... M. Rainda brother!" Mme. Chambannes murmured dreamily, leaning on the edge of her bed. Her lace-edged pillow made a soft frame for her scattered curls. Distractedly she gathered together the rest of her mail. There was an advertisement of a perfume house, a modist bill which she thrust aside with a disgusted pout, two newspapers and, under them, a closed letter-card. It was a strange card; the address was written in awkward capitals falling over each other—the suspicious appearance of an anonymous letter! Zozé tore it open slowly. Sensations of weakness vibrated along her arms. She read the following lines, traced on the gray paper in characters similar to those on the outside:

Should you have nothing better to do some morning, pass, towards 11 lock, the rue Godot-De Mauroi, in the neighborhood of number 12 bis; you will once more ascertain that the friends of our lady-friends are our friends.

She fell back, one hand over her heart as if to shield a wound; she had not a doubt, felt no hope. She remained motionless at first, her eyes closed; then she began to stammer indistinctly.

"Oh!... oh!... oh! mon Dieu!... The wicked people! What an atrocious wickedness!"

A burning sensation was in her heart, and every query she invented, every possibility seemed a new burn that made her wound deeper.

They were denouncing Gerald, of course; but the woman, the mean wretch, the unknown betrayer—who could she be?

Zozé called to her mind in turn the names of all her friends but she could not lay the guilt on any special one. All seemed equally suspicious to her. Gerald had indulged in equivocal flirtations and familiar gestures with them all in turn; in each of them she now successively thought, according to her memories, that she held the accomplice. Then came the names of others who seemed more guilty, Flora Pums after Germaine de Marquesse, Rose Silberschmidt after Flora Pums. In the end she was altogether confused, the accumulation of equivalent proofs and contradictory presumptions. She made an attempt at finding a clue by seeking to guess at the name of the writer. Names surged to her mind, names of men who desired her and who might have been capable of wishing to destroy her happiness: Pums, Burzig, Mazuccio. It would surprise her were this infamous action to come from either of these. She realized how easily she suspected them all, men and women, and a sudden bitter grimace caused her lips to contract. Phew! In what company of cads and harlots was she living then, since none of them could be free from her mistrust, since she had not once been afraid of wrongly accusing any of them? This sudden clearsight passed, however, like lightning and was clouded at once by her foaming anger. The little Mouzarkhi had no time for philosophy! She exaggerated the tone of her insults, like one in the delirium caused by disillusion; she had no love left, no tenderness, no illusion for anyone but Gerald, her beloved Gerald whom she was perhaps going to lose forever! Tears veiled her eyes. With anguish she visualized through their mist the inconceivable parting scene! She thought of herself, in the rue guesseau, on the threshold of the apartment, after the final explanation. She was turning back for a last glance at him. She came back once more to kiss him!... Oh, no, no! She did not want to see him any more; and a rushing terror caused her to draw the light linen sheet over her face. Convulsive sobs shook her sinuous form, which was plainly discernible under this burial-sheet. Suddenly she heard the clock on her mantelpiece striking ten and, with a more violent start, she threw back the coverings, jumped out of bed and rang nervously.

"Quick! hot water in the dressing-room.... My tailored costume of brown cloth.... My black coat!..." she said to the maid who came in at her call.

"What corset?"

"I do know! Any one!... Hurry up, that is all, hurry up, hurry up!"

"Does madame want a carriage?"

"Yes, tha it! A closed carriage ... or, rather, no! No carriage.... Hurry up!"

A bellicose haste speeded her on. She must be ready in time. She was rushing towards this supreme torture: to surprise the guilty ones as if it were a matchless joy; her nostrils vibrated, a savage smile lurked in the corner of her lips and her eyes shone with eagerness.

She was out at a quarter of eleven. She walked up the rue de Prony and crossed the parc Monceau. A gardener was removing the narrow sheathes of straw from round the exotic trees. The budding foliage spaced their masses which still admitted daylight; it had not lost its very pale green tints; a fresh perfume rolled softly on the breeze. The contrast of this riot of the elements saddened Zozé. She opened her sunshade, for the sun was already hot; as she walked she uttered long regretful whispers as if she were never again to see these graceful lawns nor breathe the balmy air.

She made an effort to stiffen herself against the softening reverie and called a passing closed cab:

"Listen carefully," she ordered the driver. "We are going to the rue Gaudot-de Mauroi.... When I knock on the glass, you are to stop ... not to move again.... You will keep your seat and wait.... If I knock twice, you are to start again, slowly.... If I knock three times, you start at a trot.... Do you understand?"

"Yes, Madame!" the driver said paternally. He was fat and wore a moustache; the mystery of the affair and her young captai tone amused him.

"Very well then, start!... There will be a good tip for you!"

The carriage went down the avenue de Messine.

As she approached the point of attack, Zozé saw her ardor weakening. She felt as if she were choking under heavy blows on her chest; then she fancied that her heart had become a poor little bird, and a brutal hand squeezed it. She kept her eyes closed, so as not to count the houses which were passing too fast.

A sudden motion caused her to open them again. The carriage turned into the rue Godot-de Mauroi. Zozé was barely in time to knock on the window pane. The driver stopped outside No. 9. From there, she could see diagonally No. 12 *bis*, an old house, whose gray façade merged into similar ones. But, above the door, two yellow signs proclaimed that small apartments were to let.

"Here it is!" thought Zozé with a distressful sigh. She looked at her watch and saw that it was five minutes after eleven. She put up the windows so as to hide her face behind their mock transparency. She huddled in the left-hand corner, aggressively facing No. 12 *bis* and began to look.

A quarter of an hour passed. Green-vegetable-hawkers cried their wares and pushed their heavy barrows in the silent, half-deserted street. At intervals, the cab-horse shook himself with a bored shiver that rocked the shafts; or the driver made a movement which set the harness rustling and the wood creaking. Zozé perceived these noises no more clearly than she noticed the neighboring shop, the passers-by who paused to look at her or the saddler opposite, whose face was bent down over his work behind a glass window. Invisible blinkers kept her eyes fastened ahead, as did the anxious attention which kept her body stiff, toward the small square of stones where the lovers would appear.

What were they saying now to each other, in what abject caresses were they swooning, on what floor were they, near which of these windows? Her memories helped her somewhat to visualize Gerald. But the woman escaped her. She guessed all of the perfidy, her waist, her nakedness, her breast and her arms, she could see everything but the head, all but the face! She was as one struggling in one of those terrible nightmares, when the features of one of the participants are dissolved and vanish as soon as one attempts to distinguish them.

A nearby clock announced the half hour. The delay of the two accomplices exasperated Zozé even more than their betrayal. Unconsciously, she called them forth in a vehement, and silent prayer: "Come! Come on! Hasten!" as one calls belated friends to an urgent appointment.

A sudden idea upset her. The letter might have lied! She might be the victim of a hoax! But no joy came in the wake of this idea. She could not accept its plausibility. Her suspicions had wandered in every direction, and now she could not force them back. It was as if they scented their prey and were anxious for the imminent running down of the quarry.

Again, she consulted her watch. "Quarter of twelve! Very well,... At twelve, I go in and ask the concierge!..." Then she looked up again; her head fell back tragically.

There, in front of the arch of No. 12 *bis*, a woman, dressed in a gray serge costume, was calling a cab; in spite of the white veil she wore, the thick, flowery embroidery, Zozé recognized a well-known profile, a plane-like jaw, her friend, her best friend, Germaine de Marquesse herself!

Now the carriage opposite started. It almost touched the wheels of her own. The hood was down and, under it, Germaine was arched in a resolute pose, one hand stretched on each end of her sunshade which lay across her knees. The wretch! It was indeed she! And she was not taking any notice of anything, this Germaine, so blinded was she with satisfaction!... Oh! the little Mouzarkhi never could have believed that the pleasure of surprising *these two* could be so heavy with sorrow! She almost fainted, seized with sudden cowardice, as would a woman on the operating table, at the first contact of the steel. What would the second hurt be, if the first one left her feeling so terribly rent?

But she had no time to change her mind; Gerald appeared outside the accursed house.

He was in morning dress, a black cape, a blue suit with a bunch of flesh-colored carnations that "the other one" herself had no doubt pinned on the lapel of his coat. Zozé looked intently at him, her eyes dilated with horror and love.

He glanced right and left, as if hesitating. Then he set out, in his usual lolling gait, towards the rue des Mathurins; he carried his walking-stick under his arm; his shoulders were bent forward and his hands curled, shell-like, to light a cigarette.

Maddened, Zozé forgot the agreed signals. She pulled the window down and shouted to the driver:

"Go!"

The horse started at a slow trot. Madame Chambannes knocked frantically on the glass pane and, without waiting for the carriage to stop, jumped to the pavement.

The sound of the cab stopping caused Gerald to turn round. He saw the young woman and paled with uneasiness. Yet, he constrained himself to say with a heavy smile:

"What! is it you!..."

Zozé pointed to the cab and its open door: "Get in!" she commanded, harshly.

"You wish me to get in? What a funny tone of voice you are using!" stammered Gerald, again attempting a smile.

"I tell you to get in!" repeated Zozé, herself astounded at her audacity. "Come on, get in!... I am not afraid of anything, neither of people nor of scandal.... I want you to get in!"

A band of young working girls going out to lunch looked at them and nudged each other.

"Very well!" said Gerald, embarrassed.... "All the same!... you must admit that you have a strange way of...."

"Enough! We shall talk by and by."

And, while the young count settled himself in the carriage, she told the driver.

"Drive where you like!... To the Bois.... Go towards the Bois."

They started out. Both were seasoned navigators of Paris, experts in the ways of carriage driving; they pulled down the blinds. Then Zozé cried out:

"Well?"

Then her energy left her and she burst into tears.

"What is the matter?... What is it?... I assure you I do not understand!" Gerald murmured hypocritically, as he stretched out his arm to hold her.

She avoided him with a brusque movement.

"Do not touch me!... You make me sick.... Do stop your stupid lies.... I saw Germaine.... Do you understand now?" Geral silence caused her rage to break out: "How shameful! What an ignominious affair!... With one of my own friends, with the one I loved best! Bah! you are just as worthless!... You are two bandits, two blackguards! It was natural that you should take to each other...."

Gerald attempted to come closer.

"Come, come, my little Zozé, mon petit Zozo.... Do cry.... This has no importance at all.... Yes, it is true ... and it is not nice.... But it was even more stupid than wicked.... Look here, if the rules that govern decent society allowed me to speak openly...."

"Well, what then?" said Zozé, without repulsing him.

"No!" said Gerald. "It would be disgusting.... You yourself could not wish it.... Be sure, nevertheless, that to-day was the first time and that, at once, on leaving ... do you know what I was saying to myself just now when you jumped on me?... I was telling myself that it was the first and also the last time...."

"Will you swear it to me?" asked Zozé, with a passion that gave her face, which was convulsed with rage, even a stranger look.

"I do!" Gerald replied.

She examined him tenderly, laying her two hands on his shoulders, then pushed him back far from her with an angry thrust: "I do believe you.... You lie.... You have a woma eyes!" She began to cry again. In the half light which came through the blinds, as at the rehearsal of a play, near his mistress who moaned as if she were in the last act of a melodrama, Gerald began to feel too weary to justify himself.

"Come, my little Zozé, mon petit Zozo!" he still murmured from time to time, mechanically, to put himself in countenance.

Nevertheless, the scene lasted too long; it was getting on his nerves. The proud nobleman confusedly rebelled under the love anxiety. Zoz brusque way had really hurt his feelings. He, Gerald de Meuze, allowing himself to be bullied by a mere Mme. Chambannes? No matter how docile, no matter what a charming pal Zozé was, he was beginning almost to regret the women of his own caste. Of course, among them there were a few *amoureuses*, a few sentimentalists, notorious sticklers who were known as such. But one was duly warned and only ventured into an affair with open eyes! On the other hand, what agreeable natures these people had; how easy and merry they were; and how well they understood life! Ah! neither the young Chitré, for instance, nor Mme. de Baugy, nor even that plump cherub, Mme. Torcieux, would have made so much noise for such a banal little trick! They would have pouted a while; they might have left him. But there would have been neither scandal nor sobs. Two or three sharp words at first—then a firm handshake, to make it up or to part, and that would have been all. For they knew what a man was, what a flirtation or an adventure meant. They were women of the world!...

Suddenly, between two jolts, Zozé asked in a tone of stupefaction.

"Oh! Raldo.... How could you?... How?... How?..."

How could he! Poor little one, what exquisite things she said! He repressed a smile, then, softened at once by the candor of her query, he replied:

"I tell you later ... some day, when I am absolutely sure that it can no longer hurt you...."

"Some day?... What day?" Zozé exclaimed haughtily.... "Do you suppose that I shall ever see you again?... Do you feel that it is all over?"

He drew her close to him.

"So, then, do you love me any more?"

Zozé panted, unable to answer. Tears ran down her cheeks which were contracted by a spasm of pain.

"Of course you love me, since you cry!" Gerald said, caressing her. And he went on, with more assurance. "Listen, my little Zozé.... Of course, to meet you again now, at once, to-morrow or the next day, that could only bring about more scenes, sadness ... painful interviews.... You need rest and reflection.... You must have time ... to forgive me.... Oh! I am not a brute, be sure that I guess what you are feeling.... Here is what I suggest.... I was to leave next week for Poitou, to visit my aunt at Cambres.... Well, I am going to advance my departure.... I shall leave this very night.... I stay at Cambres until the end of the month and write to you as often as you like.... And when I come back, everything will be forgotten, I give you my word on it.... Tell me, does this suit you?"

With each jolt Mme. Chambannes let her head dreamily bump upon Geral shoulder. The young man repeated:

"Answer me, my little Zozé.... Does this suit you?"

"Yes, yes!" Mme. Chambannes said meditatively. "I have an idea, too...."

"Tell me, my poor Zozé!..."

"I should be bored in Paris.... I should be too sad without you.... So, I am going to recuperate at the Frettes, until you return.... When I get home, I am going to pack my trunks and I shall leave by the 5 lock express."

"Alone?"

"No! I am going to mobilize my Aunt Panhias!..."

"Tha right! An excellent idea."

There came a pause. She felt throughout her body a lifting sensation of beatitude, a feeling of being rescued, which prevented her from speaking. She nestled quite close to Gerald, with an outpouring of avowal which was stronger than her will, and sighed languorously:

"Oh, my little Raldo! How good it is to have kept you!"

It was 2 lock before she returned home.

CHAPTER XII

MME. Chambannes had not been gone one hour when a cab stopped outside her house.

The two MM. Raindal stepped out. In order to avoid any insidious remark from his brother, the master had donned an old frock-coat. Uncle Cyprien, on the contrary, had dressed himself in his best clothes, a tail-coat, the tails of which still showed the folds which a long stay in the cupboard had given them, a pair of gray check trousers and red dogskin gloves. He was close-shaved and had replaced his thick cornel-wood stick with a thin rush cane with a gold handle and two brown silk tassels inherited from M. Raindal his father.

Firmin the butler opened the door for them; he was so surprised that he fell back a few steps. He was, moreover, dressed to go out, with a suit of English check and a felt hat.

"What! M. Raindal!" he exclaimed, as he removed his hat. "But madame is not here.... She left an hour ago for the Frettes ... and I am joining her tomorrow morning.... Did not madame warn monsieur?"

Uncle Cyprien was biting his mustache to suppress a laugh that he felt coming.

"No, madame said nothing to me," M. Raindal kept on repeating jerkily.... "I extraordinary. I hope at least there is nothing serious?"

"I do think so, monsieur," the man replied. "Madame made up her mind suddenly about 2 lock.... I ran out to Mme. Panhias and she came at once to help madame pack.... They left with Anna, the maid, as I told you, not an hour ago. Should monsieur wish to write a note I could give the letter to madame to-morrow morning...."

M. Raindal reflected. Such offhandedness left him dumfounded; and there came to his soul an ill-defined impression of anguish, of strange sorrow. At last he replied:

"No, thank you!... I shall write from home.... Where did you say madame went?"

"To the Frettes, the château des Frettes, at Villedouillet, Seine-et-Oise.... Will monsieur remember it?"

"Certainly.... Thank you."

When the door was closed the master glanced at his brother and said, with an attempt at banter:

"Well, my poor friend.... For your first visit you are not in luck!"

Cyprien nodded and spread his arms in a gesture of assent; then he straightened suddenly and remarked:

"How does it seem to you? Your Madame Chambannes does appear to be any more polite than she should!"

The master was on the point of answering when two carriages which came from opposite directions stopped at the same time in front of the house. The abbé Touronde came out of the first and the Marquis de Meuze out of the other. The two men were informed of the circumstances by M. Raindal and manifested great surprise. Neither of them had been warned; they all ventured many conjectures as to the possible reason for this strange lack of courtesy. M. de Meuze especially showed himself very shocked. He had difficulty in not cursing Gerald. What! a fellow whom he had seen that very morning, who surely knew all about it and had not said a word to his father! Really, this was going beyond all bounds of secretiveness!

"Wha to be done?" he declared. "There is only one thing left for us to do and that is for each one of us to return home.... Are you going down to Paris, M. Raindal?"

"Yes, certainly," the master replied. "Pardon me, I was forgetting.... I must introduce my brother, whom I had brought particularly to meet Mme. Chambannes."

All the men took off their hats, Uncle Cyprien purposely accentuating his salute to the abbé Touronde. Together they began to walk towards the centre, the master and the abbé walking first and M. de Meuze behind with Uncle Cyprien.

Nevertheless, M. Raindal only casually followed the words of the priest who had started on his favorite subject, the origin and dogma of the sect of the United Copts. The brutal departure of Mme. Chambannes had agitated his nerves beyond his control. What struck him as a lack of courtesy towards her other guests he construed as a real lack of friendship, in so far as he himself was concerned. Again, the adventure concealed a mystery which he wished he could fathom. What was the meaning of this hurried flight, this forgetfulness of all social obligations? What drama or what caprice had thus unexpectedly sent Mme. Chambannes out of Paris? And a certain irritation gradually oppressed him; it was not, of course, jealousy—the mere idea of it made M. Raindal laugh cynically—but it resembled disappointment, disillusion, something, in fine, that was very much like a pained surprise in his heart. He lifted his hat to wipe from his forehead a few beads of perspiration.

"You must excuse me!" Uncle Cyprien exclaimed to the marquis, after having made an unsuccessful jeering comment upon the abbé Touronde. "I prefer to be frank.... It is stronger than I.... I do like priests!..." And seeing that the Marquis remained cold and had completely closed his gray eyelids, he added rapidly: "On the other hand, I am willing to admit that I do like the Jews any better."

Thereupon they very soon proved to be in agreement. M. de Meuze told him briefly of his misfortune on the stock exchange. Cyprien reciprocated with the history of his dismissal and a short account of his theory of the two banks of the river. The marquis approved smilingly and both concluded that those of the right bank were after all a most deplorable tribe.

They were, nevertheless, the marquis added, gentlemen who must be carefully handled and who remained, no matter what one might do, the lords of the financial market.... Ah, in 1882, at the time of the *Timbale*, people had been very thoughtless. They had attacked these Jews without learning their tactics, without suspecting what their ammunition consisted of, without taking any precaution against their *ruses de guerre*; and they had been defeated, most thoroughly beaten. How could one fight more able adversaries than oneself? By divining their plans, locating all their batteries, regulating on fire by theirs, and finally rectifying the parabola according to the ambient resistance which was apparent there; such as perfidious information, the mass attacks from the syndicates, the liquidation maneuvers, false news or any other strategical piece of duplicity. Such was now the only scientific way in which men of the world were operating on the Bourse.

"Thus, as for myself," the marquis continued, giving up his military comparisons, "I am deep in the gold mines at present.... Well, you will perhaps think that I risked myself blindly in this.... Not at all.... The chance of relations brought me into touch with some of those worthy gentlemen, precisely at the Chambannes, and I can assure you that I made no bones about acting upon their particulars.... Certainly not!... And, by the way, I did not find their tips unremunerative...."

"What, you trust those gentry?" the younger M. Raindal asked with disappointment. "Yet I have been assured that many of them are not very trustworthy...."

"Who told you this?"

"One of my friends, Johann Schleifmann, one of their co-religionists, and, I may add, one of the best of men!"

"Your friend exaggerates, monsieur," the marquis said gently. "Of course, I would not trust them all.... There are some of them whom I shall not name and whom I am more afraid of than of the plague.... Nevertheless, take, for instance, to mention but one, M. Pums, the director of the Bank of Galicia. Here is a man who has been advising me for six months and without any cause for regret.... I could not swear that I do not lose every now and then ... but when I balance my accounts, I find that my operations result in profits, I may say important profits.... Please note also that this cost me neither trouble nor a proof of servility.... Pums has no desire save to oblige me.... He is not one of those viziers of high finance who make you pay for their advice at the rate of sixty humiliations to a hundred per cent.... My M. Pums is a novice! One can have him for a handshake." The marquis laughed at his own ingenious comparison. Then he went on.

"As for you, Monsieur, of course you have nothing to do with such deviltries!"

"No fear," Cyprien exclaimed. "I have invested the wretched twenty thousand francs which I had scraped sou by sou out of my poor salary in railway stock. This brings me about three per cent.... It is very little, I grant you, but it is safe and, with the help of my pension, allows me to make both ends meet.... I speculate! No, never in my life!... Then again, what would be the use? I do need it!"

The marquis fell to dreaming. He was seized with an impulse of democratic sympathy towards the fiery little official. The latter was too poor to cause the haughty nobleman to fear any unpleasant familiarity. The very distance that stood between them brought them together. He said suddenly in a sententious tone:

"Who knows, perhaps you are wrong! There are at present opportunities for a man to make a fortune in mines ... and when I see rogues and fools who become rich over night and the next moment I meet an honest man like yourself who takes no advantage of the opportunity, I feel tempted to cry out to him: 'Go on, go ahead! do not lose this opportunity!... An opportunity which can be met but two or three times in the course of a century—why, surely it is worth it.'"

"Do you think it? Do you think so?" Uncle Cyprien repeated; he was still skeptical but already shaken in his resolves. The marquis went on with that mania for preaching charity in which fortunate gamblers take delight.

"After all, what is the prospect so far as you are concerned? There is really no question of making a fortune. At the most it is a matter of bettering yourself, of gaining the means to treat yourself to a little luxury and a little comfort.... Ah, if I were you ... but enough of this.... I do want to influence you.... Whenever you feel like it, M. Raindal, come to see me.... I live at 2 rue de Bourgogne at the corner of the Place de Palais Bourbon." They caught up with the master and the abbé, who had stopped at the corner of the Pont de la Concorde. They took leave of each other. When the two brothers were left alone M. Raindal asked: "Will you come to dine with us?"

Cyprien did not hear him; he was dreamily contemplating the peach velvet patches splashed on the discolored horizon by the setting sun.

"I am asking you if you are coming to dine?" M. Raindal repeated.

"What! Wha that?" Cyprien started. "Shall I dine with you?... No, thank you.... Schleifmann is waiting for me at the brasserie.... I ca disappoint him."

The little green omnibus of the Panthéon-Courcelles was slowly climbing up the street; he shook his brothe hand rapidly.

"Au revoir.... One of these evenings!"

He climbed on top. As he turned into the Boulevard St. Germain M. Raindal caught sight of him; he was still waving his supple gold-headed stick in a friendly gesture.

"Hello! Good evening, my dear friend," said Schleifmann, when Cyprien settled down at the table next to his own.... "Have you seen the young person?"

"No, my dear friend ... but I saw one of your enemies."

He related the inexplicable flight of Mme. Chambannes, his walk with the marquis and the talk about gold mines and asked him, when he had finished: "Well, my dear Schleifmann, what do you say?"

"About what?"

"Why, this story about the mines, of course!..."

Schleifman little eyes shone fiercely and he passed his hand through his curly hair.

"I say that it is another dirty deal by means of which the Jews of the Bourse will again take in a large amount of money for themselves and raise up more hatred against those of their own race.... That is all I have to say about your mines!"

Raindal, the younger, repressed an impatient gesture.

"Sapristi, Schleifmann! Please try to understand me.... I am not asking you about the Jews but about myself.... Tell me, yes or no, do you think that I should take a risk?"

The Galicia face took on an expression of pity.

"You, my dear Raindal? You cannot be serious!... You, a *goy* (gentile), and an honest fellow, as well, you have got it into your head to have dealings with those big bears?... But they will eat you, my friend; they will chew you up as if you were a mutton chop!..."

"In short," said Uncle Cyprien with resentment, "you are opposed to this project!..."

Schleifmann sneered and shrugged his shoulders.

"But your project does exist, i pure folly.... Do as you please.... But I beg you never to tell me a word of this ludicrous piece of madness."

Cyprien remained silent, choked by anger. He resented as much the Galicia disdainful tone as the tenacity with which he dampened the sparkling hopes of riches which the marquis had lit before him. His anti-Semitic convictions were now directed, for the first time in ten years, against Schleifmann. In the stubbornness of his old comrade he discovered much less a proof of friendship than a characteristic of the Jewish pride of which his most favorite authors quoted monstrous examples! Cyprien remained taciturn throughout the evening, recalling to himself all their names. In these conditions the meeting soon languished and the two friends parted coldly an hour sooner than usual.

The next day M. Raindal, the younger, proved unable to resist the itching he felt to know the quotations on the financial market. He bought an evening paper and took refuge in the Luxemburg in order to read the reports in peace. But he was unused to them and found the transversal lines, the perpendicular columns, the quotations of "to-day" and those of "yesterday" perplexingly confusing. It was only after ten minutes of effort that he discovered the place where the "advance" was given. Everywhere on the gold mines it was considerable and almost general, showing differences of fifteen, twenty, thirty and even fifty francs.

The stocks sold up in the same way on the next day and the day after. Uncle Cyprien made a mental calculation of the amounts which he would have already pocketed but for that mule of a Schleifmann. The dinners at the brasserie daily showed more signs of these accumulated grudges.

At last, on the fifth day, M. Raindal could contain himself no longer. At half-past twelve he went home to dress and half-an-hour later stepped out of a cab in the rue de Bourgogne in front of M. de Meuz door.

The marquis in a brown coat and with a pipe in his mouth was still at his dining-table when Cyprien was ushered in.

"How do you do, my dear M. Raindal!" he exclaimed, as he pushed his chair back. "I am delighted to see you. I am receiving you without any ceremony....

You will have coffee with me, wo you? A cigar?" he added, holding out a box of fat Havanas.

"If you please," the ex-official replied.

There was a pause during which M. Raindal gravely lit his cigar, the red and gold paper band of which he had not dared to remove. He was, moreover, affected by the majestic aspect of the dining-room. The ceilings were as high as those of a museum gallery; the windows were enormous. On all the walls hung old tapestries with fading scenes, emphasized at intervals by antique chiseled copper ornaments. M. de Meuze himself, despite his brown coat and his big meerschaum pipe, well fitted into the atmosphere of high elegance which the surrounding objects gave to the room.

"Well, M. Raindal, what is your news?" he said between two puffs.

"Well, Monsieur le Marquis! Nothing of importance!" Cyprien replied with embarrassment.

M. de Meuze stared at him out of his piercing little green eye.

"I wager you came to talk business with me."

Cyprien grinned but did not deny it.

"Ah ha!" the marquis exclaimed victoriously. "What did I say?... I felt that at once.... I have but one eye but I can see as well as if I had two...."

Coquettishly he caressed the white wings of his whiskers and, going to the window, lifted up a curtain.

"Do you see? You must admit that for a first-floor apartment, mine enjoys a fine view.... The house of our lords is in full sight...."

Through the white-barred windows Cyprien saw the Place de Palais Bourbon and in front of the ancient door a little soldier dreaming near his sentry box, holding his rifle at attention. Cyprien said sneeringly:

"Ah! it is there that our lords of the cheque-book dwell."

"Yes, M. Raindal, right there ... the door facing us! This window will be worth much on the first day of the riots.... But we are gossiping. I was forgetting the object of your visit.... What was it?... You came for the mines, did you?"

Cyprien agreed that this was the case. He had come under the seal of secrecy—for, of course, no one, not even his brother, should know of his attempt—and after serious consideration.

"Quite so," the marquis interrupted. "I guessed as much.... Will you please come this way.... We shall be more at ease to talk."

They passed into the other room, a vast cabinet furnished in Eastern style with scimitars and carbines inlaid with mother-of-pearl in panoplies. He went on:

"So you wish to join the party? Nothing easier.... I am going to write to M. Pums now and, unless you inform him to the contrary, you must go and see him to-morrow about three at the Bank of Galicia, 72 rue Vivienne.... Will this do?..."

He sat down at his huge table and added, while he wrote the note:

"But, take care, no foolishness! Be cautious. The time is favorable.... But you must foresee the débâcle, the inevitable unfortunate débâcle which always occurs with speculative stocks?... Oh, we are not there yet.... But you must keep your eyes open.... Do lose your head! You had better bother Pums ten times before you give an order ... and at the slightest break, you must sell at once, sell without paying any heed to anything! Do you hear?"

Cyprien thanked him profusely and gave his solemn promise.

Once in the street, he walked briskly towards the Champs Elysées. The sky had freshened and showed a radiant spring gayety. The faces of the women he met seemed more beautiful and Uncle Cyprien bestowed gallant looks at them.

He sat in a chair facing the carriages which passed in the splendid avenue. A hopeful joy dilated his whole being. How sweet it would be if he could open his soul about this with someone! What a pity that Schleifmann proved so intractable! Once more M. Raindal was carried away by the bitterest reflections against him.

And the next day he presented his card at the Bank of Galicia and was received at once.

M. Pums at once assured him of his sympathy. The friendship of M. de Meuze and the fact that he was M. Rainda brother was a double recommendation and one too great for M. Pums not to feel very much disposed to help his visitor.

"By the way," exclaimed Cyprien, "I should be indebted to you if you would say nothing of this to my brother.... He might become alarmed and imagine that I have fallen a prey to the passion of gambling and such nonsense.... I prefer...."

"There is no need to insist," M. Pums declared. "In business discretion is the rule.... Moreover, it is quite enough that you should ask me...."

He explained to Cyprien the mechanism of buying and selling stock. He would put his visitor in touch with a broker, M. Talloire, the ban own agent, that of the marquis and of a quantity of other personages and respectable houses. M. Talloire would open an account for M. Raindal, who would then have nothing else to do but give his orders.

"Hm! Hm!" Cyprien remarked, blinking. "Shall I have to go to this Talloire myself?... It is very unpleasant."

M. Pums smiled cordially.

"Oh, it is not indispensable.... If you wish it, we can assume the responsibility of transmitting your orders in this way...."

While he analyzed the process that would have to be followed, the ex-official was speaking to his own soul. He liked little M. Pums. It would be really impossible to meet a more courteous and obliging man. As for that Jewish appearance which Cyprien had expected to notice in him, the professo brother was compelled to admit that Pums did not show any sign of it. His big chocolate-colored eyes, yellow skin and black mustache gave him the head of a creole, a Spaniard, a Turk or a rich Kirghiz. Even the very slight accent seemed to Cyprien quite different from what might be expected from a naturalized "Prussian."

"I thank you," he said, when the other had concluded. "And now, one question, please! How much shall I risk? Is five thousand enough?"

"Anything you like, monsieur. Twenty thousand francs or ten sous, according to your fancy.... You understand very well that I am treating you as a friend and not as a client.... I am only sorry for one thing, that you did not come a fortnight sooner.... With five thousands francs that I could have placed for you a week ago, a straight profit of three thousand francs would have fallen into your pocket at the settlement on the 15th...."

"Three thousand francs," Uncle Cyprien repeated sadly. "Well, i too late!... Do le think of it!... And since five thousand francs seem enough to you, please be so good as to buy me five thousand francs' worth of mining stock...."

"Which ones, monsieur?" Pums inquired gravely. "There are hundreds of them."

"I do know," murmured Uncle Cyprien. "You must advise me!... Do for me as you would for the marquis!"

Pums gave him a list of mining stocks which the Bank of Galicia and its affiliated houses were backing on the markets. Cyprien was confused by this enumeration and decided according to the prettiness or the strangeness of the names. He selected the "Pink Star of South Africa," the "Fountain of the

Red Diamond," the "Source of Carbuncles," the "Pummigan and Kraft," and the "Deemerhuis and Haarblinck," the names of which Pums obligingly translated for his benefit.

He then rose, apologizing for having claimed so much precious time. The banker retorted that he was only too glad and went as far as the outside corridor to see his visitor off. He hoped to see him again in a week at the time of the settlement, since they would have to talk it over again.

"What a charming man!" Uncle Cyprien thought, when the door was closed behind him.

He spent the following week in a fever of pleasant anxiety. The stocks were rising. But he feared he had made a mistake. He was afraid of having exaggerated the profits which, according to his calculations, were already in the neighborhood of two thousand francs. This spoiled his happiness every night.

Consequently he felt a sudden emotion when, on the morning of the 29th, as he was leaving his house to go to the brasserie, the concierge handed him a yellow envelope with the heading of the Talloire house. What did this long envelope contain? Supposing he had miscalculated? If, instead of the expected profits, it were to tell him of losses?

He walked to the high door of the house and tore the envelope open when he was behind it. It contained only a single sheet of paper, striped zebra-like with columns, figures, abbreviated words, and the trembling of his hands further increased the chaos. Two trade expressions caught his eye, on the left: Dr.; on the right: Cr. Above these he read:

M. CYPRIEN RAINDAL

His account in settlement of April 30 with M. Talloire, Broker, 96 rue de Choiseul.

"Hm! I must be cool! Do I win or do I lose?" the uncle murmured, while his eyes scanned the page. He noticed at last a little gathering of figures in a corner, with, next to the word *Total*, the mention: *Creditor*: 7700 fr.

"Seven thousand, seven hundred francs!" he muttered, his heart beating fast against his ribs. "From 7700 I take out the 5000 I put in.... There remains 2700! Two thousand, seven hundred francs profit! There must be some mistake.... And yet I must be right; whoever receives, he owes; whoever owes, he receives.... I am the creditor.... I win."

Yet a doubt lurked in his mind, despite this certainty. He wanted to free himself from it at once, to know, and it was nothing but the fear of importuning the agent that prevented him from rushing to the rue de Choiseul. This distressful feeling was met with a sudden remembrance of the

Marquis' advice, "to bother Pums ten times rather than one." The solution was clear, since Pums himself had offered his services beforehand. Uncle Cyprien jumped into a cab.

All the way, in order to prop up his own faith, he repeated in rhythmic time: "Who receives owes!... who owes receives!... Nevertheless, this axiom did not altogether reassure him. Only the jovial reception Pums gave him restored Cyprie serenity.

"Well!" the banker exclaimed, when he saw his protégé. "It seems to me that we have no cause to complain.... If my calculations are right, M. Raindal, you have made about 500 francs!"

Silently, Raindal pushed his paper forward.

"Here you are!"

"Ah!" exclaimed Pums, as he looked at the figures. "Two thousand, seven hundred francs profit!... You are going well for a beginner!... Bravo! Congratulations! Of course, it goes without saying that you are keeping your position?"

"I beg your pardon?" M. Raindal asked, with an anxious expression.

"I mean to say that I take it you will leave your profit on the same securities."

Cyprien thought a while, then asked very meekly:

"Could I not draw some of it out?"

"Anything you like! This money belongs to you. You are its lord and master.... Do be afraid.... Name your figure!"

"Seven hundred francs!" Cyprien said resolutely. "I draw seven hundred out, I leave seven thousand in.... This leaves a round sum, does it not?" Then he added in a less assured voice, "Can I cash it here?"

"Hm!" Pums replied. "It is not very regular.... Well, since it is for you, for a friend!... Just sign this power for me to cash at Talloir.... I am going to give you a check which you need only to present at our cashie office...."

Cyprien signed it.

"And we retain your confidence?" M. Pums asked as he rose. "You still wish me to direct your orders?"

"What! Are you laughing at me, M. Pums?" Cyprien replied. "My confidence.... My gratitude, you should say ... my deep gratitude! Buy me, if you please, the same stocks, or buy me any other that you think more advisable.... I am convinced that you are acting for my best interests.... Au revoir, monsieur, and thank you again!"

When he reached the street he turned instinctively towards the Bourse. The seven 100-franc notes which they had given him formed a little hard protuberance in his inside pocket, and he laid his hand on it at every step. He was filled with schemes of generous bounty. He paused a little while to contemplate the tumult of the Bourse, the shouting crowd that was perhaps to make him richer again soon. Entering the nearest tobacco shop he asked for special brand cigars and was shown several kinds. He sniffed them in expert fashion and, by squeezing them in the middle, made them crackle against his ear. Finally he bought a box at one franc apiece and added two packets of American cigarettes to this purchase.

But when he went out, he caught sight of a pipe merchan window near the shop and still on the place de la Bourse. Supported with invisible props or laid in luxurious cases, with stems that were brutally straight and stems with serpentine curves, meerschaum and briar pipes mingled their white and brown colors. Gold and silver rings encircled amber cigar cases; all of them, in their velvet cases, had the air of fine jewels destined for princely lips. Cyprien looked at them and shook his head. All at once a look of satisfaction shone in his eyes. What if he were to buy one of those pipes, a nice, fat meerschaum, like that of the Marquis, for his old comrade Schleifmann of whom, their dispute notwithstanding, he was very fond! And he entered the shop.

His selection proved to be so long, so careful an affair that it was past 12.45 by the clock of the Brasserie Klapproth when M. Raindal arrived.

"A little present for you, my dear Schleifmann!" he said, sitting down to the left of the Galician. "A little present which I have been considering for a long time.... Take it ... yes, open it; it is for you!"

Slowly Schleifmann opened the parcel.

"A pipe!" he exclaimed, as he played with the case.

"Quite so, and a pipe de luxe! The result of six months' savings in cigarettes, my dear friend!"

The pipe represented a mermaid, whose double twisted tail curled around the stem as far as the amber mouthpiece and whose seductive head had been hollowed for the bowl. Schleifmann could not conceal his admiration.

"It is marvelous ... colossal, colossal!" he repeated, using the German expression which to him signified supreme enthusiasm.... "I am going to smoke it now.... Waiter, matches!"

Uncle Cyprien watched the preparations for the inauguration with a glorious and softened feeling.

"Exquisite!" Schleifmann declared, after two whiffs. "A child could smoke it.... You are very kind, my dear Cyprien."

He took up the case and examined the lining, a coat of dark red plush with the make name stamped in gold letters. Brusquely, he knocked on the table with his fist.

"Raindal!" he shouted. "Look me in the eyes!"

"Here!" the ex-official replied, looking furtively at his friend, his face slantwise.

"You are gambling at the Bourse, my friend!"

"I!" said Uncle Cyprien, in shocked rebellion.

"Yes, you! This address tells me everything: Place de la Bourse! You are gambling on the mines!... Have a care, Raindal! This is an adventure which may cost a great deal more than you imagine!"

He replaced the pipe in its case with a gesture of renunciation.

"You make me tired, Schleifmann!" grumbled Cyprien. "You upset me considerably.... What! I take the trouble to buy you a pipe, to choose it as if for myself! And this is all I get for it: words of ill-omen!... Well, yes; there.... I have gambled.... I have even won.... I won seven hundred francs.... But it is fi-ni-shed, all finished! To-day I stopped everything.... Are you satisfied, you silly?"

"Finished!" the Galician sneered. "I do not believe a word of it, my dear fellow.... Begun, yes.... But finished, after such a profit! You take me for a fool, Raindal!"

Cyprien made a haughty grimace.

"As you like! Do believe me! I cannot compel you to believe me.... Very well, then.... I am still gambling.... I gamble until I am all out of breath.... Quite so.... And you are leaving me my pipe?... You could do anything pleasanter!"

Unwittingly, Schleifmann glanced with regret at the plump siren which, lying on her side, seemed as if asleep.

"There! I do want to upset you, my dear Cyprien!... Nevertheless, I am shamed to take your pipe.... I ought not to.... It is right."

"Do be so fussy," said Raindal, with an air of affection. "Take it back quickly ... since as I tell you not gambling any more!"

"The Lord be praised, if you are telling the truth!" Schleifmann murmured, as he lit his pipe.

The conversation once more became friendly. From time to time, Schleifmann exhaled between two puffs: "Delicious.... Colossal!" Uncle Cyprien thought that his deception had succeeded and ventured in a careless tone:

"Ah, by the way! While I think of it!... You realize that, because of this little affair, I owe a certain courtesy to the Marquis de Meuze.... Would it hurt your feelings to lunch here with him?"

"Between you and me, I would care to," the Galician grunted after a pause.

"Why not? Oh! I can guess.... The Marqui opinions! Well, first of all, if there is nothing else to stop you, you may rest assured.... I have already told him you were a good Jew."

"My dear friend, I wish you would not use that expression!" Schleifmann said nervously. "Have I not taught you that there are no bad Jews? At the most, it can only be said that there are degenerate Jews...."

"Besides," Cyprien went on, "the Marquis seemed to me very much calmed down on this subject! If you knew all the kind things he said concerning several of your co-religionists!"

"It was one of two things," Schleifmann said dryly. "Either he was laughing at you or he is a bad Catholic."

"He! He adores the curés!"

"He may adore the curés," the Galician retorted, in the same tone. "But, as a good Catholic, he cannot love the Jews.... Catholic religion means universal religion.... So long as there remains one heretic on the globe, the crusade remains open.... Wriggle out of this if you can!... And is it not natural? Religions thrive on fanaticism alone and perish through tolerance alone."

"So, you approve of the Saint Bartholomew, the Inquisition, and the Dragonnades?" exclaimed Cyprien, whose bourgeois background was shocked by the sharpness of these aphorisms.

"As of the Terror!" Schleifmann replied. "Or rather I do not approve of them, but I can explain their existence.... Such events are political measures which happen to be useful to a party.... You cannot sow the seeds of such beliefs on dry soil, by means of reasoning; they germinate only in blood and blossom only through fear."

"Accordingly, if the Revolution were to come back, you would, if necessary, have my head cut off!"

"Who knows?" Schleifmann replied, with a half sarcastic smile. "If you had become too rich!"

Although he relished a jest of this nature very little, M. Raindal affected to be amused.

"All right, Schleifmann! In advance of getting my head chopped off, you already seem to be pulling my leg, old man. I have told you, and I repeat it, the Marquis no longer harbors any appreciable intolerance. Going, going, going! Do you refuse to lunch with him?"

"Well, I am willing," the Galician replied contemptuously. "But later, say in a year, I shall be more precise and name the day; it shall be on the day that follows the smash up of the mines.... Yes, on that day, I shall be delighted to converse with your friend the Marquis about the Jews and tolerance."

Cyprien shrugged his shoulders. "One cannot be serious for a minute with you.... Oh, well! Le drop it. You refuse to join us; we can eat without you!"

Schleifmann did not reply, but busied himself with stuffing the head of his mermaid.

"What about your brother?" he asked suddenly. "What does your brother think of all this?"

"My brother? Do talk to me about him! He bores me perhaps even more than you do, my dear man! I do know what is the matter with him this last fortnight.... But I should not be so very much surprised if someone were to tell me that the departure of Mme. Rhâm-Bâhan is at the bottom of it.... You should see his temper!... and his face! In short, he is not to be spoken to."

Cyprien added confidentially: "And not a word, please, about this mining business, in case you happen to meet him! There would be everlasting sermons and warnings!"

Schleifmann promised to keep the secret. Uncle Cyprien lifted up one hand in a gesture of disgust.

"My brother! Ah! la! la! he is a bore, regular bore, these days!"

CHAPTER XIII

FOR once Uncle Cyprien had not exaggerated. Ever since the day of their disappointment in the rue de Prony, M. Raindal had been unable to rid himself of a feeling of hostility whenever he saw his brother; either because the sight of Uncle Cyprien recalled an unpleasant memory or because the master feared his brothe questions. At each visit he showed him a more bitter coldness.

The departure of Mme. Chambannes had dealt M. Rainda heart a blow from which it was still throbbing. Of course, a week later he had received a few lines from Zozé, in which she apologized for her discourteous flight; she had had some small anxieties which she could no doubt explain in person the next time they met. But the very vagueness of this postponement caused the master as much impatience as if the young woman had kept back every particular concerning her flight. Little anxieties! Surely they were not caused by Chambannes who was still away, and far from Paris. By whom then, and of what sort were they? Money troubles? A very unlikely hypothesis. Family troubles? No, since the only relation Mme. Chambannes had, had gone with her to Les Frettes. Love troubles? M. Raindal vehemently repulsed this latter solution which, in reality, excited his anger more than his incredulity. Whenever the idea of it came within the horizon of his dreams, he bent all his effort towards its destruction as if it were an absurd nightmare.

Love troubles, Mme. Chambannes! The maste friendship rebelled against such a foolish calumny. Coquettish, frivolous, childish—she might be that; but in love, his little pupil, never! Not to him could they come with such inventions, to him who knew her well, who had been studying her and judging her for nearly four months. The only young man who was in a position to court her, the tall Gerald de Meuze, hardly seemed with those languid ways and that tired expression of his, the hero who was at all likely to captivate such a vivacious, sprightly nature. At the most only a robust officer, an ardent young poet or an illustrious musician might have a faint chance, not to seduce her, but perhaps to trouble her thoughts. Not without a secret feeling of relief, M. Raindal admitted to himself that there was no such favored one about Mme. Chambannes.

Nevertheless, as he came to these conclusions a melancholy feeling suddenly brought him down from the heights again. He remembered his arrival in the rue de Prony, the empty house and the outrageous treatment accorded him. How little she must have cared for him to have forgotten him so! How very low and precarious must be his place in her affections and her thoughts. How much he had over-estimated the influence and the attraction which he exercised upon her.

He resolved for the sake of his dignity not to answer her letter, but every day that passed without bringing him news shook the proud resolution. Where was she? How did she spend her days and her evenings? Why did she not call him to her?

He would sometime lift himself up out of his misery by some sudden flight of vanity. He swore that he would never again condescend to take any notice of such trifling inquiries which proved so humiliating for a superior mind like his. He was close to the precipitous regions where floats the pure breeze of eternity; but he did not remain very long making plans alone on those calm heights. After a little while the light image of Zozé soared up to join him and he would sigh as he saw her again. A sudden clearness of sight revealed to him how strongly attached he was to his little pupil. He shrugged his shoulders, recalled his grievances against Mme. Chambannes and attempted to disdain her. The effort was vain. He wished to feel contempt and resentment, but she inspired him with nothing but regret.

In the midst of his disquietude he found no solace but in work on the new book which he was preparing: a book, as he told Thérèse, which might possibly share the success of the previous one.... I say no more now.... I am waiting for the idea to ripen.... You will see.... It is not bad....

Again he paced his study, his hands behind his back, his head bent forward as if it were reaching out towards the runaway flock of his ideas.

The provisional title of the book was: *The Idlers of Ancient Egypt*. It would be a moral study supported by historical documents rather than a work of erudition.

M. Raindal proposed to establish by means of examples that their great social moving force was the search after pleasure and especially the so-called gallant pleasures: the whole effort of human labor tended towards woman and her conquest. The refinements, especially, and all the arts often owed to her their birth and always their prosperity. It was for woman that the stones were set in gold, the silks embroidered and all the melodies resounded. M. Raindal meditated upon these developments so much that he had more than once fallen a prey to fever and headaches. At his call, the facts jumped out of their cells and rushed to line themselves in battle array as if they were well disciplined little soldiers. There was notably one chapter—Chapter VI—on *Love and Gallantry in Ancient Egypt* based on the religious legends, the toilet paraphernalia and the popular stories which had been discovered, and of which the master already possessed the main line and almost every paragraph.

There were days, however, when he conceived certain scruples concerning the value of his idea. Would not people charge him with pursuing the same attempt at scandal which his last book had inaugurated? Would they not reproach him with lingering purposely in immoral episodes? Did he even possess the gift, the necessary competency to fathom the prodigious problems of sentiment?

The first two queries M. Raindal rejected wholly in the name of the contempt which a lofty soul owes to insinuations that are prompted by jealousy.

The third one seemed to him more delicate a subject and more likely to give rise to controversies. He delighted in discussing it with Boerzell, who never failed to come every Sunday to pay the permitted call in the rue Notre-Dame-des-Champs.

"Sincerely, M. Boerzell," he asked, "do you think that a man needs to have been a libertine to properly appreciate the subtleties of sentiment? Do you believe, in short, that to speak competently of love it is necessary that a man should be a specialist in it, a professional, a practitioner, as it were?"

"Oh, master!" Boerzell replied cautiously, "tha a complex question.... I must say i one I have considered...."

"Do you think," continued M. Raindal, "that a multitude of sentiments exist which one appreciates all the better for not having felt them oneself?"

"That is incontestable!" Boerzell answered.

"You observe that in this matter one is able to retain a freshness of impression, a preciseness of view which prove to be of the highest value in scientific analyses.... One is not blinded either by vanity or by the intervention of personal recollections.... The mind retains, intact, its impartiality, its penetration, and the calm which is indispensable for regular observations...."

"Surely, master!" Boerzell admitted. "Nevertheless do you fear that a certain coldness might result from this procedure?"

"Not at all, my dear sir!" M. Raindal protested. "What is essential is that one should love the idea of the subject with which one deals, love love, if it is of love that one is writing.... The warmth of sympathy warms everything.... Our works are like our children. Only those which we do not love as we conceive them are cold and unsatisfying."

Slowly he went back to his study, while Boerzell smiled at Thérèse. In the course of their frequent conversations, the young savant had obtained little fragmentary confidences which left him no doubts concerning the worldly indiscretions of the master.

On the fourth Sunday, M. Raindal did not come to the drawing-room. He had gone out, ostensibly to visit the director of the Collège, but in reality to go to make sure that his little pupil had not returned to her house without giving him warning. The sight of the closed shutters destroyed his hopes.

Nevertheless he rang the bell repeatedly, but no answer came. Yet the first days of May had arrived! When would she come back? He walked slowly along the half-deserted streets. Everything he saw brought him some painful recollection. How often he had passed these places, with his soul and eyes still softened by Mme. Chambannes' sweetness! What a change now? How forsaken he was! To rid himself of such sorrowful thoughts or to oppose them by a physical denial from his own lips, he smiled all the way at the little girls and the little boys in their Sunday clothes, whom their parents lazily dragged by the hand.

When the master returned home, Boerzell had not gone yet but was still chatting with Thérèse. Near them, Mme. Raindal was reading a pious book. The master attempted to appear in a merry mood. The recent misfortune of one of his colleagues whose trust had been abused by forgers served him as a pretext to scoff at the learned. After all, what was the value of brute science if it was not animated by the spirit? What would his next work be, for instance, if M. Raindal did not prop it up with general and human considerations? Boerzell agreed completely and by a clever digression he brought the conversation back to the social rôle of love. The master took the bait eagerly. His nerves were voluptuously relaxed by this pleasant contest of dialectics against so subtle an adversary. The night fell before he had ended his discourse.

"You will dine with us, wo you, M. Boerzell?" he said, when Brigitte came to light the lamp.

He only let the young man go at eleven lock, dazed by the contest and so tired that he could only stammer. But this melancholy seized him again as soon as he was alone with his daughter. He hardly said good-night and rushed to his bed as if toward a distraction, an asylum of forgetfulness.

The next morning he did not rise until half past eight. There was nothing from Mme. Chambannes in his mail. Peevishly, he was splashing water over his face, when Brigitte suddenly entered.

"A telegram for monsieur...."

"My glasses. Give me my glasses, I tell you!"

He felt a commotion within himself as he recognized on the blue paper the writing of Mme. Chambannes. He opened the express letter and read:

Sunday evening.

My dear master:

I am back at last. I am anxious to see you again. Why not take advantage of the fact that the tradesmen and my friends will still be leaving me alone to make our great visit to the Louvre to-morrow morning? Unless I hear from you, therefore, let it be to-morrow morning at nine-thirty in the place du Carrousel, in front of the pavilion de Sully. How pleasant it will be to meet again!

Your little pupil,

Z. CHAMBANNES.

Instinctively M. Raindal consulted the clock which marked nine lock and he rushed to the door.

"Brigitte!" he shouted in the passage.... "Brigitte, my frock coat.... The new one.... My patent leather shoes.... My hat.... Hurry up, my good girl."

"What is the matter, father?" said Thérèse, who had come out at the disturbance.

M. Raindal regretted having shouted so loudly; he was now compelled to tell the truth.

"Oh! i Mme. Chambannes!" he replied, scratching his neck under his beard. "She has made an appointment for 9.30 for me to take her to the Louvre.... I have no time to waste, as you can see."

He noticed a smile on the gir face and asked:

"What are you laughing at?"

"I am not laughing!" Thérèse replied, having recovered her composure.

M. Raindal was upset.

"Yes, you are laughing! You ca deny it.... Go on; speak.... What were you laughing at?"

"Do you really want to know, father?... Very well! It is because to-day is Monday, and the museum is closed...."

"I had forgotten.... Yet it is true enough!... But I cannot keep her waiting...." It suddenly dawned upon him that he was being suspected of telling an untruth. He held out the special delivery and said, "You can look for yourself! The day and the hour are set down.... 'To-morrow morning at 9.30.'"

Haughtily, Thérèse brushed the paper aside.

"Oh, it is quite unnecessary, father!"

"Yes, yes! I want you to look at it...."

She threw a swift glance at the paper and handed it back to M. Raindal:

"You are right!... Hurry up!..."

"All right! I am much obliged to you!" he grumbled.

He recollected himself only when he reached the pavilion de Sully. Ten lock was just striking at the big clock above the pink columns of the door. M. Raindal sighed with relief. He was on time and that made him forget his anger at Thérèse.

The vast place stretched out before him. It was shaded and deserted in the lofty frame of its several illustrious palaces. In the distance, the open space of the Tuileries seemed to be a region of light without end, whose white reflection made the sky paler. A warm breeze came from it and at intervals bent down the green grass of the neighboring gardens. The master took a deep breath. He loved this milky and delightful aroma of the morning air in the spring. And his soul was gradually harmonizing itself with the lofty quiet of the scene.

He walked up and down in front of the peristyle, glancing at his light gloves which he was fastening. The approach of a carriage made him look up, and he saw at one of the high windows of the Colbert pavilion two clerks of the Finance Ministry who were watching him smilingly. Their inspection did not hurt his feelings. He imagined to himself the surprised admiration which the young men would feel when Mme. Chambannes arrived. Yes, of course! He was waiting for a lady! And what a lady! These two gentlemen had probably never seen in their life one so elegant and so special!

An open carriage was coming towards the pavilion de Sully by the avenue on the left. The master rushed over just in time to help Mme. Chambannes out. She had on a dark blue costume with a shot-silk blouse which sparkled at the opening of her short jacket. She placed her little white gloved hand in that of M. Raindal and gave him a candid little laugh of greeting and thankfulness.

"Well, dear master," she said, when she had paid her driver, "you are not too angry with me, are you? Were you very indignant at your little pupil?...."

M. Raindal blinked under the tender glance which pervaded him. He had grown unaccustomed to it.

"Not at all, dear lady!..." he stammered. "Above all things I am delighted to see you again.... Is M. Chambannes well?"

"Quite.... He came back last night.... By the way, he asked me to invite you to the opera to-night.... They are giving "Samson and Delilah" and "The Korrigane." We have a box on the second tier.... You will come, wo you?"

"Oh! Madame...."

"Yes, yes, you will come.... I want you to!" She looked about her inquiringly and noticed the plate with big gold letters over the peristyle:

"It is here, is it?"

"Alas! i impossible to-day, dear Madame!..." the master exclaimed, and Zozé assumed an expression of displeasure.

"For the one time that free, how vexing!... What shall we do, then?"

"I do know, Madame!... Whatever you like!"

Distractedly he glanced at the circular little open spaces where the leaves of the trees rustled in the breeze. One could not see inside them. The very access to them seemed forbidden by the thick foliage pressed against the gates. They were like two gallant theatrical property gardens, put there by mistake or merely temporarily. The master thought, "This would be perfect!" And he pointed to the nearer of these little gardens.

"Would you like to go in there for a little chat before we part?"

"It is a good idea!" Mme. Chambannes said. "These lovely squares are delightful."

The garden consisted of a tiny little lawn surrounded by four green benches carved to imitate the antique. They sat on one of them opposite the Pavilion Denon. In front of the latter a row of statues was placed at regular intervals, isolated and alike in their equalizing marble costumes. No other eyes but their lifeless ones looked upon the square.

"Ther no crowd here!" Mme. Chambannes remarked. Then she pointed to the statues with her sunshade, and added: "And to think that you will be like this one day, dear master!"

"Nothing is less assured, madame," M. Raindal replied modestly.

"But I, where shall I be then?" Zozé went on gravely.

"O, what ugly thoughts!... Was it your stay at Les Frettes which made you so gloomy?"

"No, it was not that, since, to tell the truth, Zozé had enjoyed herself very much there. Nature and solitude had made her feel better; had helped her to recuperate from Paris! For, in truth, what woman was there who did not sometimes grow weary of Paris? What woman does not in the end become satiated with visits, gossip, theaters, dress-makers, and the whole worldly surfeit of activity?... The country, with one or two good friends, like M. Raindal for instance, the rest, the fresh air cure, such seemed to be for the present Mme. Chambannes' ideal dream. And if she had returned, it was because...."

"Excuse me," the master interrupted. "Why did you leave?... Perhaps I am indiscreet in reminding you of your promise...."

"No, not at all...."

She had her two elbows on her knees in a pose of meditation and was digging the sand with the point of her sunshade.

"I left because I had troubles.... A friend in whom I had faith and who betrayed me shamefully."

"Ah!... I am very sorry for you!" said he.

She looked up to the heavens in a melancholy ecstasy. A dewy languor appeared about her eyelashes. She was transfigured by sorrow. In her little starched collar which was so modern and masculine, her features assumed, in her affliction, the air of a perverse holiness.

"And so you had a great deal of trouble?" M. Raindal said again, without taking his eyes off her.

"Oh yes, a great deal!"

"My poor friend!" murmured the master, whose voice was altered. "You will allow me to call you this?"

Mme. Chambannes nodded.

"I do want to ask you any more about your departure!" he continued. "I have hurt you unwittingly, and it would be inexcusable if I were to insist ... but, in future, if ever you are unhappy, I beg of you, do treat me as a friend, confide in me. You need not give me any details; just tell me that you are suffering, and I shall do my very best to lighten your burden, to find distractions for you.... I have so much affection for you...."

"Thank you!" she said, somewhat surprised at the urgent tone he was using. "Thank you.... How kind you are, dear master."

She had half turned towards him and looked at him with one of her most fervent smiles. Bottomless depths yawned in her eyes. Her whole face trembled in coquettish sauciness. M. Raindal thought that a flame was piercing his temples. He was carried away by delirium. With a shy briskness he seized Mme. Chambannes' hand: and, in a frantic kiss, his lips pressed upon it the avowal of love which they had not dared to utter.

"Oh! be careful!" Mme. Chambannes said, as she moved away from him.

"Of what?" the master asked awkwardly.

His forehead was wet with the perspiration of anguish. To give himself countenance he tried to laugh but he repressed it at once, perplexed and disconcerted by the young woma expression. She looked severe yet showed no anger. She expressed modest alarm rather than resentment. Her eyes remained dark in spite of a sarcastic twinkle which contracted the corners. What was she going to do? Would she be indignant, would she forgive or smile?

She rose and in a calm voice in which faintly trembled an ironical echo, said:

"Good-by, dear master. I must go home.... Will you see me to a cab, please?"

M. Raindal gave her hand an imperceptible pressure and replied, while his eyes wandered towards the statues on the colonnade.

"With pleasure, dear madame."

She passed first through the narrow doorway of the gate. M. Raindal followed her, absentmindedly playing with his gloves.

As soon as she was seated and the wheels began to move, he recovered enough daring to glance at her. She looked her usual self once more; her eyes were again tender and challenging.

"By the way, we meet to-night!" said she. "Do not forget, dear master, box No. 40...."

As soon as she was out of the Carrousel she was unable to remain serious any longer. She smiled so openly and intensely that a street urchin imitated her and cried out:

"Bon dieu, how funny it is!..."

Yes, surely, it was funny. Père Raindal in love! Who could have thought it possible? What a kiss he had given her, a kiss like a blow, it was so brutal and bashful at the same time! Poor man!... What a pity that she had broken away from that nasty Germaine! How they would have made merry together over this little story.

The memory of her perfidious friend caused Mme. Chambannes' face to darken again. She lost her pleasant mood until after lunch, when she told her aunt Panhias of her interview.

"Be careful, child!" that voluminous lady urged. "At that age, it is sometimes very dangerous!"

"For whom?" asked Zozé.

"Not for you, of course!"

Mme. Chambannes expelled a cloud of smoke from her cigarette:

"Have no fear. I shall be careful.... Who knows? Perhaps I was mistaken!"

"Perhaps!" her aunt replied skeptically.

Zozé said nothing. Once more she saw the garden of the Louvre and the ardent and timorous expression of M. Raindal. If only Gerald had been there, hidden somewhere among the bushes! She was delighted with this idea of semi-reprisals. She smoked two more cigarettes as she imagined successively the burlesque and the pathetic sides of the scene.

That evening the opera exhibited one of those spring gatherings where, in a sparkle of light, precious tones and uncovered shoulders—all the public display of luxury and beauty, of wealth and aristocracy which had apparently been a thing of the past, came to life again.

As soon as Zozé came in, many opera glasses from clubmen and first tier boxes were leveled upon her.

For she had advanced in caste the little Mouzarkhi girl. They were now putting down to her credit the two years of her liaison. If this did not create for her a link of relationship with the surrounding fashionable élite, at least it was a victory to her credit, a successful campaign which made the distance appear smaller. She was no longer the little exotic, unknown person concerning whom they had once inquired in an almost contemptuous tone. She was almost one of themselves, the little Chambannes woman, who had captured and kept young de Meuze for two whole years; and under the mask of their glasses, which hid half their faces, their lips formed smiles of good will towards her.

Then there was the presence of the old gentleman who sat next to Zozé in the front of the box; this piqued their curiosity. They had to wait for the interval in order to find out who he was.

In the meantime, the hope of the young Philistines appeared at the back of the stage. Delilah led, her black hair overloaded with flowers and multicolored jewels. They were singing in an enraptured voice a sensuous love chorus:

"Beau-té, don du ciel, prin-temps de nos jours,
Doux char-me des yeux, es-poir des amours,
Pé-ne-tre les coeurs, ver-se dans les a-mes,
Tes dou-ces flam-mes!
Aimons, mes soeurs, ai-aimons tou-jours!"

M. Raindal stiffened himself at the sharp shiver which ran down his back. Instinctively he looked at the audience. The silence had become graver and more vibrant. A voluptuous tide mounted from the orchestra to the boxes along with the languorous music. Savage lights shone in the eyes of some of the women; breasts were panting; the heavy artillery of the opera glasses was firing glances at full speed. Almost everyone in the audience, men and women, after a long day of hypocrisy, acknowledged themselves at last lovers, moved by the cynical suggestiveness of the chorus.

The master was absorbed in making comparisons. He remembered other evenings he had spent at the opera with Thérèse and Mme. Raindal, in boxes offered them by the ministry, during the summer or on the occasion of some séance of the Sociétés Savantes. What a transformation—not to say what progress—had taken place since then in his mind! How many social phenomena at that time had been still inaccessible to him, as if they had been matters of indifference or had not existed at all! That was his explanation for his yawns in the past, for the feeling of boredom and almost discomfort which he had felt at those performances. He had lacked so many elements necessary to appreciate their harmonies! To-day, on the other hand....

He looked back towards the audience. All the seats were occupied. The ballet of the priestesses of Dagon was beginning and a libertine gayety now relaxed all faces in accordance with the merry grace of the dancers.

Mentally M. Raindal took note of the change. How many shades there were in the aristocratic depravity of the assembly! How many tiny degrees there were between their previous seriousness and their present joviality!

He marked the beat of the fast Oriental rhythm which regulated the steps of the dancers, and at the same time he furtively examined Mme. Chambannes, his dear friend, as he did not yet dare openly to call her.

A slight uncertain smile hovered on her fine little face which reverie had rendered motionless. At times, however, she would seize her glasses and aim them at a box or a row of seats; then, when her inspection was over, she would throw a sort of compensating glance at M. Raindal. When the curtain went down she took refuge with the master in the tiny salon which formed a kind of boudoir behind. Chambannes stood behind them. He gave very little attention to the words of M. Raindal, who was describing, with reference to the most recent discoveries of the exegetists, the rites and the ins and outs of the cult of Dagon. Moreover, the curtain rose again before the master had finished.

The scenery represented a garden with a green bench in the foreground and to the right the villa of delights where the crime was to be accomplished.

When Delilah sat down on the bench surrounded with shrubs and Samson, panting with love, let himself fall there beside her, M. Raindal could not refrain from casting a sly glance of allusion towards Zozé. While affecting not to have noticed it, Mme. Chambannes pleasantly accentuated with a smile the dreamy look on her face. The master thanked her with a little friendly cough.

Oh! Had he been so very much at fault this morning? Considering it calmly and at a distance, he did not regret that mad kiss, that indiscreet caress which had been at least open enough to deserve respect. Why should he try any longer to hide those sentiments of his which were so sincere? Why affect indifference, when it was the very reverse which Mme. Chambannes inspired him with?... Love? Oh, no. But a certain tenderness, a certain affection, which although it was not exclusively paternal, nevertheless did not go beyond the limits authorized by the difference in age between a very young woman and a man of advanced years. What was the use of concealing by subterfuge and illusory lies, the liveliness of this inclination? Was not history full of such examples? Without mentioning Ruth and Boaz, whose romance it seemed had had a bourgeois ending, could he not mention a great number of masters who had most absolutely fallen in love with their disciples, men or women, in spite of the unlikeness of their minds and the difference in their ages? What was there, for instance, in common between the mind of a Socrates and that of an Alcibiades?...

The sweet melody which Delilah murmured to Samson followed just in time to draw the master away from such risky comparisons. The play was approaching its climax. At the fall of the curtain the Philistine soldiery silently surrounded the little house where the betrayed hero slept. M. Raindal recited softly to himself the never-to-be-forgotten stanza:

"Une lutte éternelle, en tout temps, en tout lieu,
Se livre sur la terre, en présence de Dieu,
Entre la bonté omme et la ruse de Femme...."

He went on with it, and Mme. Chambannes declared the lines very pretty. She wished to know the name of the author.

"It is from Vigny, madame!" said M. Raindal, as he joined her in the little salon at the back of the box.

Chambannes went out. They remained alone. M. Raindal asked himself whether it would do to repeat his kiss of the morning, if only to signify to Mme. Chambannes that his new intentions persisted. But finding himself still slightly irresolute, he thought it best to remain on the safe ground of literary conversation.

Just as he was beginning to tell of the tragic love affair between de Vigny and Mme. Dorval, however, the door was suddenly pushed open. A tall dark man stood at the entrance of the box. M. Raindal saw nothing at first but his black moustache and his big laughing eyes.

"Ah, M. de Meuze!... Come in!" Mme. Chambannes exclaimed, with ready ease.

Nevertheless she blushed, and between her eyelashes came such a caressing, joyous, submissive look directed toward Gerald that M. Raindal felt suddenly hurt. He wanted to join their conversation, criticize the players and praise the music. But the words refused to come at his bidding. A sudden rush of ill humor flooded his inspiration. He got up.

"Are you going out, dear master?" Zozé asked.

"Oh, just for one minute to stretch myself and get some fresh air."

He had unwittingly banged the door. He wandered aimlessly along the passages until he came to the loggias of the staircase.

"You!" Chambannes exclaimed, as he came forward to meet him.

M. Raindal replied dully:

"Yes, it was too warm in that little room.... I left your wife with M. de Meuze, junior, or rather, if you prefer, the son...."

Chambannes did not seem surprised by this revelation. M. Raindal thought him somewhat stupid. They returned together at the first ring of the bell announcing the end of the interval.

Zozé was alone in the box. She received the master with a radiant smile of welcome.

"Had a good walk?"

"Not bad!" said M. Raindal, who felt disarmed by so much charm.

Nevertheless, he preserved a gloomy aspect during the whole of the third act. He kept on thinking of Gerald. That young man he had never regarded very sympathetically. He was vague and a coxcomb and the impertinent expressions his face assumed were in no wise justified by his very poor intelligence, banal opinions, and remarkable ignorance of literature: in fact, there was nothing about him that could appeal to M. Raindal. And then— the master hung tenaciously to this memory—physically did he not recall to mind the image of Dastarac, that scoundrel of a Dastarac? Had he not been the cause of the failure of the excellent Boerzell, at the Saulvard party? There was no doubt about it. It was from this that had sprung his first feeling of antipathy. It was futile to seek any further! Consequently, M. Raindal did not attempt it.

He did not try very hard to follow the direction of Zoz glances as she scanned the huge hall. It would have been a hard task to follow them and to discover the place that she was especially seeking. Her glances were so uncertain and so fugitive; they spread their tenderness over so many people and so much space! The master made one or two fruitless attempts and then gave it up. He merely asked her in a careless tone:

"Where does M. de Meuze sit?"

"M. de Meuze?... In the orchestra, I think.... But I believe he is no longer there.... He was going to spend the rest of the evening with some friends...."

"Ah! very good!" said M. Raindal nonchalantly. "I was asking, you know, simply because...."

To be sure, Zozé knew! She bit her lips not to smile. So! her aunt Panhias had not been so far wrong. She must be careful.

The evening ended without any further difficulty. M. Raindal had enjoyed the final ballet very much; and the steps of the *Sabotière* had made him enthusiastic.

When he returned home he went to his study. Before retiring for the night he wished to set down a few moral observations which had come to him in the course of the evening. They all had a bearing upon the rôle of woman as a social motive, and they would find their place in Chapter VI.

When he had written the last words, M. Raindal gathered up the sheets. There were no less than six large pages covered with small handwriting and without a correction.

CHAPTER XIV

THE Thursday lessons had started again. Although they had not altogether banished Egypt, that subject was suffering from a gradual disgrace. As a rule Mme. Chambannes had failed to read the prescribed books. Or else a stray word sent them both into a friendly gossip concerning the little happenings of the day: a new dress of Zoz, which the master declared to his taste, her account of a dance or a play, and subjects that were even more trivial. Once they had run away from the arid regions of science, neither of the two found enough courage to return there. By common consent, they avoided the paths of conversation which might have led them back. It was only towards the end that Mme. Chambannes would exclaim:

"Well!... Another fine lesson!... If it goes on like this, I shall know a lot at the end of the year!... Ah! What a deplorable professor you are!..."

M. Raindal smiled. Then, if he had not already abused that license, he seized Zoz hand and ardently pressed his lips against it. Wisely, she allowed him but two or three such tender outbursts at each lesson. Yet in her heart she was flattered. It amused her to see this famous, white-haired, man bending over her with love. His white hair contrasted with his skin and made it look pinker, and she found this play of color neat and pleasant to her eyes.

On the third Thursday she inquired about Cyprien. Why did not M. Raindal introduce his brother to her? She was quite anxious to meet him. The master replied evasively:

"Oh, my dear friend!"—as he called her now when they were alone and in the intimacy of their lessons—"my brother is a good fellow.... Yet I doubt very much whether you could get on together.... His temperament is brusque; he is an extremist, an absurd man.... Again, I noticed from certain signs that your absence of a month ago displeased him.... I prefer, therefore, not to risk myself in explanation of which I do not foresee any favorable results...."

"Just as you say!" replied Zozé, who had only insisted out of politeness.

M. Raindal nevertheless had almost spoken the truth. Uncle Cyprien had never omitted, during the last few weeks, any occasion to flay, *en passant*, the discourteous ways of Mme. Rhâm-Bâhan.

Systematically, resolutely, and in spite of everything, he was doing his best to prevent his brother from urging an introduction. To go and hobnob with the Chambannes and their friends, that would be the last straw! To go there, where he would have to meet Pums, the marquis, perhaps Talloire, who would stupidly come and pat him on the shoulder, compromise him and denounce him with their accomplice-like cordiality, so that M. Raindal would learn of his dealings at the Bourse, his speculating in gold mines! No, thank you! He preferred to lie, to resort to the very worst stratagems, such as simulated spite, false laughter and fictitious anger, rather than fall into this horne nest! Therefore, he seized the slightest pretext to deliver his imprecations.

"A woman of the world, Mme. Rhâm-Bâhan? A woman of the world, this person who had bolted without warning and left people waiting for her, without giving them a word of apology! A woman of the world, this person who had gone away, no one knew where! A woman of the world, this person...."

"Oh please! leave me alone!" M. Raindal interrupted, unable to stand it any more. "I am not asking you to let me take you there, am I?"

"You should add that you are very wise not to do so!" Uncle Cyprien retorted, delighted with the success of his tactics.

However, apart from the little tricks which he was compelled to employ for fear of being censured, for fear of his brother and Schleifmann, he had never been happier.

He very seldom went to the Bourse; on the other hand, he now operated without any help, dealing directly with Talloire. He enjoyed the feverish pleasure of giving his own orders, following their varying fortunes and taking his profit and placing it elsewhere. Several inspirations stood behind him; there was the advice of his friend Pums, some secret intuitions of his own, and the advice of a special sheet, the "Lingot," for which he had taken a three months' subscription. Good luck had a share in it, and in time the total of his profits reached the neat sum of 35,000 francs.

He had no more than 75,000 francs to make now; that is to say, according to the least optimistic calculations, not more than four months to speculate.

Then! Ah, then, with these one hundred thousand francs in his pocket, Uncle Cyprien would discard his mask, break with Talloire, put a stop to the game and openly declare his profits. But until then, *motus*, silence, caution and mystery, in short as much hypocrisy as they wished!

Accordingly, the very choice cigars which M. Raindal smoked at the brasserie were, according to him, a present from the Marquis.

"Yes, my dear Schleifmann!" he asserted, "I found the box waiting for me when I came home."

It must have been a huge box, a trunk almost, if one could judge from the number of havanas which it kept on supplying.

And it was the same thing about the tricycle which the ex-official had not been able to resist purchasing: perhaps Schleifmann thought that it was the result of further speculation? That was a very serious mistake! It had been paid for with the remains of his seven hundred francs profit, that tricycle.... Huh! That shut him up effectively, the moralist!... Or else Cyprien opposed a stoic reply to the inquiries of his brother, his niece, and his sister-in-law:

"Where did I find the money to buy this machine, you wish to know? With my savings on cigarettes, my good friends!... What do you suppose? When you wish one thing you have to do without another. It is extremely simple."

He had added to these purchases that of a soft brown felt hat, the broad wings of which gave to his close-cropped head somewhat of a Cromwellian aspect. Thus he could be seen every day with his sombrero, his trousers gathered at the ankles, riding up and down the city on his tricycle, even when he had no further to go than the rue de Fleurus to see Schleifmann, the rue Vavin to get to Klapprot, or the rue Notre-Dame-des-Champs to see his brother.

To such short trips, however, he preferred a ride to the Bois, especially on Sundays, for there he was not troubled by his anxiety concerning the stock market.

He would go out about ten lock, following the boulevard St. Germain, the place de la Concorde, and the avenue des Champs Élysées. He wore red gloves and carried a cigar between his teeth. He pedaled with delight, bending over his front wheel, drinking in the sweet morning breeze that rushed against his cheeks. Then, as he approached the Arc de Triomphe, he straightened up, slowed down his pace and rectified his position. The avenue du Bois stretched before him, as far as he could see, the ample magnificence of its sidewalks and gardens. In the atmosphere there was already a certain heat which gave a feeling of ripeness and of summer. Under the chestnut trees near the entrance, a crowd of pretty women in light dresses chatted, standing, or sitting down with elegant gentlemen. From the distance, officers and young men approached at a canter and slowed down as they passed out of the riding track. Their horses shook themselves, stretched their necks and, if pulled back, scratched the hard ground under them. Or there would be a light-colored coach entering the avenue, pulled by four imposing horses. One could see light dresses on top of it, flowery hats, graceful women who smiled, and men with dissipated faces. Behind them in a smart herald-like attitude, his elbow lifted high and his body bent backward, a lackey would draw out of a long brass instrument raucous and triumphant appeals. One might think it the gorgeous chariot of Youth and Pleasure.

Uncle Cyprien was thrilled by this spectacle and the noise that went with it. His eyes, his lungs, and his ears drunk in the intoxication of the orgy of colors, perfumes and sounds; in spite of himself he derived from it a sensation of supreme enchantment. He rushed after the fascinating coach, caught up with it, ran alongside of it and in front of it, swelling with pride, despite the speed which caught his breath.

He passed through the gate, rode slowly under the shady trees, and stopped at a café to drink an *apéritif*. It was not until the lunch hour that he returned, still by the avenue du Bois.

Sometimes on his way back he noticed among the passers-by an old gentleman with a white beard in the company of a young woman.

"Sapristi!" he thought. "My brother and Mme. Rhâm-Bâhan, very likely.... I must be careful!... I must hurry out of this."

He affected to close his eyes as if blinded by the dust, and rushed between the carriages like one pursued. It was a superfluous precaution; an imaginary peril! M. Raindal had also taken good care to look the other way.

These Sunday morning outings were Mme. Chambannes' own idea. She had discovered this clever way of publicly showing her friendship with the master. And although this exhibition took place only one or two Sundays a month, Zozé derived much gratification for her vanity from it. Smiles and sarcastic grins which she noticed as she passed only increased her satisfaction.

"You may laugh, my friends," she thought to herself, "you may joke, but, nevertheless, you envy me very much!"

Most of the time Chambannes or her Uncle Panhias joined the couple for the sake of appearances. At other times, Gerald, either on foot or on his bicycle, came and stopped a while to exchange a few words with them.

Despite the unpleasantness of such meetings, M. Raindal was far from disliking his Sunday walks. They brought relief to his week and with the reflection of their splendor seemed to illuminate the gloomy stagnation of the days that followed until he came again for his Thursday visits.

They were like a supplementary holiday to him, a semi-monthly festival, and had it not been that he dreaded his family, he would have come every Sunday.

Besides, what documents, what precious observations he was able to accumulate there, for use in his book! These refined young men and attractive women—were they not the living representatives of the voluptuous élite which persisted through the centuries? Did they not constitute the sacred battalion of pleasure which, at every period of history, led the chorus of elegance, issued the decrees of fashion, and dominated society by means of their charm, grace, and beauty? It needed but a simple effort of transposition for him to discern in them the coquettes and the men about town who had been the contemporaries of Rameses or King Tuthmosis!

Thus, in the course of his walks, M. Raindal took good care not to forget his severe duties as a historian. Whenever he was not looking at Mme. Chambannes, he was transposing and gathering in his memory a thousand significant details. The ladies caught his attention more than the men. He sought the eternal in their enticing gestures and their alluring glances; he did not find it there, but, nevertheless, drew satisfaction from them. He had passed several of them so often that they were clear in his memory. Whenever he recognized their silhouettes at a distance, he prepared himself to stare at them. His new gloves, which he held in his hand against the knob of his stick, spread their fingers like the stiff petals of a lotus flower. His blue cheviot coat, gray trousers, black felt hat, his button of an officer of the *Légion onneur*, and his beard, silvery and well-kept, gave him the appearance of a manufacturer grown old in the midst of wealth, of a rich conservative faithful to his sound principles.

Towards twelve lock they went back to the rue de Prony. Luncheon was a long affair. The blinds were pulled down and allowed only a yellowish light to filter through. Flowers placed on the table exhaled their harmonious fragrance. And when, moreover, Chambannes lit his cigar and Zozé the Turkish tobacco of her cigarette, the whole atmosphere fulfilled the overwhelming desire for a siesta which the master felt in the semi-darkness. His eyes were burnt by the sun and his legs tired by his walk; he struggled between his desire to look at his pupil a little longer and the weight of sleepiness which pulled his eyelids down. On the verge of giving way, he would rise and take his leave.

As soon as he was out, however, his heart was tormented by regret. He reproached himself sharply for his stupid drowsiness, for having wasted those sweet moments by his physical slackness. It would not have taken much to make him go back on the pretense of having forgotten something or to make an inquiry. But what inquiry? Self-consciousness and shame prevented him from going back. He went on his way with an increasing petulance. No sooner had he reached his home, in the rue Notre-Dame-des-Champs, than his exasperated bitterness turned to hatred. What an unlovely district! What tomb-like buildings! As soon as his lease ran out, they would see! He certainly would not renew it.

Through the door of his apartment sounds came to him of conversation and laughter. Thérèse was in the drawing-room with Boerzell, who still came regularly every Sunday.

Once, as he came in, M. Raindal heard the name of Dastarac pronounced.

"What!" he said, in surprise. "Are you speaking of that wretch?"

Thérèse replied:

"Yes, surely, we were speaking of Dastarac.... I have told M. Boerzell all about it.... I have nothing to hide...."

"Of course not!" the master assented.

"And do you know what monsieur was telling me?... That he has turned out very badly—our Dastarac.... There is a story of very unsavory debts, embezzlement, and false securities. In short, he has been put out of the University and compelled to run away to Belgium.... M. Boerzell will explain this to you better than I could."

The young savant told all the details of the affair.

"Well!... A pretty gentleman!..." exclaimed the young girl in a tone of burning contempt when Boerzell had finished.

"Nothing surprises me from that fellow!" declared M. Raindal. "Just the same, we owe M. Gaussine a fine debt of gratitude!"

He did not complain that day of the length of the hours. Comforting thoughts occupied him until dinner-time. So far he had never dared, under any circumstances, to sound Thérèse concerning the visits of Boerzell. He stood in fear of reprisals and oft-repeated conventional inquiries concerning the Chambannes' household. However, now that Dastarac seemed to be annihilated, crushed as it were, to the disgust of Thérèse herself, why should not the sympathy which he noticed existed between the young people follow its normal course? Why should they not, from being comrades, become husband and wife? And then, besides the joy of getting his daughter married, what an opportunity for the master, and what a liberation! No one would remain as a witness of his outings but Mme. Raindal who, entirely occupied with her religious duties, was an easy-going woman totally without severity, provided her faith was not interfered with. No longer any control; no more watch set on him; no further need to invent new lies or preserve silence! M. Raindal promised himself that he would keep his eye on this affair with caution and diplomacy so as not to spoil it.

Yet an oft-recurrent anxiety seized him again after dinner. He was thinking of the summer and the forthcoming vacation, those three months which he would, doubtless, have to spend far away from Mme. Chambannes. As he recollected his impatience, his recent fears during one single month of privation, he felt a sudden sensation of choking anguish. Where would she go? To what seashore or mountain resort? How many miles away would she be? And with whom?

He had discreetly put these questions in the course of many lessons given to his little pupil. She had replied vaguely. She affected not to have made up her mind yet and to be still hesitating between Les Frettes, the seaside,

Switzerland or some watering-place. She would decide on her choice at the time of a certain trip which George was shortly to make to Bosnia. She sighed as she said that. A melancholy shadow veiled the tenderness of her eyes. She turned the conversation to another subject.

His dear little friend!... Who knew but that some torment similar to his own oppressed her gentle little soul? Who knew but that she also was afflicted by the idea of the approaching separation?... M. Raindal was not so far lacking in modesty that he imagined himself alone the subject of all her possible regrets. However, he did not abandon the idea that perhaps he could claim a share of them. And he was quite right, too.

It was indeed true that Mme. Chambannes darkened whenever the master questioned her. But the baseness of Raldo was the only cause of her sorrow. This problem of their summer vacation was now debated at each of their meetings. Gerald, whose treachery had only strengthened his despotism, clung to a project of settling down at Deauville with his father for the month of August. There were invitations, "de la jolie femme," pigeon shooting, polo playing, and racing—in short, everything called him there. Against the attraction of so many pleasures, Mme. Chambannes' silent tears made no more impression than drops of rain on a window-pane.

"You can come there," he told her. "I sha prevent you from coming!"

She shrugged her shoulders. Could she not foresee the torments she would have to endure at Deauville, without friends, without relations, and separated from her lover!... Could she not in advance see herself separated from Raldo and the set which he frequented by that impalpable barrier, more efficient than an iron railing, which everywhere surrounded the flock of good society? She would be exposed to the snobbish glances of those women, the insulting echoes of their joy, the spectacle of their flirtations, and the social humiliation which can only be measured at close range.... Zozé, for the sake of her love, and to safeguard her passion, preferred a thousand times to go into retreat and abandon it for a time. These sacrifices pierced her heart beforehand. She took to crying silently, weeping intermittent tears after holding them back too long, and, between kisses, in the middle of an embrace, they would unexpectedly wet the cheeks of her Raldo.

How could she be revenged on him, how reply to his pitiless selfishness? Ah! Zozé was at last beginning to find out that there is no equality in love. Otherwise, would she not have punished the recent treachery of Gerald with an immediate betrayal? That was continuing now; would she not reply with some barbarous plan, say, to choose for her holiday some place where one or the other of the men who were in love with her happened to be going? There was Dieppe, for instance, where Givonne was going, Bagneres, where Pums was to take a cure, or Dinard, where Burzig, as an authentic

Englishman, had taken a little villa. None of these reprisals satisfied her. She soon convinced herself that Gerald would not be disturbed by any of these. What, therefore, was the use of her going to those fashionable resorts which, owing to their similarity, would forever carry her dreams back to Deauville? Would it not be much better for her to go and hide at Les Frettes, to seek slumber for her mind and forgetfulness in that peaceful spot, to plunge herself into the emptiness of country life till her wicked Raldo came back?

She chose this solution in the first days of July. Gerald promised that he would join her there at the beginning of September, which was the time set for Chambannes' return from Bosnia. Zozé was to leave on the 20th with her Aunt and Uncle Panhias. Moreover, she would not be left altogether alone, since the abbé Touronde was in the neighborhood and the Herschsteins and Silberschmidts also.

"And, after all," Gerald remarked, "a month is only four weeks.... And four weeks are very quickly over."

Mme. Chambannes agreed. His nonchalance brought a grimace of contempt and a tremor to her lips, but her pride made her attempt to smile.

Then came the following Thursday when, without saying anything about Gerald, she informed M. Raindal of her preparations.

"Ah!" he stammered, blinking, his eyes so full of sorrow and so imploring that Zozé felt at once moved by it.... "Ah! you are going to Les Frettes?... Oh, very well ...!"

"What about you, dear master?" said she. "What will you do with your summer?"

"I?"

He tried to remember, but his mind would not work. At last it came back to him, and he replied:

"I?... We?... We are going to Langrune, as we do every year.... How long are you going to stay at Les Frettes?"

"Oh, a month, two months perhaps, maybe three.... It all depends on Georg business."

"Three months!" repeated M. Raindal, whose mind had been struck by the cruelest of the three figures given. And he added with sincerity: "It pains me very much, my dear friend!"

At the same time he had seized Mme. Chambannes' hand and greedily pressed his lips upon it. She sighed with pity. Poor père Raindal! How heavy his heart must be!

She thought to herself, "Am I wicked!... Yes, I am to him what Gerald is to me, tha all!" Then, at the thought of the latte name, a fresh idea struck her. After all, why not?... It would be a very innocent revenge, a companionship and a relaxation which were as good as any. And so, with a little smile, she asked, as she drew away gently from under the lips of M. Raindal the hand which she had forgotten:

"Listen, dear master, what would you say about spending a few weeks at Les Frettes?... Would that upset your habits too much?"

M. Raindal contracted his forehead.

"I?... No! not at all!" he said, with the sensation of a comforting river bathing his heart. "But, there is my wife, and my daughter."

"Why, they would come, too!"

"Do you think so?" the master asked doubtfully.

"Of course, unless they refused, unless they have reasons to decline."

M. Raindal remained silent for a time. His face showed his discomfort. He rebelled against the need of denouncing his domestic tormentors. At length he exclaimed:

"Reasons! Why, they have none ... not the slightest!... Yet you know them a little.... My daughter is a savage; my wife is a bigot.... One is always on the watch in the presence of such people. Anyhow, my dear friend, I shall try, and you may guess what zeal and strength of affections...."

This eloquent peroration seemed to give him a sort of justification for kissing Zoz hand once more. The enthusiasm of his promise bolstered up his hopes throughout the evening. Besides, he had never, as yet, faced the contest straightforwardly. He had rather avoided it, postponed it by means of patience and cunning. Who knew what might not come out of an open battle, if he let loose the whole mass of those grievances and desires which he had repressed for so many months!

CHAPTER XV

THE next morning, however, he waited until the end of the lunch to try the first assault. As Brigitte served the coffee, he said:

"Children! I have an invitation to transmit to you.... If you do not like it, you are quite at liberty to decline!... But, first of all, I beg you, please listen to me to the end...."

While he spoke, with lowered head and unconsciously scratching with his nails the oil-cloth on the table, Mme. Raindal darted horrified glances at her daughter. Thérèse replied to them with a reassuring mimicry of her lips and eyelids. When M. Raindal had finished, she said in a very even tone, without any suggestion either of anger or fear:

"Mme. Chambannes is very kind, father.... Nevertheless, so far as I am concerned, I find her invitation unacceptable. And I should be very much surprised if mother did not agree with me!"

"Oh, quite!" Mme. Raindal approved, with a nod.

"May I ask what your reasons are?" the master asked, in a tone which he tried to make appear unctuous.

"My reason, and I am only giving you my own," Thérèse said with a similar air, "is this, that Mme. Chambannes, be it said without offense, is no company for us."

The master still held himself in hand:

"What do you mean?"

Thérèse replied:

"It seems to me clear enough...."

M. Raindal got up and walked around the table breaking a toothpick into shreds in his hands.

"Very well! I promised you that I would leave you free.... You are free.... I do not go back on it...." Then he raised his voice and went on. "Nevertheless, *sapristi!* it is impossible for me to put up with your insinuations.... Mme. Chambannes is a lady for whom I profess the greatest sympathy, and I am not afraid of acknowledging it, the most lively regard. I can not allow such abominable and unfounded charges to pass unchallenged." He mastered himself with a supreme effort and added, a little more gently:

"I beg you both, you and your mother, to speak out frankly.... What is it you have against Mme. Chambannes?"

Silence fell upon them. Brigitte, frightened in this atmosphere which she felt was heavy with the spirit of contention, had promptly dashed back to the kitchen. On both sides, they were holding their fury in leash, holding back the words of abuse which rebelled, ready to spring. "Well!" the master insisted. "I am waiting for your explanations ... for yours, Thérèse, since your mother does not answer me."

Mlle. Raindal replied seriously:

"Father, it is well understood, is it not, that we have no intention of hurting you, nor of commenting upon your friendships, that we are only speaking for your own good and for our own?"

The master grew impatient:

"Yes, yes, go on!"

"Very well, then! I assure you that Mme. Chambannes is not a woman with whom we can have anything to do, especially not a woman whose hospitality we could possibly accept.... Do you wish me to dot my ?"

"Do so! Do be afraid...."

"We ca go and live with a woman who amuses herself with a lover almost publicly...."

M. Raindal nearly choked. He drew in a deep breath:

"A lover," he exclaimed, "Who?... And who told you."

"Nobody! My own eyes told me. I had but to look and see.... Moreover, it seemed to me that her friends were all of the same caliber.... I could not, at any price, associate with such women!"

"Your eyes!" M. Raindal said, following his own idea. "And, according to your eyes, what is the name of the young man in question?"

Thérèse replied: "I have said enough.... I shall not add a single word...."

The master threw a glance of defiance and hatred at his daughter and then shrugged his shoulders, saying:

"I am sorry for you.... Your unworthy calumnies have not even the excuse of good faith, of being the result of an error.... You are the victim of personal spite.... You resent Mme. Chambannes' beauty and her charm.... You are an envious girl and a fool!"

"My dear!" begged Mme. Raindal.

"Leave him alone, mother!" Thérèse said, her fingers trembling on the edge of her plate. "Father does not know what he is saying any more.... All I wish is that he were as clear-sighted as other people, that he could perceive the abyss of ridicule towards which he is rushing, and dragging us with him, too."

M. Raindal, exasperated, struck the table with his fist, and called his wife to witness:

"Do you hear how she dares to treat me?... She has lost her reason.... She is mad...."

"Am I mad!" Thérèse exclaimed.

She ran out to her room and returned almost immediately, throwing three newspapers on the table.

"If I am mad, I am not the only one.... Read this! I take it that they are not all mad, those who write for these sheets...."

Her trembling hands pointed to certain paragraphs on the open pages which had been marked with a pencil.

With a gesture of contempt, M. Raindal snatched at the nearest of the three, and read:

"Who said that women were no longer interested in history? Surely not our old friend La Crois-Chammerilles, who told me yesterday the following anecdote:

"'For the last six months, one of our prettiest exotics has been taken up with ancient history. And every week, one of our most noted savants comes to her house to give her lessons.

"'As to the period of history of which he teaches her, and as to the name of the illustrious professor, seek them in the neighborhood of the Institute and remember also one of the greatest literary successes of last autumn.

"'Ancient history—old story!'"

M. Raindal gave one push and the other two newspapers fell to the floor.

"Do you dare to soil me with such infamy?"

He stamped with his heels on the papers:

"There, tha what I think of your filthy rags!... Pshaw! To think that my daughter, my own daughter, collects this filth, and in my own home constitutes herself the auxiliary of my enemies!"

He fell back on his chair. Thérèse rushed to him:

"Father, father!" she implored, kneeling down beside him, "forgive me.... You have misunderstood me.... I failed in showing you proper regard, I was not careful enough ... but you know that I love you, that I am quite incapable of wishing to cause you any pain."

M. Raindal looked at her with a softened glance. She insisted:

"Kiss me ... forgive me my quickness of temper.... I swear to you...."

Gently he forced her to her feet and set her on his knees as if she were a little child:

"All is forgotten.... I forgive you.... There, do cry, i over.... It is of no importance."

Her voice checked by sobs, she went on:

"I swear to you, father ... it was for your own good...."

"What good?" said M. Raindal, and his arms relaxed their embrace. Thérèse replied diffidently:

"The good of your reputation, of your name.... You do not realize, father. You are blinded by your friendship.... But you are on the way to compromise both...."

M. Raindal jumped roughly to his feet and replied sarcastically:

"So, I compromise you.... I am bringing dishonor upon you?... Upon your name? It is quite true.... Tha it, for the last thirty-five years, I have practically worked for nothing else but that.... Ha! Ha!... It is pure truth!"

He grew very excited and began again to walk around the table.

"Yes, you are very much to be pitied for having so compromising, as you say, a husband and father!... A man who has piled up turpitude upon turpitude, whose life is but one mass of madness and debauchery.... A man...."

Thérèse interrupted him:

"There, you are getting angry again, father.... You are jeering at us.... You misinterpret my words intentionally.... What I said, and I maintain my position, was that you could not but hurt yourself by preserving this intimacy with Mme. Chambannes.... I told you so because it was my duty, and because the time had come ... and nothing will prevent me from saying it again...."

M. Raindal stopped and crossed his arms over his chest. His glance challenged in turn his wife and Thérèse.

"Well, now," said he, "what is it you want?... I should think it was time to explain yourselves!... You wish me not to go to Les Frettes?"

"That, to begin with!" Mlle. Raindal replied firmly.

"To begin with!... The words are pleasant sounding in themselves, but I am willing to oblige you!... Let the 'to begin with' pass.... And then, after that?..."

"Then," the young girl said, "we would like you, without breaking with Mme. Chambannes, to decrease the number of those regular calls, those fixed dinners of yours, because, rightly or wrongly, people are talking and gossiping about it...."

"And where is it that they talk, if you please?"

"Everywhere!... At the college, at the Institute, among your colleagues, and even in the newspapers...."

The master smiled bitterly.

"Ah, you are well informed!... It is probably M. Boerzell who...."

"He and everyone else, father.... He and all the allusions, the wicked words with which people delight in wounding us, among our relations, our acquaintances, when we pay or are being paid visits...."

M. Raindal retorted with a broadside of noisy sarcasm:

"Evidently the danger is more serious than I thought. One must not neglect the warnings of so many kind earnest people. One must be cautious and put the brake on.... From now on, I place myself in your hands.... You yourselves will regulate the days and the hours of my visits in the rue de Prony.... If necessary, Brigitte can take me there and bring me back. I am so weak, so inexperienced, so childish!"

He went on in that tone for several minutes. By a phenomenon of auto-suggestion, the whole of his late-come virility was in a state of excitement and increasing revolt against this control, the details and the episodes of which he was himself creating. Every point raised was like a new sting that goaded him further, and poured into his veins a quick, warm poison which over-heated his sufferings with its own energy. He saw himself deprived in future, and forever, of Mme. Chambannes, forever interned far away from her, a prey to the worst torments of separation and perhaps of jealousy. For, supposing that Thérèse had spoken the truth!... A sudden anguish whipped his heart. His imaginary regrets almost reached a paroxysm. He changed his tone suddenly, and in a voice that was hurried and hollow, and which sounded the revolt, he said:

"Enough of this jest!... It is quite enough.... Oh! I know, for a long while I have had some idea of all the wicked thoughts and shameful suspicions which you were piling up against me!... Your plots, your sneers, your confabulations, and even your silence, which was more insidious than all the rest—none of those things has escaped me!... If, a minute ago, when you opened your souls to me, I showed some surprise, it was due less to the unexpectedness of it than to disgust.... Really, I did not believe that I could find so much mud and villainy in them.... Pshaw! Let it be so!... I know neither what your inspiration is, nor what your idea is based on, and I do wish to know.... But what I do wish and what I insist upon henceforth is that I shall be master in my home and free outside of it. What I want and insist upon is an end to your hypocritical grimaces, your aggressive silence, and all those sly maneuvers that are only an imitation of docility and shock me more than your insults of a little while ago.... Finally, I want confidence, esteem, and the respect to which I am entitled by my age, by a continuous life of steady work, and I may even say to have no false modesty, by my rank and my own worth.... If I cannot obtain these, we shall give up our life in common, since it would be unbearable for all of us to continue it.... This is clear, is it not?... I shall not come back to this point.... And to begin, this very day, I have the honor to inform you that, with or without you, I shall go and spend a month at Les Frettes.... You may consult with each other, make up your minds.... You have ample time, for Mme. Chambannes is not going for ten days.... However, until then, not a word on the subject, not a remark.... I will tolerate none. Yes, or no. I will not put up with more."

He walked towards his study, adding, as he placed his hand on the door-knob:

"I do conceal from myself how regrettable such a situation is. You have no one else to blame for it but your two selves, and your secret hostility towards me.... Everything has an ending, even patience.... And for the last six months, you have strangely overtaxed mine!"

He disappeared. Then, as if he wished to barricade himself against any attempt at conciliation, his key turned twice in the key-hole. M. Raindal had locked himself up.

"Well, my poor child!" Mme. Raindal whispered, her eyes shining with tears.

Either because she was afraid of being heard or because she instinctively imitated the hollow voice of her father, Thérèse replied quietly:

"What can I say, mother!... It is lamentable.... I did think that the evil had gone so far.... Our intervention has come too late!"

"I know it, dear," the old lady sighed.

Thérèse remained silent, leaning on the table, in an attitude of angry reverie.

"What is to become of us?" Mme. Raindal went on, in a kind tone. "If we shut our eyes, that wicked woman will take him away from us. If we cross him, he will leave us. And we are alone, absolutely alone, without anyone to advise us and defend us...."

"Possibly not!" the young girl replied, looking up.

"Have you anyone in mind?"

"Yes, Uncle Cyprien.... I do see anyone else who can scare father.... I am going there now, at once.... I shall work him up, rouse him to white heat.... And, I should be very disappointed if, with such heavy artillery, we could not overcome the resistance of father!"

The comparison made Mme. Raindal smile in spite of her tears:

"If you hope to succeed with him, go there now, dear! Alas! we have no time to waste!"

Thérèse bent over her and kissed her:

"Do cry, dear mother!... Courage!... I have an idea that we have not lost yet!..."

"May God hear you, my poor dearest!" murmured Mme. Raindal, rolling her eyes with a prayerful expression towards the ceiling.

Her Uncle Cyprie door was ajar when Thérèse reached the sixth floor. She knocked, asking at the same time: "May I come in?"

"Come in, come in!"

From the passage an odor of kerosene was already perceptible. Uncle Cyprien sat on a stool, a towel across his knees, cleaning his tricycle, which stood wheels up and saddle down, like an overturned carriage.

"I you, nephew!" he said, speaking through a corner of his mouth, the other being obstructed by an enormous cigar.... "Take a chair.... Yol excuse me, wo you? When I clean my machine, I get all mixed up if I stop in the middle of it.... Have you found a chair? Very good.... Well, I must say, I did expect you!... Nothing unpleasant, I hope?... Your father is not ill, is he?..."

Thérèse replied:

"Ill? That would be so serious in comparison!"

"Sapristi!" Uncle Cyprien exclaimed, opening his eyes wide. "You frighten me! Worse than being ill, what is it? Good God, what can it be?..."

" going to tell you, Uncle, but I need all your devotion and all your attention...."

"They are yours, nephew!... I am listening while I work ... or I work while I listen.... For you, my ears, and my eyes for my machine!... But, be quick, because you frighten me with your solemn face."

While his niece spoke, accordingly, M. Raindal, the younger never once looked up from his work. He rubbed and polished and oiled; his hands ran among the oil-cans, black rags, greasy bits of flannel, screwdrivers, and wrenches; at first sight, one might have thought him a sheep-shearer practising his art upon a tricycle.

"Unfortunate!" he merely murmured at intervals, his head still bent down. "Very unfortunate!... Most unfortunate!..."

Nevertheless, he was making up his mind very coolly, under the cover of his busy appearance. Although his losses were small, they had, during the previous week, reached the total of his profits. The liquidation of the last eight days showed no profit, and this was almost a loss for a speculator who was, like himself, accustomed to profits. Moreover, other mining stocks had undergone violent fluctuations. The market showed signs of a need for caution, if not for alarm. Business slowed down and the fall had affected several stocks which had until then risen daily. This consideration gave food for thought to Uncle Cyprien. Was it really a favorable time to take sides against his brother, to urge openly the necessity of a break with Mme. Chambannes? Did he not risk, if he took such a decided attitude, alienating the powerful sympathies which he enjoyed with the opposite camp—that is to say, the Chambannes and the whole band behind them, the Pums, the de Meuzes, and the Talloires, in short all his friends of the Bourse, and all his advisers? The point deserved to be settled only after proper consideration.

"It was then," Thérèse concluded, "that the idea came to me to seek your help.... No one but you can save us, because you are the only one who has sufficient authority over father to pull him away from the dangerous path in which he goes deeper every day."

"Unfortunate! Most unfortunate!" M. Raindal, the younger, repeated.

There was a pause. Uncle Cyprien was busy dropping oil from a little can into one of the oil-holes.

"You are saying anything, uncle!" Thérèse went on, disconcerted by his reserve.... "Why do you speak?... You share our opinion, do you?... Surely this scandal must cease.... We must tear father away from those people!"

"Fuff! nephew," said Uncle Cyprien, as he rose, folded his stool and put his tricycle on its wheels again.... "You asked my advice, did you, my sincere and friendly advice?... I shall give it to you with brutal frankness.... My own advice is that this affair is exceedingly delicate.... Of course, your fathe behavior seems to me unfortunate, and even deplorable; I would give anything to have him change.... But between that and going to a man of his age, a man of your fathe standing, and saying to him: 'My friend, I forbid you to go to Mme. So-

and-so any more ... and henceforth you shall not go ... '—between this and that, there is a difference!"

"And so you refuse to reason with him, to have a serious talk with him!" Mlle. Raindal said, pushing back her hair.

"I do refuse," the ex-official corrected her. "I am merely explaining the difficulties, almost the impossibility of the mission which you wish me to undertake.... Moreover, your father is not so easy to get on with; he is quite likely to send me about my business and to tell me that his affairs are no concern of mine.... And after that, there would be nothing left for me to do but to pack my things and break with him!"

He seized the handle-bar of his tricycle and led the machine around the room to watch the result of his cleaning operations. Then he added:

"To resume, you understand me, do you?... I do refuse.... I only lay the problem before you.... Do you think in your soul and conscience that I stand any chance of success?... If so, this is just the time to put my hat on and go to him.... Otherwise, it would be better for me not to expose myself to an unnecessary rebuke just for the sake of doing it.... Think it over!"

"It is all thought over, uncle!" Thérèse replied, suppressing a contemptuous smile.... "I am beginning to agree with you.... It is more seemly that you should not figure in this unpleasant affair...."

M. Raindal threw a suspicious glance at his niece.

"Oh-ho! mademoiselle, we are peeved, it seems, ... I am still at your disposal.... But, take my advice, do get excited, ... consider this question calmly.... And l bet you anything you like against a box of cigars that, before two days are past, you will be admitting that your wicked old uncle was right!"

He took her in his arms and kissed her forehead.

"Besides, who said that this infatuation would last?... Your father lost his temper because you opposed him, and the Raindals have a perfect horror of being contradicted.... We are like milk soup!... It falls down as soon as it is removed from the fire.... If you were to come to me this evening and tell me that everything is settled and that your father is going to Langrune with you, why! I would not be so very much surprised!..."

They reached the hall. Thérèse gave his hand a slight touch.

"Oh, what a cotton-hand!" M. Raindal protested. "Will you please shake hands better than that!"

Thérèse obeyed him.

"All right!" he approved. "Tha better! Au revoir, nephew ... and no spite, either, please."

Thérèse went down holding herself on the banisters. Her legs almost gave way under her. Her ideas were confused in an overwhelming impression of defeat and powerlessness.

When she reached the outside door, she stopped, hesitating. She did not try even to define her sensation of isolation, nor to elucidate the gross defection of her uncle. She felt stupefied, paralyzed, and forever vanquished.

She walked slowly towards the rue Notre-Dame-des-Champs. The passers-by looked at her, surprised by her disordered appearance, staring eyes, and expression of hidden sorrow. Love-trouble?... With those yellow cotton gloves, that faded alpaca dress, and that straw hat bought at a bargain-counter—and moreover, not pretty herself! No! Rather a discharged governess....

Without taking any notice of their glances, without even seeing them, she walked close to the walls, as if she needed a support in case she were to lose consciousness. Suddenly she came to the rue Vavin, and a vision, a ma name brought her to a sharp stop: Boerzell. Why, yes! There was the supreme resource, the supreme protector against the threatening catastrophe, against the ruin which threatened to strike her home very shortly!

A ray of hope enlivened her face, worn out by anguish. She hastened. Five minutes later she was in the rue de Rennes in front of Pierre Boerzel door.

Hearing the bell, he came to the door himself. He was in his shirtsleeves, and without a collar, because of the heat; his plump white neck showing freely above his shirt.

He gave a surprised exclamation on recognizing Thérèse, and quickly smoothed his hair down:

"You, mademoiselle!... I hope there is nothing wrong?"

Thérèse smiled with difficulty.

"No, M. Boerzell!... A service, a piece of advice I have come to seek from you."

"Will you allow me, mademoiselle?... Let me show you in...."

As soon as they were in the front room, which was his study—a tiny little room, where books and pamphlets covered the table, the chairs, and the divan—he apologized for the exiguity of the place: "You see!... I am very much limited as to space here ... and there are even more books in my room.... I shall have to move one of these days!"

Hastily he cleared the divan and said:

"Please sit down, mademoiselle.... What is it?"

At the same time he hurried to his room. He came back very shortly, having fixed his collar and tie and donned a coat.

"There!... I am at your service.... What can I do for you, mademoiselle?..."

With a thousand reticences, Thérèse took up her narrative. Boerzell followed her attentively, nodding his concern at intervals. But the selfish welcome which her uncle had given her roused him to an expression of indignation:

"That is too much!... Really, it is disgusting!"

"Yet, it is the case!" Thérèse said. "You knew some of our anxieties already before this mornin scene. Now you know everything!... I came to you as a trusted friend.... I have absolute faith in your discretion, your judgment, and your affection.... Answer me straightforwardly.... What would you do in our place?"

Boerzell lifted his arms in a gesture of despair:

"Ah! mademoiselle!... You will tell me that I am choosing a very bad moment to reproach you ... yet you must agree that, had you been more indulgent and merciful, we should not find ourselves in such a distressing position to-day!..."

"How is that?" Thérèse asked.

"Well! I kept my promise, I kept it religiously.... I never spoke of marriage to you.... Many chances offered themselves to me for doing so.... I took advantage of none of them.... I was counting on your own heart to release me some day from my oath.... The more I came into your intimacy, and the more my hopes were strengthened.... Well! I deplore my patience.... I am sorry for my faithfulness.... If I had overcome them, I may presume that we would be married by now ... and once I were your husband, I could take a part in your family dissensions, I could discuss matters with M. Raindal; I might have persuaded him, caused him to change.... But to-day, as things are, what can I do? Nothing ... nothing, even less than nothing!... At my first words, M. Raindal would show me the door. Ah! mademoiselle, here you have a case, alas! a very painful one, where this marriage which you scorned so much might have proved of use to you!"

He walked up and down the room, knocking against the table and the chairs, which he put back in place each time.

Thérèse murmured:

"Outside this marriage, do you see any other solution?"

"No, mademoiselle!" Boerzell replied feverishly.... "I am neither related nor allied to you.... I have no hold on your father." He sighed deeply: "And to think that I would throw myself into the fire for your sake! I would sacrifice everything for you, anything that you might ask me to—and see now to what I am reduced!... To sending you away as if you were a beggar, a stranger come to beg from me!... I have not even the consolation of giving you my advice left.... Your father is the master.... You have nothing to do but to bow, and to let him go if he so wishes."

Thérèse was worn out; her head leaning against the back of the divan, she began to cry in her handkerchief.

"And now you are crying!" pursued Boerzell. "And I am compelled to let you cry.... If I only dared to come close to you and to take your hands in mine without your permission, I would at once become hateful to you.... A friend, yes, but a friend with whom one keeps on distance, and whom one would treat as the very opposite of a gentleman if he made the slightest show of love!"

"No, M. Boerzell!..." Thérèse stammered between two sobs. "You are exaggerating.... It is true that I have been hard to you.... But I like you very much ... very much more than I did."

He paused to look at her. She eyed him with sympathy in her gray eyes, which were full of tears. With an unconscious movement of tenderness, she stretched out her hand to him. He fell back a step, he was so surprised; then he seized Thérès hand and, without kneeling down, without any such demonstration usually made by a lover who has just been accepted, he said in a halting voice which betrayed the intensity of his emotion:

"What! mademoiselle!... Am I mistaken? Do I understand the meaning of your words? You might be willing, you are consenting?"

"I do know," sighed Mlle. Raindal, oppressed by discouragement, and withal touched by his anxiety. "Later, perhaps.... I shall see...."

"Oh, thank you!" Boerzell exclaimed, as he pressed the feverish hand of his visitor ardently. "Thank you, mademoiselle.... You will see.... You will see how much I shall try to make you happy and contented...."

He looked at her kindly, with little shivers of gratefulness running along the corners of his temples. But suddenly his face darkened and he gently let go the young lad hand:

"And yet, no.... That would be to take advantage of your present state ... of your disturbed condition. I refuse a consent which I could extort from you in the midst of your sorrow and your tears.... Our marriage can only be accomplished through your own free will, and in the complete mastery of yourself. Later, as you say ... later, when you have recovered your calm and your clear sight, if you still hold the same sentiments toward me, you know what happiness you will give me, if you accept and become my wife.... Until then, I seek nothing from you but your friendship.... We are not heroes of novels nor fools nor madmen.... Our union must not be brought about by a subterfuge, by some surprise, or by a lack of reflection that might carry us away.... I would rather renounce you forever than to know I had conquered you by such vulgar means.... In the days to come, whatever may happen, I can assure you that neither you nor I will regret our wisdom of to-day. Am I not right, mademoiselle?"

He stood in front of Thérèse and sought his answer in her eyes. She endured his persistent look for a long time, then replied in melancholy accents:

"You are the very incarnation of common sense!... You are the best and most loyal of friends.... Just as you say!... Let us wait.... That, as a matter of fact, is more worthy of such old wise people as you and I.... Nevertheless, I would like to show you my gratitude. I do want to leave you now, after the words that have passed between us, without giving you some proof of my friendship...."

"That is quite easy, mademoiselle!" Boerzell replied quietly.

"In what way?"

"Allow me, whatever happens, whether M. Raindal goes there or not—to accompany you at Langrune. This vacation of yours which was to separate us was a cause of serious pain to me.... More than once, I was on the verge of asking your leave to come.... I delayed my prayer for fear of displeasing you.... I am bolder now.... Tell me, may I?"

Thereupon Mlle. Raindal stretched out her hand once more:

"What a thing to ask! M. Boerzell! I shall be delighted!...."

He felt bold enough this time for a kiss of thanksgiving. Thérèse thoughtlessly complained of being thirsty. He ran out to his room and came back with a tray. In an instant he had prepared a glass of sugar and water in which he poured a few drops of rum.

"A bachelo home, a savan home!" he grumbled jestingly, as he stirred the mixture.... "No cordial ... no smelling salts ... nothing that is needed for receiving ladies!"

He corrected himself at once:

"Pshaw!... There, I am again alluding to marriage.... I had forgotten that my promise was on again...."

Thérèse drank greedily, her eyes smiling at him. The clock struck three and she started.

"I was forgetting my poor mother!... Good-by.... Thank you again with all my heart!... Till next Sunday then? Perhaps we shall have good news!..."

"It is my dearest wish, mademoiselle!" Boerzell replied skeptically.

He leaned out of his window to watch her go. She walked with a virile and well-balanced step; she made her way among the passers-by holding her head somewhat haughtily as only those women do who have a consciousness of their own charm, or a pride in their thoughts. Boerzell felt instinctively that it was no longer a young girl who was walking away from him: it was rather a sort of leader, a mother by right of intellect—the true head of the Raindal family.

She turned into the next street and was no longer visible to him.... He closed the window. He felt his breast swelling in a glorious satisfaction. Their behavior, the cordial chastity of their interview seemed to him to stamp them out as people who were far from being vulgar.

"We have been very chic!" he summarized, falling back into his student dialect.

Then he sat down at his table once more, his eyes dreamy, as if he were voicing a wish:

"If she only would!" he murmured.... "What a companion for me! What a wife!... She is a man ... a man in the finest meaning of the word!"

CHAPTER XVI

M. RAINDAL reached the station fifteen minutes before the departure of the train which was to take him to Les Frettes. He paced the platform, thinking.

Most of the carriages were empty. On the deserted platform he saw not a porter, not a truck; it stretched out, an endless carpet of asphalt. The glass roof refracted a dark, heavy heat. It was that hour of semi-rest, between the end of morning and the beginning of afternoon, when everything seems to be dozing in the railway stations, apart from the engines, the men, the wagons and the goods.

M. Raindal walked with his head down, his hands clasped behind his back, his big white panama hat set slightly at the back of his head. One by one he recalled the previous days, the painful ten days' siege from which he had come out at last victorious, although confused, worn-out and wounded. At times he sighed at the thought of it.

The week had surely been a painful one! Twenty meals of sulky silence, shifty glances and contrite looks! In between, never a word; a speechless war of resistances which clashed without coming to a close contact; a strained parody of ease in the midst of utter discomfort. Then, on the eve of his departure, one hour before the women were to leave for Langrune, the last battle had been fought: Thérèse and Mme. Raindal had abdicated all pride, affectionately begged M. Raindal to follow them, and attempted to give him a supreme counsel. A little more and he would have given way. His refusals were softened; the chains of his promise were breaking apart. A careless admission on the part of Thérèse had changed the issue of the battle.

"Well, I admit it, father!" she had said in answer to the maste charge. "We might, after all, have shown ourselves less openly hostile to Mme. Chambannes, less cold perhaps when you described her receptions to us."

That admission had moved him to a new resentment, bringing back an angry memory of all their previous malice.

"Ha! you acknowledge it now!" he exclaimed. "Now that you see me firm in my decision, now that you realize the extent of your faults.... And you wish me to add to those one more discourtesy, you want me to break my word to Mme. Chambannes who is waiting for me.... Too late! You should have thought of all this sooner."

He had gone on mumbling indistinct and vindictive recriminations. Intimate arguments supported him. What if he were to listen to these two women— would it not mean that the same thing would have to be gone through again on his return? No, they stood in need of a little lesson, of an exemplary warning!... Brigitte had closed the debate when she came in to announce the arrival of the carriage from the station. They had exchanged icy kisses from the tips of their lips, with hurried promises to write every week and to meet again in September. The door had banged. The sound of heavy wheels came from the street. M. Raindal had been left alone, delivered, saved from going to Langrune.

Still walking up and down, the master sighed. He had now no great illusion concerning the seriousness of that parting. How many *ménages* survived such outbursts! The malice of outsiders took a share in them and exasperated the disagreements. Grievances were sharpened by distance and were sharper on return; when people met again, they were almost enemies.

Why! Should he have submitted to the tyranny which his wife and daughter tried to impose upon him? Should he have sacrificed a precious sympathy, an exceptional friendship, to their envy and prejudice? Ought he to have blindly bent himself to their orders, as if he were repenting of some guilt, instead of opposing them with the firmness of his innocence?

"Passengers for Mantes, Maisons—Lafitte, Poissy, Villedouillet, les Mureaux, take your seats!" proclaimed a guard.

M. Raindal climbed into a carriage. An old attendant closed the door after him. The master noticed in the man a likeness to Uncle Cyprien. He grunted:

"Another one who will not bother me any more!"

He settled in a corner of the carriage, took off his hat, his relaxed frame all ready for a doze. The thought of Cyprien kept him awake a few minutes. He had, until the last minutes, dreaded his brothe lectures, anathemas and curses. But no such outbursts had come. On the eve of his departure, Cyprien had dined with them and expressed no violent opinion whatsoever on hearing from the maste own lips of the dual vacation which was to split the family. All he had done was to risk a harmless jest: "So then, my friends, you are to be bifurcated! Bah! If it suits your taste.... It does rest one, after seeing each other all the year round."

He had seemed almost ill at ease, kept his eyes on his plate and only reassumed his good humor when they had left the table.... A queer fellow, Cyprien, a foamy brain, any suspicion on his part was out of the question.

This contemptuous judgment fully satisfied the master. He gradually fell into slumber and did not wake up until he reached Villedouillet station.

Mme. Chambannes was on the platform, wearing a dress of batiste, embroidered with pink flowers, and white kid shoes. She waved to him with her sunshade, then followed the train until it came to a stop. Standing at the entrance of his carriage, she smiled at the master as he climbed down the stiff steps.

"So your wife and daughter did not want to come?" she asked maliciously, after the first words of greetings had been exchanged.

"No, my dear friend! I could not persuade them.... Besides, I did insist very much.... The sea air is very good for Thérèse."

"They must hate me! You must admit it!"

M. Raindal blushed and affected to chuckle.

"Well, well! I would not like to say that this departure took place without some objections on both sides.... These two women have their own views ... and I have mine.... You know, they do always coincide."

Then he added more boastfully:

"However, they are in the habit of respecting my will and, after all, the parting was better than I had feared, despite the regrettable scene which I mentioned briefly to you in Paris.... At all events, here I am.... Is that the only thing that matters?"

There was a pause. Zozé, a sarcastic and thoughtful expression on her face, stood outside the station. A yellow-painted governess carriage, with a bay pony, its mane close-clipped, stood against the curb. Firmin, who stood at the head of the pony, discreetly greeted the master.

"Here, Firmin!" said Mme. Chambannes. "Keep M. Rainda check.... You will look after his luggage and bring it along in the trap I ordered from the livery man."

She settled herself in the carriage, sitting sidewise, facing the tail of the horse. She took up the reins. The master sat opposite her. Zozé caressed the flanks of the pony with a light touch of her whip. The carriage ran down the inclined station-yard, pitching at the shock of the uneven stones. A few lookers-on stood on the edge of the pavement and smiled half-jeeringly as they watched it go.

In less than fifteen minutes the carriage entered the graveled avenue which led to the front steps of Les Frettes. Trees made a frame on each side of it; suddenly the house appeared. It was a large modern building with white walls broken at two or three windows by brown blinds.

There was a wide lawn in front with beds of roses, dahlias and mixed phlox in the corners. Behind, the park began at once. It was dark, thick-leaved, endless apparently, and ran for a long distance alongside the state road separated from it by a wall.

Right and left of the house, more trees linked their branches, hiding the country beyond, forming a thick enclosure as far as the back of the building, around another lawn which was like a little field and contained a tennis court with the net hanging slack. To "enjoy the view," as Mme. Chambannes said, one had to go up to the second floor.

"Your room is on that floor, dear master, and on the side looking right over the tennis lawn.... A superb view, as you will see."

M. Raindal followed her up the stairs, which were filled with an odor of iris.

Zozé pushed the window open. A great gust of soft wind entered. The master leaned on the balcony and for a long time contemplated the scenery.

Beyond the trees began the immensity of the apparently limitless lower plain. The villages with their belfries seemed like so many topographic points marked, as on a map, with childish signs. To the left, the little hills opposite curved their slopes in a chess-board effect of yellow, brown and green vegetation. At the bottom one could not see but one could guess the presence of the Seine river, a loop of which sparkled like a pruning-hook.

"Is it pretty?" said Mme. Chambannes who, with her plump elbow, touched that of the master on the railing of the balcony.

"Very beautiful!" declared the master.

And he murmured, turning his glance to Zozé:

"I am very happy, my dear friend, very happy to be near you!"

She thanked him with a candid smile on her profile. In this full light, the clearness of her complexion was enlivened. It showed subtle shades finely superposed in a diaphanous blend. The light of day penetrated her batiste blouse and a pale rose reflection breathed under the material. M. Raindal was enumerating all these charms to himself. Unwittingly, he was little by little pressing his elbow against that of the young woman. He was even going to seize the hand of his little pupil—always a perilous operation which he never risked unless moved by a sudden audacious impulse—but the door was unexpectedly opened.

Aunt Panhias entered, escorted by a servant who carried M. Rainda trunk on his shoulder.

From that time, until the next morning, the master and Zozé were never alone. When the trunk was opened, visits began: Mme. Herschstein, Mme.

Silberschmidt, with one of her cousins from Breslau, and, at five, the abbé Touronde.

They all gathered at that time, in the shelter of a shady glade which opened on the park, not far from the entrance and on the side of the main path. It was surrounded with lime trees and forest trees not yet grown to their full height. In the center of this circular space stood a mushroom-shaped stone table. Tea was brought in, with cakes and iced fruit in champagne which Zozé served with a small gilt ladle.

The women sat in comfortable reed armchairs which presented this inconvenience, however, that they squeaked under the weight of people who were too heavy. M. Raindal preferred a strong rocking-chair, the balancing of which amused him.

The conversation was kept up, light and easy, until the return of Uncle Panhias who came back from Paris about 6.30. The abbé Touronde, as he left, secured the maste promise that he would come and visit his orphanage in the course of the week.

When the dinner was finished, M. Raindal asked leave to retire. He was, he said, tired out by this first day of settling down. Mme. Chambannes encouraged him to go and rest.

He inspected his room, however, before going to bed. Everything had been arranged with a perfect refinement of country elegance: from the furniture of ash-wood with copper handles to the bed and window curtains of English cretonne and the sachets of lavender scattered about the drawers and on the shelves of the mirrored wardrobe.

The bedclothes smelt of iris, a coarser iris, but more wholesome than that personally used by Zozé. M. Raindal sniffed persistently at this unusual scent which bathed his body; then he blew out his candle.

He was going to sleep. The sound of footsteps above caused him to open his eyes in spite of the utter darkness about him. Who was it? His little pupil, his dear friend? What a flattering and rare pleasure it was to sleep under the same roof with her! The master tossed about several times in his bed. A thousand tempestuous and uncertain images showed Zozé to him. He sighed and grew impatient in this captivating sleeplessness. The fresh air, very likely, the stimulation of the fresh air! At last, he made up his mind about it. Lying on his back, he contemplated, without resisting them, the procession of his feverish reveries. They were beginning to assume a more distinct shape than was altogether seemly when fortunately sleep came and swept them all away.

The next morning, about ten, Mme. Chambannes proposed a ride to the master. They left the house, with Anselme, the coachman, who sat, despite the bumps of the road, stiff and respectful, in the corner of the little carriage, near the case destined for umbrellas.

The morning was clear and fresh, of that August freshness, still cool between the previous da heat and that of the coming hours, but a summer freshness all the same, reassuring and with no chilly signs of any forthcoming cold spell.

Zozé drove with high hands, her eyes free, turning aside according to the conversation, while the pony trotted with all its speed, swinging his back.

Twenty minutes later, they reached the road which climbed under trees towards the tiny forest of Verneuil. Instinctively, the pony slowed its pace. Huge horse-flies scattered under its feet, others stuck greedily to its neck and its fat shiny flanks.

The wood showed a diversity of the most harmonious colors. Broken by daylight here and there, it would seem all white with rows of slender silver birches. Further on were spaces that were wholly pink, invaded by the wild briar. A dark mass of pines dominated everything, clarified only by the growth of the young, light green, pine-needles. The wind had scattered many of the older ones and they lay drying in the dust.

On returning, they stopped by the side of the road which cut the wood. Anselme spread out a rug on the ground, and the master sat there with Mme. Chambannes. Zozé apologized for taking out her cigarette-case. In the country, etiquette might be relaxed, might it not? And then they were in a little wood where they could meet no one.

Hardly had she said this when two young cyclists appeared. They were pedaling in a leisurely way, side by side. At once, M. Raindal angrily recalled his intolerant brother Cyprien.

The two young men winked slyly at each other, indicating Zozé. "Pretty!" the nearer of the two said distinctly.

This familiar remark further provoked M. Raindal.

"Cad!" he said, when the two cyclists had passed on.

"Why?" asked Zozé, blowing out her smoke. "One must not take offense for so little, in the country."

Those three words constituted her favorite motto at Les Frettes, a permanent justification for all the fantasies of dress and behavior which her gloom and her idleness invented.

She took advantage of it, the next morning, to dispense with Anselm services for their ride. The coachma presence had obviously paralyzed M. Raindal.

"A very good idea!" the master said approvingly, as soon as they had started. "Besides he was of no use at all, that fellow."

Thereupon he seized his little pupi hand so brusquely and violently that Notpou—such was the almost Egyptian-sounding name which Mme. Chambannes had bestowed upon her pony—shied with fear, under the pain from his suddenly pulled bit.

"You must keep quiet, dear master?" Zozé chided, as she brought the animal back to its pace. "You are scaring Notpou.... Yol have us tipped over!"

"It was such a long time!" M. Raindal stammered.

She smiled indulgently. Suddenly emboldened, the master asked, in the absent-minded tone he used on such occasions:

"And the Messrs. de Meuze?... Did you have any news from them?"

Mme. Chambannes replied, making an effort to repress the blood she felt rushing to her face:

"None!... I believe that they are at Deauville until the end of the month, as I told you last week.... They were to arrive there the day before I left Paris."

M. Raindal, his hands hanging, directed a studious look at her.

"In that case, they are not coming here?"

"Not that I know of, during August," Zozé replied, having almost conquered her blush. "After that, it will be the shooting season.... So ... you see!"

"Quite!" the master murmured, while in his heart he ragingly abused Thérèse.

Ah! how he wished she were here, for an instant only, so that she could hear this! That was the way people made accusations and spread calumny, without proofs, acting upon suspicions and uncertain jealousies! "A woman who publicly gave herself a lover!" M. Raindal repeated to himself. Publicly! A lover! Where?... At Deauville, perhaps! (For, gradually, the master had narrowed down his suspicions and centered their watchfulness upon the head of Gerald, the only young man, after all, whom Mme. Chambannes saw frequently.) Yes! At Deauville, fifty leagues from Les Frettes, neglecting his love affair for a month and even more! A fine lover indeed!... How mean and unfair people were! He let out a contemptuous laugh.

"Are you laughing, dear master?" Mme. Chambannes inquired.

"I am laughing," he replied between two kisses, "I am laughing at the wickedness, or more exactly at the stupidity of mankind!"

The daily schedule soon became regular. Whenever the heat did not prevent it, the morning was spent in driving.

They eschewed the fashionable places beyond Poissy, in the neighborhood of Saint Germain. They preferred to follow the course of the Seine, driving towards Poutoise or even Mantes, an uneven, hilly and often imposing region which attracted the master, as it had Mme. Chambannes.

There the wind rolled its ample currents over plateaux and hills, carrying a strong taste reminiscent of the sea. Sometimes, at the top of a shut-in road that climbed under the shady trees, an unexpected perspective disclosed enormous expanses, forests, cross-roads, the breadth of the river, a big village, oxen in a field, vine on a hill-side, in short, the whole unexpected complexity of the provincial countryside, far from Paris and its suburbs.

The master and Mme. Chambannes would leave about nine and not return until time for lunch. Some days, in order to prevent idle gossip, they took the abbé Touronde with them. M. Raindal and the priest occupied one seat and Zozé, who was driving, the other.

One Thursday, the three of them went as far as Mantes, where the master wished to purchase a pair of brown shoes; their arrival caused a sensation. The strange carriage, the piquant attractiveness of Mme. Chambannes, M. Rainda white hair and the black robe of the abbé impressed the curious with their cumulative effect. In front of the bootmake shop, urchins surrounded the carriage. Neighboring shopkeepers came out on their steps and passed jocular comments. This affair and the popular emotion it caused were summed up in a short anonymous paragraph in the *Petit Impartial de Seine-et-Oise*. Although names were not given no one could mistake the meaning of the allusions, from the heading, *Suzanne*, to the bitterness of the writer towards "certain ecclesiastics, friends of the orphans" who were paying for the abbé Tourond holidays.

As a result of this unlucky experience Mme. Chambannes henceforth avoided the towns.

These drives, moreover, were less of a pleasure than a mere pastime between the hours when she read Geral letters—when any came—and those when she wrote to him.

Every day, after lunch, she shut herself up, to write him long pages, cleverly composed so as to stimulate his inert tenderness and his somnolent jealousy. In the meantime, M. Raindal, who had gone up, seemingly to work, enjoyed a nap on the floor above or imitated his hostess by writing a few words to his family. It would have made a piquant comparison to put their two letters side by side. Zozé purposely blackened her own character, multiplied the questionable details, the recital of episodes where her coquetry won her admiration, the masculine homage, the fervent glances of M. Raindal, of the abbé, of a passer-by, of all the men. The master, on the contrary, exhausted all examples in order to whitewash her of everything suspicious, to establish her child-like candor, her virtue and undoubted purity.

They did not meet again until nearly four lock. Then, according to the temperature, they remained in the garden or made visits in the neighborhood, either to the abbé Touronde, whose little orphans M. Raindal inspected twice, the Herschsteins, or the Silberschmidts.

Never did the time lag for the master, unless it were when Zozé left him alone with her Aunt Panhias, having herself to call somewhere in the village, give orders, or change her dress. His only compensation was that he could talk about his little pupil. He confided to Mme. Panhias his own observations concerning the changing moods of Zozé. Some mornings she seemed a prey to utter weariness, without any notable event justifying these fits of sadness. To what could he attribute them? Mme. Panhias, who had secretly noted the coincidence of such crises with the non-arrival of letters bearing the Deauville post-mark, replied evasively:

"It is her *natourre* to be like this! How can it be helped?"

"It may be so!" M. Raindal approved. "Quite so!... A dreamy nature!... A nature essentially melancholy!"

And he promised himself to neglect nothing that could bring distraction to his little pupil.

He even consented to play tennis with her, one afternoon, for fear of disappointing her. Zozé was on one side, M. Raindal and Aunt Panhias together on the other. Rather because he was all out of breath than for fear of compromising his own dignity, the master gave it up after a few minutes. His success in that game had been mediocre. Moved by a feeling of self-denial, Zozé did not repeat the attempt.

She also meant to show solicitude. She was sorry for poor M. Rainda family worries, of which he had given her a few significant illustrations. Whenever the master opened a letter from Langrune in front of her, she never failed to inquire whether his ladies showed less malice.

"Phew!... Icy.... Always ice-like!... Inquiries as to my health.... News of their own.... Compliments for you.... Kisses.... Hardly ten lines.... Read for yourself!"

She scanned the page, remembering Geral letters—notes whose laconism hardly exceeded that of the maste relatives.

"Yes, dear master!" she sighed.... "As you say, humanity is very stupid!"

On such days, out of pity for his sorrows which were so similar to her own, she was less rigorous towards the furtive kisses with which M. Raindal sought out her hands, gloved or bare, on every possible occasion. She racked her brains to order delicate dishes which she knew would please him. Then, the dinner ended, if he did not fall asleep, she read to him in the drawing-room—a newspaper or a volume of history. She read timidly, doing her best, with incorrect intonations, little gir errors which almost melted the maste heart. Or else—height of delights—she accepted his arm for a walk in the garden, along the lawn, in front of the terrace. When the sky was cloudy, M. Raindal, under the veil of obscurity, daringly kissed the young woma hand. Once he almost risked a nearer kiss, on her neck, taking advantage of the half-décolleté evening dress which Mme. Chambannes wore. But, on the verge of executing the movement, he was seized with such a fear that he stopped dead on the spot.

"Are you ill, dear master?" Zozé asked.

"No!" he replied, starting again. "I was listening to the wind in the branches!"

When he reached his room after these nocturnal frolics, he had difficulty in going to sleep. Reflections bubbled in him in foaming cascades. He counted up the number of kisses Mme. Chambannes had tolerated since the morning: one in the Verneuil wood, another in the park before lunch, another in the afternoon, in Zoz own room, where he had gone on the pretext of asking for a book, a fifth and even a sixth one in the evening, below the terrace.... He modestly admitted to himself that these were childish calculations and not devoid of vanity!

But what weight have metaphysical considerations against the overwhelming reality of our joys? The latter know no other limit than the variations of our feelings. If they reach exaltation, we should not dismiss their enthusiasm with contempt; if they fall or diminish, what philosophy can lift them up again? Thus M. Raindal meditated, with a growing scorn for speculative pleasures.

He often reached a state of extreme frankness, in the course of those solemn examinations, when his naked soul spoke to his mind, as a wife to her husband. It was quite true! M. Raindal did not attempt to deny it; he was slightly in love with his pretty little pupil. At her approach, he felt himself blush; he felt those emotions and internal flutterings which, according to general opinion, are signs of infatuation. To be sure, it was a harmless love, a flame that could not scorch, the last radiation of his heart! What danger did he run in rejoicing at those crepuscular lights which life, in a last act of kindness, sometimes kindles again on the road that leads to the grave? What wrong did he do when he drew from those illicit kisses a sensation of renewed youth, a continuous denial given to the fatal decline of his years?

These grave thoughts saddened him. He deplored being so old; he regretted that he had not known his dear friend Mme. Chambannes sooner. Again, not to mention the forthcoming departure which would separate him from the young woman, how many hours near her had Fate in store for him?... Under a rush of bitterness, he would sit down to write to Thérèse, to attempt a new project. August was drawing to an end. M. Raindal, from words Mme. Chambannes let fall, was inclined to conclude that a prolongation of his visit would please his hostess. In the course of many chats, she had seemed to indicate that the arrival of the two ladies in September would not be unwelcome to her. What did these latter say to that? Would they join the master, instead of returning to Paris, during those "days of intense heat" which threatened to persist? M. Raindal did not intend to force their hands. Nevertheless, he was of the opinion that their ill-humor had lasted too long, and it did not seem right that they should a second time refuse such cordial advances.

He went to bed revived by the hope one acquires through the mere voicing of on desires. And, the next day, when he saw Zozé again, all smiling and fresh in a light morning gown, like a nymph of dawn, the last vapors of his melancholy fled away.

"Where are you going, dear master?" she cried merrily from her window.

He looked up and made friendly signals to her with his hand.

"I am going to the stables to take some sugar to Notpou.... After that I shall go to the post-office to mail a letter to my family!"

"Hurry up, dear master! I shall be ready in half an hour."

He looked back, five steps away, placing his hands above his eyes. She was still smiling, leaning on the balcony. The wide sleeves of her gown had slipped apart and showed the white flesh of her arm, folded on the balustrade.

"If only those women agree to come!" thought M. Raindal, as he walked towards the stables.

One morning, as he returned from mailing the fourth letter to them in one week—three having been left unanswered—he caught up with the village postman on whose route the château was.

"A letter for you, monsieur!" the man said as he saluted.

The master slowed down. It was a letter from Langrune. The Raindal ladies admitted that he was right in his remarks concerning the heat. Consequently, they would delay their departure and not return to Paris until about September 15th. Of Les Frettes, of Mme. Chambannes, not a word was said.

"Fools!" the master murmured with disappointment.

But his satisfaction was stronger. After all, this gave him the desired postponement, the right to remain at Les Frettes. Who knew but that the two women, had they been coming, would have made him uncomfortable with their humiliating surveillance! As to their coldness, their hidden enmity, he would see them on his return, and subdue them, cost what it might!

He walked so fast that he met the postman coming out of the door of the château.

In the middle of the terrace, the stone balustrade of which ran all round the house, Zozé sat dreaming in a wicker armchair. In front of her some opened letters lay on a little table beside the tea tray.

"Anything new, dear master?" she asked. "The postman told me he had given you a letter.... Was it from your family?"

M. Raindal stammered confused explanations.

"Well, then, when will you be leaving?" asked Zozé calmly.

He looked at her with a somewhat disappointed expression.

"Eh! I am not going, *mon amie*.... Since you are willing, I shall be happy to stay."

He glanced to the left, then to the right, and seized Zoz hand, bending over her.

"I, too, have some great news now!" the young woman declared, suppressing a gesture of enervation while M. Raindal completed a heavy kiss. "First of all, I have a telegram from George. He is coming back on September 1st, Monday ... in three days!"

"Ah!" M. Raindal said carelessly. "Good! How is he!"

"Very well! You may read his telegram.... And then...."

"And then?" the master repeated, oppressed with anxiety.

"Then? Well, I have received a letter from the Messrs. de Meuze who inform me that they are coming to spend a week at Les Frettes."

M. Rainda lips twisted. He attempted an emphatic objection:

"But you assured me...."

"Yes, that they would open the shooting season.... They are going to do that, in the Poitou, where it does open until the 12th."

"That is different!" murmured the master in a tone of defeat. "When do they arrive?"

"Monday, also!"

The master drew in his breath and asked, in a firmer voice:

"The same day as your husband?"

"Yes!" Zozé replied, watching him from the corner of one eye. "That is to say, George will arrive at nine. Uncle Panhias will meet him at the Gare du Nord, and he cannot be here before eleven. The Messrs. de Meuze arrive in the afternoon.... After all, George will be here a few hours later!"

"Tha right; a few hours later!" M. Raindal repeated, at all hazard.

He laid a hand upon his forehead, complaining of a sudden headache. The sun, no doubt ... or his haste in returning.

"With your permission, I shall not go out this morning!" he said. "I prefer to rest."

Smiling, Mme. Chambannes watched him depart. Then a sudden sulkiness brought down the corners of her lips. After all, there was nothing for her to laugh at. Everything was taking an ugly turn. The master had taken seriously her banal words of courtesy to him and the regrets which, in a moment of anger, she had formulated concerning Gerald. Old Raindal was going to "stick to" Les Frettes for another fortnight! Thereupon, George was coming back from Bosnia! The marquis and his son arriving at the same time—as agreed. She had no hope that Raldo would agree to hurry their arrival! Barely one evening to see each other again, find each other again! And this, besides, would have to be before old Raindal, who was already sulky and would keep his eye on them! What ill-luck, what complications and difficulties!

During the three days that followed, Mme. Chambannes apologized for being in a sad mood. She did not feel very well and her nerves ached.

M. Raindal affected to be sorry and full of goodwill. He, at most, risked a kiss or two, to keep himself in countenance. But he was not feeling very gay himself. Courteously, Uncle Panhias accused him of that fact. The master feigned surprise. No, really, he had no reason whatsoever for being sad; and to prove his care-free state, he chuckled, beating his chest:

"Ha ha! I not gay! Ha ha! Why should I not feel gay? Ha!"

Geral image passed, more clearly, before his mind; the maste little laugh stopped dead, as if broken in two by a sudden shock.

CHAPTER XVII

ON Monday evening, after dinner, the company went to the drawing-room to take coffee.

Zozé was christening a pale blue muslin dress, the low cut of which revealed her neck, encircled with a double row of pearls. The Marquis was in evening dress and white bow; Gerald, in a dinner-jacket, wore a tea rose in his button-hole. An air of festivity seemed to emanate from them both.

The tall French windows of the room were opened; they led straight out onto the terrace that surrounded the house. Through the space between their two sides could be seen the lawn, the flower beds and the thick mass of the trees of the park. The day was, as it were, retiring with regret. Its lingering gray light seemed to dispute with the night, in the air, over the warm charm of the end of the evening.

"A beautiful evening!" said M. de Meuze, who was smoking a cigar on the balcony.

Seated at the back of the drawing-room, facing the window, M. Raindal was reading the paper near a lamp. Mme. Chambannes and Gerald were chatting in the left-hand corner, on a little cretonne divan. Aunt Panhias passed the coffee cups, grumbling the while against her husband who had insisted on staying until after dessert. Had anyone ever heard of such absurd stubbornness! When one had to meet somebody, was it not the least one could do to give up his dessert? And she pestered Zozé to find out about the hour of the trains, calculate the delays due to transfers and decide whether Uncle Panhias would arrive on time.

M. de Meuze came in again and interrupted her complaints.

"Please excuse me, ladies," he said. "The journey has tired me out.... I am going to put my old body to bed!"

He went towards M. Raindal to shake hands with him.

"Hush!" he whispered, turning back to the young people. "Science is asleep.... Peace to his rest!... Good night, dear madame!"

Zozé gave him a friendly nod.

"Oh, tha nothing!" Aunt Panhias declared, in a hushed voice. "Our good M. Raindal is caught with that almost every night!"

She went out with the Marquis, having a score of orders to give for the comfort of the new guests, for Chambannes' return, and for the dispatching of the carriage.

"Alone at last!" Gerald murmured softly, in a tone of banter.

"Not so loud, my darling!" implored Zozé, as she pressed his hand.

"Why?... He is asleep!"

Zozé, without releasing the hand of her Raldo, frowned as she examined M. Raindal. Then she rose and pulled the young man after her.

"Come! Let us go on the terrace.... I shall feel safer."

Then she sighed: "Oh! my own Raldo! What a bore that he stayed!... And you know.... We have him here for another fortnight!"

"Yes, you told me! Well! If he is in our way, wl lead him a chase, the old kangaroo!... It ca be very hard to do that."

They were leaning on the white stone balustrade. With extreme caution, M. Raindal opened his eyes. From where he was, he had only a side view of Mme. Chambannes, her vase-like pale blue dress, her fine profile turned to the right.... That was so, no doubt, because she was speaking to Gerald whom he guessed was very close to her, elbow to elbow, as he himself had leaned over, up above, in the lighted room, on the day of his arrival! He held his breath back in order to try to hear them. He could distinguish nothing but a gentle melody of confused voices, a cascade of softened syllables, whose meaning was broken by the invisible partitions of the air.

At times, the young woma profile shook or plunged into the darkness. The conversation was cut short by a dead stop. M. Raindal, his hands stuck to his armchair, contemplated with a feeling of distress the pale dress, the headless trunk of his little pupil. Why did she bend so? For what mystery did she incline her whispering, laughing lips?

Suddenly, a tall shadow passed behind Mme. Chambannes; Geral silhouette, even his rose and his moustache showing distinctly. Nimble steps went down the front steps. The pebbles of the paths in the garden squeaked. Now, there came, at intervals, a low voice in a monologue. Her head immobile, Mme. Chambannes seemed to listen to him; her finger before her face made gestures of refusal.

Forgetting all caution, M. Raindal opened his eyes very wide. Zoz brusquely turning about caused him to close them again, but barely in time. What was happening? She came into the drawing-room, looked for something—hearing a rustling of silk and lace, M. Raindal assumed that it was a scarf—then went out again on tip-toes, turning round an instant as she reached the French windows.... Then he heard her heels on the steps and on the gravel of the path.

"This is going rather far!" the master murmured, as he rose and stretched himself.

He listened. Everything was silent outside. Where had she run away? Yes, to the garden, to walk with young Gerald.... But if they were walking, how could he explain the silence? Had they, by any chance, gone beyond the customary limit, as far as the lawn, perhaps even beyond that? An unlikely liberty! Yet M. Raindal wanted to make sure of it. In his turn he came to lean on the white stone balustrade. In disorderly bounds his heart beat against his ribs, and this continuous hammering extended to his left arm like a hollow internal alarm-bell. His eyes scanned the garden.

The silence persisted under a sky covered with stars. A faint bluish light revealed every part where bushes, trees or other opaque obstacles had not resisted their fragile rays. Thus, the lawn showed in all its outlines, even to its slight slope and the flower beds. The path that edged it also sketched out clearly its coils of gravel. The darkness began only beyond that path, at the high wall of the lime trees, which scattered the perfume of their late blooms far through the damp atmosphere.

As a rule, M. Raindal delighted in that sugary perfume. He would inhale it greedily with mouth wide open and nostrils palpitating. But now, all his body, with the exception of his eyes, was petrified with anguish. He had no strength, no life, no consciousness but for the one aim, to scan the shadows, to search the darkness with his greedy eyes, his eyes that longed to see.

No one on the lawn; no one in the path ... not a sound on the gravel! Then they were hiding in the park, the wretches!

The master took no time to answer this terrible query. He straightened himself brusquely; like an automaton, whose very stiffness is unsteady, he went down the steps.

In two strides he was on the lawn; the soft earth deadened the sound of his feet. He gave a sardonic chuckle, a kind of victorious cough. At least, moving this way, on this soft ground, he would not be heard coming.... Oh!... Where was he going in his infatuated march? What could he do, or say, what could he imagine, in case he were to meet them at the turning of a path? He had scarcely thought of that; a savage sorrow was burning him, ceaselessly, and urged him forward like an animal maddened by fire. He felt nothing, neither the perfume of the lime-trees, nor the freshness of the grass which wet his ankles, nor the hateful aspect of his own pursuit, the shamefulness of his cunning! He was approaching ... he reached the park, he was going to see!

He ventured into the thickest part of the wood. The carpet of dead leaves exhaled slowly towards him its pungent odor of eternal and ever renewed decay. Supple branches cut his face. Roots rose under his feet. He went on, his eyes half closed for fear of thorns; perspiration dripped from his forehead; his hands were stretched forward to feel his way through the darkness and foliage.

He stopped suddenly. From the left, from the place where he thought were the glade of the lime-trees, the spaced trees, the mushroom-like stone table and the wicker chairs, a murmur arose, a sort of duet of violent and languorous voices. They ceased an instant, then renewed their murmur. He had an impression that his heart was shrinking, vanishing out of his body. He paused a minute, because his legs gave way under him.... Then he took up his march again, panting, bent in two like a gorilla, his hands almost touching the ground. As he crawled nearer, the voices became more distinct. Suddenly, he almost fainted. Now he perceived everything, even the familiar sound of those voices. It was an exchange of invocations so shameless, of apostrophes at once so bestial and so tender that he was utterly stupefied. Ah! only Queen Cleopatra, perhaps, could have ever fallen to that depth of shamelessness!... M. Raindal did not have the courage to look, to see. A panicky rage swept him away. He felt a frantic need to run, to escape the tortures of that infernal wood. He rushed out in a mad, furious race, now fearless of making a noise, not caring whether he betrayed himself or not, smashing the branches that stood in his way, taking his revenge on the bushes, sweating, galloping with the noise of big game running under wood before the dogs. Out of breath, he stumbled onto the lawn, and the dahlias received him. He rose quickly, his knees heavy with damp earth. He took up his march again, at a more moderate pace but yet hastily.

He did not run but his legs nervously set a fast pace, finding relief in that hurried gait. When he reached the steps, he brushed his clothes with his sleeve, instinctively. A remnant of clear sight made him dread Aunt Panhias, her curiosity and possible inquiries. The drawing-room, however, proved to be still empty. The master rushed to the hall and swiftly climbed the stairs.... At last he was in his room. With a far resounding kick he closed his door. His trembling hand turned the key twice in the keyhole. He fell, exhausted, on the edge of his big bed, which had already been prepared for the night.

His lassitude did not calm him. A boiling anger surged in his veins. His hands made gestures of destruction. He would have liked to hold Mme. Chambannes, to break her as he had the branches in her park, to crush and annihilate her.

His little pupil! His little pupil! Was it she? Was it those candid lips that had uttered such abominable words. At the memory of each word, he felt a new blade piercing his heart.... No! his judgment was prejudiced and rebelled against so much infamy; his memory must be lying!... His little pupil!... His dear friend! Simultaneously, he united the basest insults with these terms of endearment. He evoked Thérèse, recalling to his mind her hatred for Zozé, and wishing that she were near him now so that they could hate the guilty one together.

Ah! Thérèse had not been wrong about the shallowness of this Mme. Chambannes, her depravity and her mediocrity. In one meeting, she had appreciated her better, fathomed her and sentenced her more accurately than he had done in a hundred meetings. For she, Thérèse, did not love her, while he, alas did!

"Yes! I loved her; I love her still!" he murmured fervently, as if to deny in that remorseful admission all the puny disguises, all the artifices of prudery which had sheltered a passion that was without courage.

The sound of shutters being closed and footsteps coming up interrupted his meditations. He hoped that Mme. Chambannes would come in to ask him how he was. What should he say in reply? Should he fall at her knees, pitifully stammering words of love? Or should he repulse her with a scornful reply?

He did not have to choose, because Zozé did not come to him. Instead of her coming, the echoes of the park took up once more in the mind of the master their vile, diabolical concert, the duet of their ravished accents.

Oh! what atrocious, what repugnant words! M. Raindal compared them with the Latin footnotes of his book. At a distance of twenty centuries, they were almost the same words, the same follies as those which Cleopatra, in her worst ecstasies had stimulated in her lover, Antony the rough soldier! By means of what miracle of universal and immutable perversity had this infamous vocabulary been shamefully transmitted from the Queen of Egypt to the maste little friend? How many amorous couples must have repeated and preserved it, from generation to generation!

Then, suddenly, a clear intuition rose through the discard of those historical parallels. M. Raindal understood; he explained to himself at last the work of his little pupil ... his professor rather, his little teacher who had, from the first day, little by little, taught him the meaning of a refined existence, material enjoyment, the tangible reality of all those terms which he had in the past carelessly used in the written sentences of his books, as the symbolical pieces of a lifeless chessboard!... Pleasure, love, luxury, elegance, ardor of the senses, beauty, grace, passion, tenderness—these had been to him as so many inert syllables, until Mme. Chambannes brought them to life for him.

And the last lesson, the end of this apprenticeship—had it not been completed just now, out there among the high trees where, perhaps, she might still be, enraptured, and forgetting him in the arms of another man!...

The hitherto unknown torture with which this vision inflicted him brought an exclamation of horror to his lips. He rose from his bed, blinking. He beat the air with his fists in a sudden threat. For a few minutes, he lost the thread of his meditations.

He crumbled down, quite exhausted, in a cretonne armchair; in his mind he was living again his whole career, the succession of those virtuous years whose righteousness had once exalted his pride. How dull and trivial that narrow little path which he had walked at the cost of so much hardship and so many efforts seemed now! It reminded him of one of those out of the way side-paths which one walked, on holidays, to avoid the joy of others.... Near that vision, he dimly perceived, as in an ancient print, the noisy kermesse of Life, singing groups, bouquets, drunken orgies, women with men, the furious exuberance of the mob of revelry.... Meanwhile he was pursuing, apart, his own road and that step by step, seeing only the next da march when one was completed, applying his efforts merely not to deviate from this path, his zeal not to be diverted.... What cared he whether they enjoyed themselves and lived on the other side? Was he not aware with scientific certainty how vain and vulgar were the pleasures which satisfy the mob? Did he not know that they left nothing but disgust behind them, to what sottishness they brought one down, and finally what a very small thing was Woman (*mulier*) in comparison with a superior mind?...

Woman—he had really known but one, his own. Apart from a few indiscretions during his life as a student, indiscretions that were forgotten as soon as committed, he remembered his life as a young man, his four years spent in the desert under Mariette Bey, his imperturbable chastity, that precocious contempt for love which caused even the "Great Bey" to tease him. When his comrades left the cantonment and went to the nearest town to see the dancing Bayaderes or spend a nigh leave with some native girl, M. Raindal had, as a rule, discovered some pretext not to join them, some special work to be finished, a papyrus to be deciphered or a sudden indisposition. "Sapristi! Raindal, you must rub the rust off yourself, my dear fellow!" the Great Bey declared, in that sarcastic voice of his. "You will end by making us believe that you have a liaison with a mummy!" The young savant would laugh, promise to follow his companions, but recant at the last minute. The Bayaderes bored him. Since then, apart from his wife, no one! Not one adventure, not one memory, no graceful image, none of those dear phantoms whose one particular beauty—her hands, her smile, her finesse in lovemaking or the sweetness of her eyes—flatters one, with its secret companionship, till death.

Here he was now, hoary and disfigured by age, unable to attract anyone, panting with love at the time when pleasure should be given up, enamored of a young woman who loved another! What a punishment! What agony!

How long would it last? How long would it remain to show him the joys he had missed, thanks to pedantic vainglory and proud self-confidence?

He walked to the chimney. Standing before the mirror, he twisted his features in stranger grimaces to convince himself even more that his decrepitude was beyond hope. Ah! yes indeed, he had a pretty complexion, fine teeth and wrinkles, puffed skin and a nice flabby face, everything in short which he needed to seduce a young woman!

The wheels of a carriage crunched the gravel of the path. He heard voices raised in appeals and much laughter. George had arrived.

M. Raindal had a sudden desire to go down. He would allege the return of Chambannes and the wish to welcome his host; then he could see Zozé once more. His hand was on the handle of the door, but a scruple of pride kept him back. No, that would be too cowardly! He stayed upstairs.

He heard doors being closed. Silence again fell over the house. M. Raindal felt as if his heart had been stabbed again. He was thinking about the husband who was with his wife now.... His shoulders shook in a nasty sneer. Phew! he was not jealous of that unfortunate Chambannes! Really, there was nothing to envy him for! To be the husband of a brainless little fool, a worthless creature who, a minute ago.... He did not finish his thought. His eyes were bloodshot; brutal curses rushed to his lips; he was choking. M. Raindal opened the window.

The night was cooler. On the distant plain, trains passed at intervals, winding their coils of yellow lights on the horizon. Some roosters in the neighborhood, deceived by the false paleness of the sky, sent to each other, through space, their dauntless greetings, to which dogs howled in reply.

M. Raindal gravely contemplated the blue stars. Each was to him a sun with satellites gravitating round it. He asked himself how many sorrows, identical with his own, must be making men moan at that same moment, on those obscure planets. He reasoned, made calculations, intoxicating himself with lofty thoughts. He invoked Human Sorrow, the Sufferings of the Worlds, the Universal Complaint—the conventional pity, the lip-charity, the egotistic and hypocritically tender hygiene, all the declamatory remedies which books teach to alleviate personal sorrows. But he derived no solace from them.

Poor thinker, poor master, poor Man! Yes, he could indeed call to his help the spectacle of the heavens, the astronomers and the philosophers; he could call on Newton, Laplace, Kant and Hegel! He could swell himself up and make himself feel greater!

The fact remained that he still harbored within his own breast an atom of flesh which was more sensitive and real than all those vaunted infinites which were powerless alike to cure him and to dominate him.

What was there left to him in this overwhelming catastrophe? His family? He had, in the last year, lost even the desire to cherish them. His work? He hated the results of it, its lying mirage, its evil routine.

He closed the window, renouncing the stars. He sat on his bed once more and began to cry.

Ended were his illusions! Gone his old ma fatuity! He would leave the next day. He would not be a witness of *their* humiliating amours. Never again would he see his dear little pupil. And he wept.... It was at last a sincere sorrow, without evil spite, without any parody of vanity, a humble sorrow which acknowledged itself and loved its tears! In this M. Raindal found peace and finally sleep.

On the morrow, however, when he went down to the garden about ten lock, a sudden commotion reopened his secret wound.

"Yes, monsieur, madame has gone out," Firmin assured him. "She has gone out for a drive with M. de Meuze."

"Which one?" M. Raindal almost shouted.

"With M. le Marquis.... M. le Comte and monsieur are still in their rooms."

"Ah! very good!" M. Raindal said, recovering his ease.

He sat in a rocking-chair, in the shadow of the terrace and affected to be engrossed in reading the paper.

But his set eyes were not on the lines. An internal passion was following other ideas, other words, the little parting speech, a few mysterious and firm sentences in which he would announce his intention to leave. He had mastered the greater part of it when the close-cut mane of Notpou emerged from between the trees.

From the carriage, the Marquis gave a cordial salute to M. Raindal. Oh! there had been no delay! no hesitation! The master was thoroughly ousted, deprived of his power! Even Geral father, this old marquis, had taken his little pupil away from him; even of him he felt jealous! Go! He must go as soon as possible! His own suffering necessitated this prompt sacrifice.

The master rose to his feet. He was watching for Mme. Chambannes' first glance, for her fatigued expression and the lowering of her eyes with which she would undoubtedly greet him. Zoz physiognomy disappointed him. She walked up to him, smiling as usual, her eyes free and easy under her veil, raised up, like a headband, level with her eyebrows. She offered him her white-gloved hand without constraint, as she had the day before, as on the previous morning, as if neither the night, nor Gerald, the scene in the park, as if none of those shameful things had come between them! He gave her hand a timid pressure and sat back in the rocking-chair.

"Will you allow me to say a few words to you, dear madame?" he asked, looking at his brown leather shoes.

"With pleasure!" Mme. Chambannes answered deliberately, as she pulled an armchair beside that of the master.

She sat down and caressed the master with one of her warm looks: "I am listening, dear master.... Have you any trouble? Not from your family, I trust?"

Still smiling, she took her gloves off. Then she lifted her arms, like two graceful handles on each side of her face, and with difficulty pulled out the long pin which held her sailor hat.

"You are mistaken!" stammered M. Raindal, his eyes still unresponsive. "It is precisely of Langrune that...."

His hands hanging loose, his wrists contracted. The ingenuous air of Mme. Chambannes revolted him as a last challenge to his credulity.

"Well?" asked the young woman.

He dared to stare at her. What! Those lips were still fresh after so much defilement! No trace of it had polluted the clearness of her eyes. Not even a shudder; not a blush! Did lies then wash out everything in their foul waters? A renewed anger roused M. Raindal. His caution was shaken. The prepared words vanished. Looking straight at her, his hands grasping the armchair as if better to spring, he declared roughly:

"I am going!"

"You are going!" Zozé exclaimed, in a tone of well-simulated wonder.

M. Raindal recollected somewhat the words that had to be used.

"Excuse my rudeness, my bad temper.... I received this morning from Langrune such a pressing letter that I must give in to the ladies' wish.... They claim me over there and I am going.... Rest assured that I am very sorry!"

There was a pause. Zozé thought it out. Now that she was sure he was leaving, why should she not preserve her assumed innocence, the persistence of which could but draw off his suspicions? It was with an imperceptible smile that she said:

"I believe you, dear master, although you surprise me."

"I ... surprise you, dear madame?" M. Raindal asked sullenly, his heart beating more rapidly.

"You see, I was downstairs this morning when the postman came.... He gave me all the mail and there was no letter for you!"

M. Raindal preserved a challenging silence, disdaining to clear himself, not denying his deception.

"Come, dear master!" Zozé went on gently. "Since there was no letter, what is it that makes you leave us? Has anyone upset you? Have we hurt your feelings unwittingly? Please, tell me who it is, I beg you."

Her eyes looked all around, as if she were trying to discover the culprit, the naughty, wicked unknown one who had upset her dear master. M. Raindal watched her for an instant, his lips convulsed with disgust.

"Who? Tell me who it is!" he repeated to himself. This was really too much of an imposture, altogether too impudent! He pushed back his armchair. His jaws were parted, ready to bite, ready to let out the whole burden of questions, outrages, reproach. But, in a supreme effort, he mastered himself. He paced up and down before Zozé, in a short space of ten feet, and said in a voice broken by his fury:

"Do not ask me anything, dear madame! Nothing ... it would be useless!... I must go and I am going.... I can say no more to you.... I do not know if you understand me, and I wish that you would not.... Yes, I wish that with all my soul!... Alas, on the contrary, I am very much afraid that you have understood...."

"But, dear master!" Zozé protested.

"All right, dear madame!... You do not understand me?... All the better.... You will later, when you think it over.... The only thing I ask you is that you should avoid any struggle for me.... Lend yourself to my little stratagem: you know, the letter received ... the letter which I did *not* receive.... Because my resolution is irrevocable.... I shall leave this afternoon.... To remain here one single day would be humiliating to me.... I cannot!... I cannot!"

He was choking. Zozé rose to her feet and caught his hand, which he made no attempt to withdraw.

"I do not understand you, dear master.... You are free.... I have no right to detain you.... But I beg your pardon if I have offended you!" she said with emotion, not more than half of which was feigned.

M. Raindal turned his head away. He did not wish her to see his eyes, which were full of tears. He released his own hand from hers and pretended to be examining the lawn, the park, the clouds.

"I thank you, dear madame.... I have nothing to forgive you!" he said, coughing as if he wished to force back a new rush of tears which made his voice hoarse. "I shall leave this afternoon by the five lock train.... Do not bother about me.... Please only let me have Firmin.... He will help me pack my things.... Hm! Hm! Hm!"

He kept on coughing and then became melancholy.

"Hm! Hm!... When I am gone, when I am no longer here I hope that you will think sometimes of your dear...." He corrected himself,—"of your old master who, on his part, even from afar, will not forget you...."

The solemnity of this promise completed his confusion. Hurriedly, as if stricken with a sudden indisposition, he ran into the drawing-room, then through the hall and up the stairs.

Zozé ran behind him, chirping, in her softest, tenderest intonation: "Dear master!... Dear master!... And in Paris.... In Paris ... we shall meet again, sha we?"

He only replied when he was at the top of the stairs, his voice clear once more, intending to leave no doubt, afterward, in the minds of those in the house:

"To be sure, dear madame.... I shall transmit your message to my daughter.... Besides, we can talk about it again at lunch, before I go."

As soon as he reached Paris, M. Raindal informed himself of the trains for Langrune. There were two: an evening one which arrived there in the night, another one in the morning which would reach Langrune in the afternoon. To inform his family of his arrival by telegram would alarm them. He chose not to leave until the next morning, and to spend the night at the nearest hotel. Slowly he walked towards the station yard, where the setting sun distilled a mist of gold.

An endless procession of people passed him, on the pavement and under the arcades. It was the departure of the suburban workers who returned at night to the open fields, and of the smarter population of the villas of the Seine-et-Oise region. First came clerks marching briskly, by twos and in step, their hats on the backs of their heads because of the heat; then the bourgeois, who held carefully beyond the reach of shocks their packages of dainties tied with red strings; young women in light dresses with white gloves like those Zozé wore; well-groomed men who stood up in their open cabs, to jump out more quickly.... All of them were going towards a place of rest, perhaps towards love, to the peace of the country, the beautiful night under the trees, to the priceless happiness which M. Raindal had just deserted.

The maste sadness and weariness were increased by this. He sat down on the terrace of a near-by café and ordered an absinthe.

His eyes burned, for he had wept again in the train, careless of all pride, unable to resist his pain. Zozé had fallen in with his wishes by not accompanying him to the station. The parting had been public, before Aunt Panhias, the Marquis de Meuze, Gerald and Chambannes all gathered together. The master had purposely come down late in order to shorten the cruel instant. Vain calculation! He had had to wait fully five minutes on the steps, before them all, to smile, speak and answer questions.... What a martyrdom it had been! If only he had been able to kiss Zoz hand, to kiss it with fire, with intoxication, as before ... to take a last taste of that forsaken delight!... But they were looking! It had been, instead, a cold and superficial kiss on the fingers of his little pupil, and it had seemed to him that his very lips were surprised! Well, these torments had been slight, compared to those that would soon follow!

To-morrow he would be at Langrune, miles and miles away, compelled to explain his return, a prisoner of his family, exiled on a gloomy seashore! To-morrow, he would be once more Mme. Rainda husband, Mlle. Rainda father, *M. Raindal, of the Institute*, an austere old savant, with no one to make his life pleasant, with no clandestine friendship, no little pupil, no secret distraction, apart from his books—books to write, books to read, books to review!...

"Books, books, always books!" he murmured, in a sickened tone.

And a thought intrigued him; it was to stay in Paris and find some means of avoiding Langrune.

The clock of the station struck seven. He paid the waiter and walked towards the boulevards.

Where could he dine? He remembered the name of a restaurant, in the place de la Madeleine, the cooking of which Chambannes and the Marquis had often praised before him.

He sauntered in that direction. The room was still half empty. He ordered a choice dinner, with such dishes as Zozé preferred, a bottle of *Saint-Estephe* and a bottle of frappé Champagne which was placed before him in a silver vase. His absinthe encouraged him to these libations. Since he had drunk it, he felt livelier and less sad.

He ate abundantly and applied himself to drinking. His ideas became lighter and seemed to penetrate one another. It was a pleasant confusion, and made him giggle at times. Towards the end of the dinner, he conceived the project of a drama, a myth in dialogue form, which would be entitled *Hercules*. He would show Vice, under the guise of a woman—who in the maste mind resembled Zozé exactly—entering the house of the now aged hero. And the latter would lament, would weep over his departed youth, and would implore the gods to give it back to him.... The drama developed according to this theme, in lofty axioms and lyrical plaints.

This was a much more likely conception than that which represented Hercules choosing, in the prime of his youth, between Vice and Virtue. Did such a choice offer itself in real life? Of course not; one walked on with the one, misunderstanding the other, and vice versa. What libertine did not some day regret the hours spent in debauchery? What man of intellect did not deplore, at some fatal moment, the fact that he had lived in ignorance of the forbidden pleasures? Rare were the men, who, by divine grace, mixed the practice of both in a fair proportion.... There would be, besides, in his myth, avenging blank verses against Vice, against Mme. Chambannes!

M. Raindal rose and shook the crumbs off his waistcoat. In a shaky hand he took his felt hat and walking-stick which the headwaiter handed him. Then, his eyes somewhat cloudy, he walked up the boulevards. Darkness had fallen. The merry crowd of nocturnal walkers rubbed elbows on the pavement. A late summer breath bent the tips of the withering chestnut trees.

M. Raindal once more thought of Zozé, of the lime-trees and the park. A thousand seductive images zigzagged under his burning cranium. He felt like embracing, hugging, loving someone.

When he passed the door of the Olympia, the posters attracted him. He saw women in tights, equilibrists and a young person in a low-neck dress, standing in the middle of a group of trained dogs. Above the posters the name of the establishment, made up of red electric bulbs, scintillated in ruby-colored letters. Girls went in, alone or by twos. Through the half-open swinging doors came confused whiffs of lively music.

M. Raindal hesitated. Then, with a gesture as quick as a pickpocke, he tore from his button-hole his button of an officer of the Légion onneur. He marched straight to the ticket-office, then disappeared inside.

CHAPTER XVIII

THE next morning, towards eleven, Mlle. Clara Laneret, better known in night cabarets by her nickname of *rlandaise*, bent over the banister of her staircase to watch someone go down.

"Eh, monsieur!" she exclaimed suddenly, discreetly recalling him. "You will come again, wo you?"

The "monsieur"—that is to say, M. Eusèbe Raindal, member of the Institute of France, officer of the Légion onneur, author of the *Life of Cleopatra* and of several other important books—the "monsieur" replied in a weak voice, rendered even more hollow by the distance of the steps:

"Yes, yes, certainly, I shall come back!..."

What a disgrace! What turpitude! He had followed that brunette girl, missed his train, lost his self-respect altogether! Ah! if his family, if Zozé were to see him on that sordid staircase running out, pursued by the tenderness of Clara rlandaise!... And now, where was he to go? What could he do till the hour of his train?

He stopped on the edge of the pavement, trying to read on the high enameled plate, the name of the street—rue ms ... rue msterdam—which he had forgotten. His head was heavy, his tongue pasty and he longed to resume his sleep.

"I might go and see Cyprien," he thought, stiffening himself against slumber.

He called a cab. But when he reached the house in the rue ssas, Uncle Cyprien had gone out on his tricycle.

"Not three minutes ago," the concierge assured him.

In fact, two hundred meters away, in the rue de Fleurus, Cyprien was at that very moment stopping before the house where Johan Schleifmann lived.

He put his tricycle—his "beast" as he would have said—under the arch and asked the concierge to keep an eye on it; then he began to climb the stairs.

"Have you come to fetch me for lunch, my friend?" Schleifmann asked, when he had opened the door to him. "One minute, please! l put my frockcoat on and go with you!"

They walked into the study, a light, spacious, garret, the red tiles of which were half covered with two straw mats.

M. Raindal the younge expression was both amused and ceremonious. He sat in an old armchair and declared, as, with a stage gesture, he took off his wide, brown sombrero:

"No, my friend, I have not come to fetch you.... I have come to talk to you...."

"What has happened?" asked Schleifmann. "This has happened, my dear fellow, that ... that I am presenting to you a man who is done for, absolutely done for!"

And he added, while the Galician lifted his arms in a gesture of surprise.

"Yes, Schleifmann! I have gambled in gold mines and I have lost...."

"I was sure of it!" the Galician exclaimed, stamping angrily on the red tiles. "How much have you lost?"

"One hundred and ten thousand francs, my dear friend!... Yes, there is no need for you to open your eyes so wide.... I said it: one hundred and ten thousand francs!... At the last settlement, on the 15th, I had only lost fifty thousand francs.... Thanks to the help of M. de Meuze, who had written to his friend M. Pums, the father of your pupil, I made arrangements with Talloire, my stockbroker—for I have a stockbroker, is it comical enough, eh! I, a stockbroker!—I made arrangements with Talloire, I say, for him to carry me over; in other words, an operation which allowed me a delay for settling up and permitted me to gamble again.... You know?... Good!... I gambled again.... The smash came, more terrible than ever, organized by the whole Black Band.... I was stubborn; I gave orders right and left.... Result: sixty thousand francs added to my losses!"

"Oh, my poor Raindal, my poor friend!" the Galician murmured, shaking his head.

"That is not all!" Uncle Cyprien added. "I have asked to be carried over again.... Nothing doing! Pums did not receive me, and Talloire kicked me out.... I wrote to the Marquis, who is holidaying at Deauville; no reply!... Therefore, this afternoon, unless I have paid up, I shall be 'executed' at the Bourse, and, this evening, I shall execute myself at home!... Tell me, Schleifmann, am I done for or am I not?"

The Galician took a turn round the room, with his usual dragging gait, grumbling:

"Devilish idiot! Devilish idiot!" Then he asked brusquely. "What about your pension, Raindal?... You could perhaps borrow on that?"

"Child!" exclaimed M. Raindal, the younger, paternally. "Do you think that I have waited for you to think of that? Guess what I have been offered for my pension by the usurers: fifteen thousand francs, fifteen paltry thousand francs, not a damned sou more!"

The Galician thought. Then after a time he said:

"Listen, Raindal!... I have put five thousand francs by.... With your fifteen thousand, that would give you twenty.... Do you want them?"

Cyprien came over to press his hand.

"You are a very good friend, Schleifmann," he said.... "I am very grateful to you.... That *would* give me twenty, yes, that is to say, a little less than twenty per cent, enough to make arrangements which would cause some men to call me an honest man, and others—a thief. But after that, my friend! After that, how should I exist? I would not have a penny, not a sou.... I would need to look for a job and, what is more difficult, to find one.... No, you see, I would never have the patience.... I prefer to end it at once!"

"You are speaking foolishly!" Schleifmann protested. "To end it!... Why should you?... What a lazy rent-holder you are!... Devil take it, you could work!"

"Work!" grunted Cyprien.... "I would work if I were given work to do!... A man of my age, who has been hammered on 'Change.... You know, that is not precisely a good recommendation!"

Schleifmann scratched his thick gray hair, thinking fast. At length, he asked:

"Come, my dear Cyprien!... I have an idea.... Supposing you were allowed to carry over, would you be able to re-establish your finances?"

"I can promise nothing!" Cyprien replied. "But there would be a chance.... This crash will not last.... People affirm on all sides that it is due to a maneuver of the Black Band.... Before the end of this fortnight, everything may be changed.... At all events, if one has to blow up, it would be finer to have fought to the end...."

"And, of course, you would gamble again?"

"No, Schleifmann! I would not gamble again.... I would maintain my position, as they say ... my splendid position, and I would wait for things to turn up!"

"Will you swear it to me on the head of your niece, Mlle. Thérèse?"

"I do like this oath idea very much!... Well, let it be so!... I swear it, upon the head of my nephew.... But why all these preambles and questions?"

"Well, here is my idea!" Schleifmann said solemnly. "Where is M. Pums at this hour?"

Uncle Cyprien consulted his watch.

"Noon!... He must be at the Bourse."

"Very good! I am going to see him.... I shall attempt to get him to have you carried over.... He is not a bad fellow.... At the time of my affair of the reforms, you remember, Cyprien, do you, he was one of those who received me with the least roughness. Again, he left me his son as a pupil, his overdressed gummy son.... Well, I have some hopes.... What do you say?"

"All right! If I am carried over!" Cyprien said skeptically.

"Let me go down, then.... A cab, quick!... Huf! Huf!"

Downstairs, Cyprien asked the concierge to take his "beast" back to the rue ssas, and the two old friends climbed into an open carriage.

They were silent for a few minutes; then M. Raindal said with sarcasm.

"The one time in my life that I have had anything to do with the Jews, you must admit, my dear Schleifmann, has brought me no luck!"

"And M. de Meuze?" the Galician replied aggressively. "M. de Meuze who led you to this, is *he* a Jew?"

"No, tha true enough," Cyprien admitted. "He is not a Jew.... But he is Judaized, which comes to the same thing."

"And I, a Jew, who always told you not to touch that dirty business, how about me?"

"You! Tha different! You are a good Jew!" Cyprien interrupted.

As usual, when he heard that remark, Schleifmann could not dissimulate an angry gesture. M. Raindal regretted his lack of tact and attempted to turn the matter; he gave a mass of minute directions and topographic particulars touching the plan of the Bourse and the place where Pums was to be found.

"By the way," he added, "take care of the clerks' pranks! True, they will probably not be very much in a mood for joking to-day.... Nevertheless, be careful of their funny tricks! The first day I myself, went to the Bourse, why, they slipped a paper arrow under the collar of my coat; on it was written in large letters the word: *Topper!*... I know that it has no importance.... Just the same, it is sometimes very annoying at the moment!"

The carriage stopped before the gate of the monument.

"I shall wait for you here!" Raindal shouted after the Galician as he walked away. "Good luck for us both, and courage, my dear friend!"

Up above, under the colonnade, or top of the steps, was the mournful Bourse of the days of *débâcle*. Not a laugh, not a chat, no outburst of merry voices. The faces were ghastly pale; the bravest attempted a joke, twitching their features in lying smiles which were more hideous than grimaces. Over that lugubrious silence came the vociferations of the agents, the outbidding downward, the monotonous shouts of the sales, sales at any price. They were all selling.

An unfortunate mistake led the Galician right into the midst of the agents who were dealing with the gold mines.

Politely he removed his hat and stood before a fair young man who had ceased shouting.

"Excuse me, monsieur," he said. "Will you be good enough to tell me where I can find M. Pums?"

The other looked at him, dumfounded.... M. Pums, on such a day, at such a time! As if he had nothing else to do! Wait, wait a bit, old man, they are going to give it to you; thel show you M. Pums!... And, of a sudden, on a wink from the blonde young man, with repeated shouts of "M. Pums! M. Pums!" a frantic rush sent the unfortunate Schleifmann forward.

"M. Pums! M. Pums!" The Galician passed from hand to hand, from group to group, thrown from *Gold* to *Cash*, from *Cash* to *Gold*, from *Gold* to *Values*, from *Values* to *External*, from *External* to *Turkish*. All of them, despite the tragic hour, despite the anguish of that da operations, sought relief for their nerves in that brutal game, relaxed their hearts and arms by molesting the old intruder.... "M. Pums! M. Pums!"

He landed in a corner of the circular hall; his gold-rimmed spectacles all awry, his hat thrown on the floor in a final cuff.

A little messenger, in a bottle-green livery, took pity on his distress.

"Here, monsieur!" he said, picking up Schleifman hat. "You want M. Pums!... I work at the bank.... M. Pums is at his office, 72 rue Vivienne."

"Thank you, youngster!" the Galician stammered. "Thanks very much, my boy!"

Slowly, looking back at every step for fear of a treacherous blow, and polishing his poor hat with his sleeve, he walked down the steps.

The hall of the bank was crowded with solicitors when the Galician entered. There were agents, bucket-shop brokers, financial go-betweens of all kinds, some seated, their eyes on their shoes, in a defeated attitude, others standing talking by groups in corners or near the windows, with the measured accents one uses in the room of the dying.

Alone, the usher in green livery, seated behind his oak rostrum, seemed indifferent to the cares of those about him and read placidly the serial story in the *Petit Journal*.

He barely moved his eyelids to decipher the card which Schleifmann pushed before him and fell back to his paper, saying, "Very good, monsieur.... Please take a seat!"

"I do not want a seat!" said Schleifmann, who was holding himself in hand. "I am asking you to take my card to M. Pums, and at once, do you hear?"

"Impossible, sir.... *Monsieur le sous-Directeur* is attending a conference. He has given orders that no one should come in until he rings...." Then he added, pointing to the gathered agents and brokers: "Besides, all these gentlemen here are ahead of you."

"I do know whether these gentlemen ..." and here the Galicia voice became more haughty, "are ahead of me.... But I ask you once more to hand my card.... You will tell M. Pums that it is a serious matter, that a ma life is in danger."

The usher stared impudently at Schleifmann. That dramatic language, that silk hat brushed away, that tie all in disorder, and that foreign accent—some poor devil, some Jewish beggar, no doubt. He did not even condescend to answer and took up his reading again.

"I say, did you hear me?" stammered Schleifmann, incensed by so much insolence. "Yes or no, are you going to take my card in?"

"When M. Pums rings, sir!" the usher reiterated, curling his mustache, his body still bent towards the paper. "I cannot go before he does."

"You cannot!" Schleifmann almost shouted. "Very good! We shall see...."

He walked towards a tall door painted brown which he supposed to be that of Pums' office.

"Where are you going?" the usher asked, barring his advance with outstretched arms.

The Galician gave a sharp push of his shoulders and threw the man aside. "I go where it pleases me! Get out of here, damn you!"

Some of the dealers hurried to the call of the usher and surrounded Schleifmann, questioning him. Their intervention completed the Galicia exasperation. He had a sudden vision of the recent scene, a jostling mob, fists shaken, ugly faces. All that might be coming again! His voice became threatening.

"What are you butting into this for?... We are not at the Bourse here! Leave me alone; the first man who lays a hand on me I will kick in the stomach!"

"What! You, Schleifmann!" said Pums, who opened his door when he heard the fracas. "Is it you, talking about kicking people in the stomach?"

The Galician took off his hat and said in lower tones:

"Yes, ... it was I, M. Pums.... They wanted to prevent me from seeing you.... And it is an urgent matter. As I was telling that ill-bred usher, it is a matter of a ma life!"

"But, at the present moment ..." the assistant director protested.

"When a ma life is at stake, there is no such thing as a moment, M. Pums! Believe me.... Let me speak with you. Some day, you will thank me for this!"

"All right!" said Pums, darting a sly wink of apology and connivance at the agents.

Schleifmann followed him in and closed the door behind him.

Pums sat at his desk of purple ebony; Schleifmann opposite him, his back to the door. He laid his hat on the table.

"I shall be brief, M. Pums," he began. "In a word, as I told you, it is a matter of a ma life.... This man—I shall not conceal his name any longer—is my best friend, M. Cyprien Raindal, brother of M. Raindal of the Institute.... His situation you know already.... If he does not pay up, he is smashed.... And, I may add, if he is smashed, he will kill himself.... I came to ask you to have his account carried over...."

"I would do it with pleasure, M. Schleifmann...." Pums murmured in German, preferring to use that tongue in delicate transactions.

"Allow me!" Schleifmann retorted, also in German and because of an analogous preference. "Allow me! I am not through yet.... You will ask me what interest you have in saving my friend Cyprien.... I will tell you.... It is a sacred interest, it is the interest of your own race, of your family, of your children, of your grandchildren, of your great-grandchildren...."

"Sorry to interrupt you!" said M. Pums, drumming his desk impatiently. "We are right in the middle of a panic.... I have twenty persons to see.... I beg you; you promised me to be brief ... be so!"

"I shall!" said Schleifmann.

And he started an interminable discourse. His thesis was that Pums, who had guided Cyprien in his first speculations, owed him support at the hour of his failure. What, at the most, would this help which would be rather moral support cost him? Not more than a risk, a mere signature. Even if he were to lose the sum which he would thus endorse, would he be thereby impoverished, incommoded in his train of life, he whose actual fortune was estimated at three millions or more? On the other hand, what a glory for Israel, what a noble tradition in the family, what a magnanimous example attached to the name of Pums, this legend would become as it passed from lip to lip: a rich Israelite, generously saving from misery, from suicide, a little ex-official, a Christian, lured to his ruin by a taste for lucre and by gambling!.... Such acts, as they multiplied, would do more for the Jews than a thousand gifts to the poor, a thousand sanitary foundations celebrated by the press with much din of praise. Such acts would carry further than charity. For they would have originated from a higher source, from humanity, from justice itself....

The Galician ended at last. Pums looked up with a slight jerk and leaned back in his armchair.

"My dear M. Schleifmann," he announced in a doctoral tone, "I pay homage to your intentions; you are an excellent man but, allow me to say it, you understand nothing of business...."

A quick blinking of his eyelids accentuated all that was unfavorable in that verdict in M. Pu estimation. He then went on:

"No, nothing, absolutely nothing.... For instance, you imagine that you know what your frien situation is? You do know the first word of it. If M. Cyprien Raindal had listened to me, if he had been satisfied to follow my advice, his losses would be insignificant, about like those of the Marquis de Meuze, his protector, seven, eight, perhaps ten thousand francs at the most.... But your friend wished to show his cleverness.... He followed his own ideas. *Il st enfilé*, as we say in the slang of the Bourse.... And, to-day, he faces the result.... Whose fault is it? Mine or his, tell me?"

"M. Pums," the stubborn Galician replied. "I did not come here to talk business to you.... You are right, I know nothing about it.... I came as a Jew and a friend to talk *heart* to you, to talk justice, to enlist your aid for this brave fellow of whom I am very fond.... If you do not give it, it will be a pity and it will be very sad, because he will die of it!"

"Very regrettable," Pums said, "but not certain.... And then, frankly, M. Schleifmann, think it over.... You are asking too much! He is not a relation, this M. Cyprien Raindal, not a friend, at best an acquaintance.... To help him, to be obliging to him—why, it seems to me that I would not begrudge my time.... But in order to save him, I should have to assume his liability in my own name.... I have no choice between the means.... The panic is general.... No one at all is allowed to carry over his account. The Bank of England itself refuses to allow it.... And, according to you, I should personally pledge myself for one hundred and ten thousand francs on behalf of a man I have seen three times in my life?... No, that is not reasonable.... At every séance of the Bourse, there would be ten like him to save.... My fortune would not be sufficient...."

He grew more animated, stamping around the table, his thumbs in the shoulder-holes of his waistcoat.

"And why should I do this? In order that people should speak well of the Jews, burn incense before Israel.... Go on! I do care a rap for the Jews.... I have no prejudices.... Every man for himself.... Let them look after their affairs.... I have no hundred and ten thousand francs to throw out of the window like this!" He came to a stop before Schleifmann. "Bah! do you imagine that I am making anything out of this mining business?... I am caught like the others.... I am losing huge sums, the very eyes out of my head."

Involuntarily his big round eyeballs showed, in their self-denouncing projection, that he had not lost everything yet. Schleifmann at least did not seem altogether convinced, for he answered Pums, insinuatingly:

"Yet, the fall is instigated by the Black Band.... And the Black Band—they are your friends!"

"My friends?" repeated Pums, suddenly all abashed. Then he recovered his self-control and added: "Oh, yes! nice friends! You may speak of them.... Wretches!... Imbeciles!... Men who stupidly lead the market to ruin, who know nothing but the rise and fall of stocks! Ah! clever work!... I congratulate them!"

Schleifmann did not give up the thread of his arguments.

"Nevertheless, these imbeciles, these wretches, you will see them again, tomorrow, or the next day...."

"What are you talking about?" Pums exclaimed, to mask his hesitation.... "Shall I see them again?... Well, yes, I presume so.... But I guarantee you that I shall tell them what I think. At this moment, see, if I had one of them handy...."

"*Alzo! wie gehts!*" a cordial voice cried out in German behind Schleifmann.

Pums did not finish his sentence. He had taken on a sinister pallor; his chocolate-colored eyeballs were even more haggard and prominent, as if they were on the point of jumping out of their sockets. Schleifmann turned round and recognized Herschstein.

The head of the Black Band entered by a side door, his hat on his head, smiling, without knocking, as if he were at home, as master; brilliantine shone in silvery eddies in his patriarchal gray beard.

When he caught sight of Schleifmann, he recoiled prudently; his venerable face took on a different expression and he murmured modestly: "Ah! you are busy!"

Pums, who was diligently sorting some papers, did not reply. Schleifmann examined them both in turn, a flame of contempt in his eyes.

"Eh, M. Pums!" he commanded sarcastically. "I am waiting.... Here is one of them.... Go ahead!... Let him know what you think of it.... Tell him! Ha! You have forgotten! Patience, M. Herschstein.... It will come.... M. Pums has a heartload to let out for you!... He is trying to find.... Sit down!"

"What does this mean?" Herschstein asked, icily.

"I shall explain, my dear friend!" stammered Pums. "We were talking of M. Raindal brother, who is losing on the mines.... M. Schleifmann is joking...."

"Am I joking!" the Galician said, smashing his fist on the table so violently that the ink came out of the inkstand. "Truly, here is ground for joking indeed!"

He eyed them both.

"So! you are in league!... So, 'it goes!'... You, M. Pums, you make up a pair with M. Herschstein.... And you, M. Herschstein, you come to give account!... Congratulations! It must have been a fine massacre!... Write it down, M. Pums. I shall dictate: Profits of September 2nd: M. Cyprien Raindal, one hundred and ten thousand francs.... Hah! M. Pums, how much of that do you get? Ten thousand? Fifteen thousand?" He chuckled, then suddenly his face fell under an intolerable sadness.

"Malediction!" he groaned, prowling about the room. "Malediction and misery!... Yes, ever since Sinai, there has been the same eternal misunderstanding!... God gives His People supreme intelligence and His People prostitute it to the basest works, and then God exacts vengeance because His People ignore Him! It is the whole history of Israel, all their unhappiness.... Malediction! Malediction!... When shall this cease?... You are not a fool, M. Pums, nor you either, M. Herschstein!... But you believe, do you, that the Lord has given you this power of mind so that you can manipulate the markets, and pile up gold.... Madmen that you are! I see the hand of the Lord over you!... It was because they had betrayed His law that your ancestors went to Babylon, to Nineveh and to Egypt! And for the same reason, you will have to go elsewhere!"

He stretched out his arm towards mysterious far distant places.

"Yes! the Lord will make you sleep under tents once more and, with you, there may be some who are innocent, meek and lowly ones, toilers ... unless, beforehand, they all break away from you!"

"Enough, M. Schleifmann!" dryly declared Herschstein, who was gradually recovering his arrogance. "Enough of your jeremiads! We know your ideas.... You are an anti-Semite, a renegade! It is well known!"

Schleifmann lifted his arms again and looked up at the ceiling.

"A renegade!" he repeated, "Anti-Semite!... Adonaï! Adonaï! Hearest thou what this man is saying to me?"

"Moreover," added Pums who, like Herschstein, had recovered his ease, "moreover, when it comes to people being expelled, you might very well be before we are, M. Schleifmann! For we are French, we ... while you...."

A frantic laugh cut him short. Schleifmann exploded with bitter merriment, a prey to a fit of wild hilarity.

"French! You French!" he exclaimed, between two sobs of laughter. "But you are neither French, nor German, nor Austrians, nor anything at all—least of all Jews!... Your Jewry oppresses you under your clothing.... It oppresses you in drawing-rooms, in clubs, everywhere you go! It makes you itch, like a haircloth.... You wear it without good grace, without good nature, without pride! You only acknowledge it with regret.... It makes you pale!... You are unacquainted with its most elementary dogmas.... And, were it not that you fear it might hurt you in your business, I wager that, to-morrow morning, you would all seek to be naturalized as Catholics!"

"We do not argue with possessed people!" cried Herschstein, whose forehead and cheeks were striped with livid lines.

"With whom do you argue, if you please?" Schleifmann vociferated. "With dross like yourself? For I tell you, in the words of Ezekiel: 'You are all dross, all dross of brass, of lead, of iron; you are all dross of silver.... And the Lord shall precipitate you in the crucible to melt you under the breath of His anger!'"

He had given the Hebrew text. Now he gave it in German, and it was such a volley of harsh, thundering syllables that Pums began to take fright. What would the agents and the clerks in the hall nearby think of this noise? He decided to try audacity and said haltingly:

"That will do, M. Schleifmann!... Enough scandal!... I ask you to retire.... Shut up and get out, or damn it all, I will call the police!"

"Ah! that would complete the day!" Schleifmann exclaimed. "No! but do it; do it, so that I can laugh a little more!... Have me removed to the police station for a religious brawl!... Have me arrested!... Jeremiah was arrested twice.... Hamasiah also and Micah as well, and many others.... It is natural.... No, I stay right here, if only just to see it happen! The police!... Ha! ha!"

"He is mad, raving mad!" Pums murmured, his face convulsed.

"Not at all," Herschstein said in an attempt at irony. "You have got it right.... He is a prophet, my friend, a great prophet!"

"Alas, no, M. Herschstein!" the Galician retorted simply. "I am too old; I have passed the age.... I regret it.... Until the social question is settled for everyone in a scientific fashion, as my master Karl Marx wished it, it would do you no harm to find, on Saturday at the Synagogue, instead of your rabbis who flatter you, a sort of Sophonia who would say to you: 'Lament! ye dwellers in the market-place! All who traffic shall be....'"

Again the avalanche of Hebrew and German poured forth. Pums, his nerves overtaxed, closed his ears. Herschstein contracted his hand upon his Moses-like beard. Then a light of hope came to his anxious eyes. He had found an objection.

"What about the Christians?" he said victoriously. "Do the Christians traffic?"

"It is no concern of ours what the Christians do!" Schleifmann thundered, cutting the space with a broad forbidding gesture. "They have their God to punish them and socialism to reduce them!... But you ... you are the people of the Lord!... You owe a spontaneous example to the others! You must be *better*!... enjoy less and suffer more!... Such is your destiny! your difficult glory!... They are unique in the world! You can only avoid them by meeting worse sufferings! You are the people of the Lord!"

Messrs. Pums and Herschstein would have readily deprived themselves of belonging to that people! To show the example to the others, they! Why they, more than the others? No, this time, upon their honor, they failed to understand. And that rain of quotations, that prophetic storm which was still raging! Better leave the place to him, better find some pretext for a flight.

Pums winked rapidly to warn Herschstein and then said deliberately:

"You came to sign those papers, did you?"

"Yes!" Herschstein replied, winking back at him.

"Well, then, will you come this way?..."

He opened a door at the back and kept his hand on the handle, pluckily protecting the retreat of his ally.

"I leave you here, M. Schleifmann!" he said. "The exit is opposite.... As to your lessons to my son, there is no need for you to trouble about them any more. Send me your bill and we shall end it there.... *Au plaisir!*"

Schleifmann, stupefied by this flight, stood still, with his mouth open. He racked his mind for a biting word, for a last deadly venomous apostrophe! Then he came close to the door through which Pums had disappeared.

"You are the chosen People of the Lord!" he clamored frantically.

He went back into the hall, threw a challenging look at the usher and, recollecting the anxiety of his friend Cyprien, hurried down the steps.

"Well?" M. Raindal asked, with a suppliant movement of his jaw.

"Nothing!" Schleifmann replied. "Nothing!... The scoundrel would not do a thing!"

"I could have sworn to it!" Uncle Cyprien sighed, sliding down despairingly.

Schleifmann sat beside him in the carriage and asked, "Where shall I drive you, my dear Raindal? To the brasserie?"

"No, Schleifmann! I am not hungry.... Better take me home!"

They started. The Galician narrated his interview.

Uncle Cyprien listened in silence, his body crumpled up, his eyes dull, his face rigid. Schleifmann was still relating when they reached the pont des Saints-Pères.

"And I am not telling you a quarter of it, my friend!" the Galician concluded, still in the fever of his epopee. "I am forgetting some of it!... True, I did not obtain anything!... True, I lost a pupil!... But I have told them what I thought of them!"

"You may have told them what you thought of them, my friend," Cyprien remarked judiciously. "But that does not prevent my being done for, the most undone of all men!"

He made a motion as if to stride out of the carriage. Schleifmann pulled him back.

"Ho! Cyprien! Wha the matter?"

"I feel very much like chucking myself into the Seine.... It is right here, under my very nose.... It would save me a trip!"

The Galician shrugged his shoulders philosophically.

"Do be foolish, Raindal!... Be serious, my dear fellow! Your brother is not your brother for nothing!... Hl pull you out of it! He will arrange this affair!"

"If he arranges it as you have done, be it said without reproach, Schleifmann, I am sorry for my creditors!" Raindal retorted calmly.

He said not another word until they reached the rue ssas. But while Schleifmann paid the driver, Cyprien felt a sudden sensation of weakness.

"Schleifmann!" he called out.

"I am coming!" the Galician replied.

There was a dull sound. A brown sombrero rolled into the gutter. M. Raindal had sunk, bent in two, on the pavement, all his nerves relaxed, his limbs flabby—a bundle of lifeless flesh with a face of chalk-like pallor.

Near the bed where they had laid Cyprien, still inanimate, Schleifmann wrote feverishly.

"Here!" he told the concierge, who was finishing putting the patien clothes in order, "when you go to the drug-store, you will please send this telegram to M. Eusèbe Raindal, the brother of M. Raindal."

"M. Eusèbe Raindal!" the concierge protested. "But he is in Paris, monsieur!... He called this morning, just after M. Cyprien had gone, and he told me to inform his brother that he would come again this afternoon."

"Ah!" said Schleifmann, surprised. "Very well, then; no telegram.... Go straight to the rue Notre-Dame-des-Champs! Listen, do frighten the poor man.... Tell him that his brother is ill."

"Yes, yes! Monsieur may rest assured.... l tell him that as he ought to be told."

Nevertheless, M. Raindal was stammering with emotion when, half an hour later, he entered the room.

"What? What?" he asked, forgetting to salute Schleifmann. "Cyprien is ill ... gravely?"

"You can see for yourself, monsieur!" the Galician replied. "A stroke!... He fell in the street. My own physician, Doctor Chesnard, has just been here and suggests that it is an embolism. He is coming again to-night. Cyprien had gambled in mining stock and lost enormous sums."

He added more details. The master interrupted him with distressed exclamations.

"Is it possible!... Had I but known!... Oh! poor fellow!... poor fellow!... Why did he hide it from me?"

When Schleifmann had told him all, there were a few minutes of mutual embarrassment. The two men had at no time felt any affinity for each other. Schleifmann considered M. Raindal a narrow-minded man, timorous and dried up with erudition. He did not deny the merit of the maste works but reproached him with keeping out of the great contemporary problems. M. Raindal, on the other hand, had always disliked Schleifmann, whom he charged with stimulating the subversive instincts of his brother. Now, compelled to sympathize over a pious duty, they both would have liked to destroy those ancient grievances which their loyalty blushed to keep back. M. Raindal was the first to be emboldened enough to fib. He spoke most cordially.

"M. Schleifmann! Circumstances have been such that we have not become fast friends.... But I knew your affection for my poor Cyprien; I knew the wide range of your culture, the reliability of your character; you may be sure that I have always felt the most earnest esteem for you."

The Galician replied with tactful praise of M. Rainda books.

The discomfort disappeared. It vanished altogether when the concierge came back with drugs, mustard plasters and leeches. Both busied themselves nursing the patient; they had no leisure until the evening.

At the approach of night, Uncle Cyprien awoke from his torpor. He opened his eyes and looked absently about the room. Gradually he appeared to remember.

"Ah, yes!" he murmured. "The Bourse! The smash!"

He tried to stretch himself. A resistance on his left side caused him to frown. He felt his left shoulder with his right hand, which remained free.

"Ah! I am paralyzed, somewhere there.... Tha nice!" he grunted.

Again he inspected the room with the same infant-like stare of his mobile, toneless eyes. The presence of Schleifmann and his brother, who were watching him at the foot of the bed, caused him a momentary perplexity. Who were those men? He hesitated, having the impression that he knew them without being able to call them by name. "Eusèbe ..." he uttered at last. "Sch ... Schleifmann!"

M. Raindal went forward, stretching out his hand. Uncle Cyprien smiled sadly and said in a hoarse voice, stammering a little:

"Heh! What a state they have put me in, these fellows!... I fell on the pavement.... Did Schleifmann explain to you?"

"Yes, my dear, fellow! Do get yourself tired!"

"And the money?" the ex-official went on. "Did Schleifmann tell you that, too? Do you know that I owe one hundred and ten thousand francs. A nice thing for a Raindal!... To die leaving one hundred and ten thousand francs' debts! If poor Father had seen such a thing!"

"Hush, reassure yourself!" the master said. "First of all, you seem to me on the road to recovery...."

In reply Cyprien touched his dead shoulder.

"As to your debts!" the master added. "I will make them my affair. I have saved ninety thousand francs and I give them up to you without much regret.... My salary and what I get for my books and articles will amply suffice for all of us to live on and even to pay, a little each year, the unpaid balance.... Well, I hope that your mind is relieved."

"Yes, thanks! I thank you!" Cyprien replied distractedly, the leeches and the mustard plasters pricking him terribly. Then he forced himself to add: "Just the same, poor Eusèbe.... I have very often teased you, worried you! How many jokes have I not played upon you? But if I had been told that I would ruin you one day, I, Uncle Cyprien, with my hundred francs a month, my board at the brasserie and my garret at five hundred francs a year, well!... No, No! It is incredible! To think that all this happened because, because...." His impotent thoughts wandered through the complications of his adventure; then he went on after a pause: "Yes, because ... because, to annoy you, I wished to go to that Mme. Rhâm-Bâhan and there met the ... the marquis ... the marquis de...."

He moved his eyelids, but a weight seemed to dominate them. He fell asleep again, with an uneven breathing, sometimes imperceptible, sometimes snoring and galloping like the wind on a log fire. His cheeks became purple. His throat rattled with a scraping noise. Congestion was beginning. On his return, Dr. Chesnard assumed a face of ill-omen. He made a new prescription and ordered more violent revulsives.

As he was leaving, M. Raindal suggested for the next day a consultation with Dr. Gombauld, his colleague of the Academy of Medicine.

"Well, monsieur!" Dr. Chesnard said contemptuously, shaking his small, bald, gray head.... "I am only a district doctor and have no ambition. I shall speak to you quite frankly. Gombauld or no Gombauld—it will make little difference. An embolism is an embolism. There are not ten thousand treatments for such a case. There is only one, and it is that which I have indicated.... Of course, if a consultation appeals to you, I see no inconvenience in having it."

The meeting was fixed for noon.

They arranged a bed with a mattress and blankets in the front room, on the green rep couch. Every other hour the Galician, after watching the patient, went to stretch out upon it.

M. Raindal could not sleep. When his regret for his little pupil did not torment him, it was remorse, scruples of his conscience, the need to absolve himself. The halting words of Cyprien rang in his ears, like the repercussion of an endless echo. "All this because I wanted to go to that Mme. Rhâm-Bâhan and met there the ... the marquis!" Surely that was false reasoning! A childish conception of the relation between cause and effect! But the particle of truth which perfumes every error nevertheless spread its venomous aroma in M. Rainda soul. Evidently, he was not responsible for the mortal accident which had struck his brother. Had he been informed in time, he would have made the hardest sacrifices in order to tear the poor fellow away from the wheels of stock-gambling. Yet, who knew if, but for his intervention, for this fatal love which held him, who knew if Uncle Cyprien would have ever met "the ... the marquis?" Who could say but that this love, guilty already of so many faults against sane morality and the sentiments due to others, had not its share also—small but real—in the present calamity?

M. Raindal continued to sigh about it. He was wet with perspiration. At last, fatigue got the better of insomnia. He only awoke at eight, to open the door to Thérèse and Mme. Raindal. Behind them, the bearded head of young Boerzell saluted him.

Summoned by telegram, the women had traveled all night. Their hair in disorder, their faces sprinkled with coal dust, where drying tears had traced white lines, expressed better than their voices the anguish of their night journey. M. Raindal kissed them both with an unusual effusion of tenderness, then led them, himself in tears, to the room of Uncle Cyprien.

The latter was still sleeping, his sleep alternately tumultuous and lethargic; his skin was more purple and blacker in places than the day before, at the beginning of the crisis. Mme. Raindal knelt down beside the bed, her hands crossed. They waited for the doctors, commenting on the drama. The doctors came precisely at noon. The consultation was short. Dr. Gombauld approved his colleagu prescriptions. For the rest, he refused to foretell: nature would decide.

"What did I tell you?" Dr. Chesnard said contemptuously, on reaching the door.

And he promised to return in the course of the evening.

When he did return, the only result of his visit was that their alarm was increased. The physician left, refusing to give an opinion as to the issue of the night.

An hour later, delirium took possession of Uncle Cyprien. At first, there were nothing but vague exclamations, inarticulate complaints. But they soon became more precise. He named people, insulted certain enemies, all the immemorial enemies of Uncle Cyprien, the whole troop of grafters, *youpins*, *calotins* and *rastas*! It was as if they were dancing with triumphant laughter a Satanic round about his cot, breaking his chest with heavy boots, at times, for he took on attitudes of defense or of fear as if he were under the iron shoes of a horse. To exercise this evil rout, he tired his lungs with words of abuse, with insults taken from the vocabulary of his favorite author. His forefinger threatened; his fist hammered the empty space. Suddenly, it seemed that the saraband was scattered. By a chance turn of his memory, one preponderating image effaced the malice of the others: the image of an illustrious statesman, of a minister renowned for his fight against Boulangism. That legendary figure appeared before the bed and, without bending, it reached Uncle Cyprien with the hands that completed its enormous arms.

"Oh! Oh!...." M. Raindal, the younger, roared out in terror. "Here is the old Pirate now!... Oh! those arms!... What arms he has!... Will you go away, old Pirate! Will you let go of me!"

The imaginary grasp was stronger than his cries. In vain he put his hands to his throat. He was choking. He fell back in a coma.

He stayed in it all the evening, all night. The family waited in the next room and took turns watching the patient with Schleifmann, Boerzell and a medical student sent by Dr. Gombauld. At eleven, when the women and Schleifmann had fallen asleep on couches and chairs, M. Raindal signaled with his eyes for the young savant to come to him.

"My dear M. Boerzell," the master whispered softly, "Thérèse has told me everything this afternoon.... It seems that, while at Langrune, you came to an agreement. For my part, I am very glad of it.... But you know what disaster has befallen us.... Without speaking of poor Cyprien, it is complete ruin for us, and Thérèse will have neither dowry nor expectations of any kind. I wanted formally to warn you, knowing by experience what are the expenses of a *ménage*, ... children to be brought up, expenses...."

"I am very much obliged to you for your sincerity, dear master!" Boerzell interrupted him, in the same tone. "However, these sad events have not modified my intentions towards Mlle. Thérèse...."

He paused, ever careful of measure, of truth and exactness, then added: "I shall not go so far as to tell you that I am indifferent to these money considerations.... On the contrary, it is certain that a dowry and some expectations would have been a precious help to my wif comfort and the education of our children.... But our marriage can easily take place without this help. I feel that I am full of energy, and the prospect of a little more mediocre work is not enough to move the young and vigorous man I feel myself to be.... Therefore, I maintain my request, dear master!"

Schleifmann left the room to join the medical student. M. Raindal and the young savant shook hands affectionately; then, each on a chair, their chins in their hands, they fell gradually asleep.

Towards dawn, the interne woke them all up. The agony had begun. It proved a long one. Uncle Cyprie insurgent soul rebelled against death as it had rebelled against life. Choked by blood, he wished to breathe, to live still; his well arm repulsed the asphyxia with an imperative gesture which seemed to express his indignation.

Finally he lost his breath. He distended his purple face, his twisted lips in a supreme effort and fell back, defeated, immobile, delivered.

Mme. Raindal threw herself on her knees and prayed with abundant tears. Schleifmann, one elbow resting on the marble mantel-piece, his hands over his eyes, quietly chanted some Hebraic words. Thérèse sobbed on her fathe shoulders.

The interne opened the window and pushed back the shutters through which there already came some golden rays.

With the fresh splendor of the morning brightness an outburst of chirping penetrated the room.

It was the sparrows of the Luxembourg which sang merrily on the branches, unwittingly chirping a last good-by to their old friend, Cyprien Raindal.

CHAPTER XIX

ON the morning of the burial, Thérèse was in her room, busy sorting papers they had found in her uncl room, when Brigitte knocked at the door.

"A lady, mademoiselle!" the maid said. "Mme. Chambannes, I think."

A frown appeared on Mlle. Rainda velvety eyebrows.

"Did you tell her that monsieur and madame had gone out?"

"Yes, mademoiselle! But she said that she would like to see mademoiselle. She is in the drawing-room."

"Very well, l go!" Thérèse replied.

She threw a rapid glance in the mirror, to examine her dress and her hair, as a woman does on marching to a decisive encounter. Her stiff crêpe collar like the neckpiece of a suit of armor kept her head more erect and made her physiognomy more aggressive and severe. The corners of her thin lips arched in an aggressive smile. Ah! Mme. Chambannes wishes to see her! Well, all right! She would see her and hear her too! She was going to have her wishes, that lady, and perhaps more than that.

Thérèse opened the door of the drawing-room. Mme. Chambannes, in a black dress, black gloves and a black hat, rose slowly. Each made a ceremonious salute, from the back of the neck, with an accompaniment of watching looks and glances which already felt each other in the semi-anticipation of a contest.

Thérèse opened the door of the drawing-room, to take a seat. Mme. Chambannes murmured hesitatingly!

"I wished to tell M. Raindal how sorry we were about his loss."

"Thank you, madame!" Thérèse said, dryly. "My father is at the chapel.... I shall transmit your condolences to him, as soon as he comes home."

She fell back into silence. Mme. Chambannes went on, more timidly:

"We learned all about it through one of our common friends, the Marquis de Meuze.... Your uncle was not very old, was he?"

"Forty-two, madame."

"Still young!" Zozé remarked, urged to exaggeration by the fierce looks of Thérèse.

She walked towards the door, but stopped halfway: "Will you be kind enough to tell M. Raindal that I shall come to visit him to-morrow?"

Icily Thérèse replied.

"Do not take this trouble, Madame.... My father will not receive."

"Not even his intimate friends?"

"No, madame!... His intentions are formal.... There will be no exception for anyone."

"Not even for me?" Zozé insisted, with a mock sweetness that was really a challenge.

Her languorous eyes seemed to smile, to elaborate on the question: "I, you know, I, Mme. Chambannes; I who took him away from you.... your father; I who hold him, who make him do what I want."

The provocation caused Thérèse to become very pale. "Not even for you, madame!" she said with self-restraint.... "Father has decided to keep very strict mourning and I trust that no one will attempt to make him change his mind."

"So then, you will prevent him from seeing his friends?"

Thérès trembling fingers were opening and shutting on the back of an armchair. "We shall not prevent him from doing anything at all, Madame.... I am surprised to hear *you* using such expressions.... You must have learned in the last six months that our wishes are of little importance against those of my father...."

"What do you mean, mademoiselle?" Zozé said, with that impertinent phlegm which is often the only resource of worldly women when engaged in a discussion.

"I mean," Thérèse replied haltingly. "I mean to say, or rather you are compelling me to say that, for the last six months, you have taken my father away from us, you have led him away, engaged him in a grotesque *affaire*, the details and aim of which I know nothing of, but the worry of which has never ceased horribly to torment my mother and myself...." "But, mademois...."

"Oh! If you please, madame!" Thérèse interrupted firmly. "You have sought an explanation. Allow me to finish.... Yes, you found it quite natural to disunite us, to monopolize this poor man, to drag him in your train, out of vainglory, out of I know not what vain fantasy and without any excuse.... To-day, this catastrophe brings him back to us.... You should find it natural that we should protect him and that, seeing him rescued, we do not wish to lose him again. Was it due to my uncl death or to other emotions with which I am unacquainted that my father seemed, on our return, very weary and much aged. He who is usually so courageous in the hours of sorrow, weeps at every opportunity, he has sudden fits of heavy sobs, like a child.... He needs quiet and a well-regulated, peaceful life. Gradually he will return to his family and to his work, and you to your pleasures, which his absence will not appreciably diminish, I should think."

Zozé blushed imperceptibly under the bantering tone of Thérès last words. Mlle. Raindal took advantage of her confusion and added:

"Leave him to us now, madame! I assure you, it will be better thus.... It will be both straightforward and charitable!"

They studied each other in silence for a while and the scorn in their glances seemed a mutual reflection. "Not at her best in mourning dress, this Mlle. Raindal!" Mme. Chambannes thought to herself. Thérèse saw nothing on the charming face but signs of baseness and stupidity.

The sound of a key slipped in the keyhole caused them both to lower their eyelids.

"Will you excuse me, madame?" Thérèse said, with a curt nod.

Without pausing for an answer she walked to the hall, closed the door of the room and whispered in a short enervated voice, while M. Raindal put down his gloves and walking-stick: "Father, Mme. Chambannes is here!"

"Where? Where did you say?" M. Raindal stammered, his forehead purple.

"In the drawing-room!" Thérèse replied, eyeing him sharply. "Do you wish to see her?"

"Ah! It would be only decent, it seems to me.... What do you think?"

He sought anxiously in his daughter eyes a permission, an approval.

"If you like, father!" Thérèse said less sharply.

"Very well, then!" the master concluded, but he did not budge. An involuntary look in his eyes begged the girl to go away, not to remain treacherously on watch behind the door. She understood his distrust. Why oppose him, why upset him in the course of this test whose issue, favorable or not, would at all events be significant. She gave him a friendly look and said:

"Au revoir! I am going back to my room!"

He entered the drawing-room, closing the door behind him after having made sure that the hall was really empty.

"My dear master!" Zozé murmured tenderly, as she advanced towards him.

At the same time, either as a last maneuver to avoid defeat, or from an impulse of filial compassion, she threw herself in his arms.

He did not resist. He pressed her against his chest, kissed her haphazard, on her cheeks, on the hair of the neck, sobbing, stammering, not knowing any more what it was he was crying over, his lost brother or his destroyed happiness.

"*Ma chère amie! ma chère amie!*" he faltered, without tiring of tasting the hitherto unknown joy of holding her in his arms.

She released herself from his embrace which she considered too long and, after the first words of sympathy, asked him quietly:

"Is it true, my dear master, what Mlle. Thérèse has just told me?"

"What was that?" M. Raindal said, mopping his eyes.

"That you do not want to see me again, that you want to break away from us?"

The master did not reply. Once more he burst into tears.

"Why do you want to?" Zozé insisted, as she sat near him on a low stool.

"Because...." M. Raindal sobbed out, unable to finish.

"Because of what?" Zozé asked, helping him as if he were a schoolboy balking at a confession. "Speak frankly to me.... Am I not your friend?"

He contemplated her greedily, with shining eyes where his tears had caused the many little red veins to show more vividly. His words were exhaled rather than spoken:

"Because my affection for you has taken a turn ... an unfortunate turn, alas an excessive turn, I might even say a guilty turn...."

She tried to evince surprise despite the calm of her face.

"How, so, dear master?"

"Yes, yes!" he pursued more distinctly, as if relieved by the admission.... "You know it well enough, my dear friend.... You have known it since the day of my departure from Les Frettes, you remember?" He collected his thoughts and shook his head. "Is it not sad and ridiculous at my age, eh?... At my age!... Old and decrepit as I am!... Bah! it is not your fault.... I bear you no grudge.... But, I beg of you, do come here again.... Leave me alone.... Let me cure myself, if I can!... It will be more charitable!"

Almost the same words that Thérèse had used, an instant before and, indeed, almost the same tone! Mme. Chambannes, who was, at bottom, not heartless, felt herself thoroughly upset.

"Good-by, then, dear master!" she sighed, and offered her hand to M. Raindal.

"Good-by, my dear friend!" said the master, whose face was twisted with pain.

Passionately he pressed to his lips her little black-gloved hand, truly a hand of funerals and eternal parting.

"Good-by, good-by, since you wish it!" Mme. Chambannes repeated.

"No, I do not *wish* it!" M. Raindal specified. "I *must* wish it!"

She passed out, disappeared on the stairs, with her cadenced gait that the master so much admired.

"It was necessary!" he said aloud, when the door was closed.

Returning to his room, he evoked famous parting scenes, historic adieux: Titus and Berenice, the *Dimisit Invitus* ... and also Louis XIV and Marie Mancini.

Then suddenly his strength betrayed him. Despair, held back by his literary memories, rose to his throat in tears. He collapsed on a chair, his handkerchief over his eyes.

"I shall not see her again," he whispered dramatically. "I shall never see her again, ... never ... never!"

He did, nevertheless, see her again, a few hours later, at the Cimetière Montparnasse, while a delegate of the Atheists' Association pronounced the eulogy of Uncle Cyprien, in front of the gaping tomb.

There were not many people, owing to the season, few women especially. All those who had come wore black, but the black garments of Zozé among theirs seemed like a quee dress. Her grace, her smartness were still triumphant in mourning. Her fine small face, paler than usual near the dark material, had a pleasant seriousness which would have made the master smile, had he not wept so much.

His dull glances went successively from Zozé to the grave and from the grave to Zozé, while his tears ran confusedly for both.

The delegate, on concluding his speech, laid on the marble a vast crown of red goldilocks.

The family lined up with Schleifmann in a little side alley and the audience passed on file, murmuring their condolences. M. Raindal, without seeing anyone, pressed the hands of all, those of the indifferent like those of Zozé,

Chambannes, the Marquis, even Gerald and the abbé Touronde, who was somewhat ill at ease among so many free-thinkers. Then the procession ceased. All walked to the entrance gate.

Schleifmann lingered behind, prowling about the grave of his friend Cyprien. Once free from onlookers, he gave two twenty-sou pieces to one of the grave-diggers. Then, after the rite of Israel, scratching the ground of a nearby tomb-garden, he three times threw a handful of earth and gravel across the sepulture. The pebbles resounded on the wood of the coffin. In reply, the Galician murmured a Hebrew verse.

His eyes looked up to the heavens. Their fervent glance seemed to desire to pierce the mystery of the clouds, into the inaccessible region of destinies. He no longer cursed. He was merely seeking a reply.

Why did the Lord tolerate such iniquitous ruins? By what formidable designs did He associate His people with the accomplishment of such misdeeds? When would He at last raise up in His Temple, among His priests, someone, with a free and daring voice—to remind the Jews, the proudest and the meekest, of the solemn trust of purity and justice which they once received at the foot of Sinai?

No sign answered these silent queries. The clouds pursued their peaceful promenade on the blue background of the sky.

Schleifmann dragged his weary feet to the gate. In the curly locks of his gray beard his lips unconsciously mumbled: "Cyprien!... Cyprien!..." He remembered the good times spent at Klapprot, the progressive building up of the old theory of the Two Banks of the River.... A most uncertain, a most contestable theory, if one liked—but a theory which, nevertheless, contained a small portion of the truth! Then, how valiantly he would utter it, poor Cyprien! With what gayety, what fire, what conviction, and what presentiment perhaps! Now, alas, there would be no more Cyprien! Henceforth, Schleifmann, my dear fellow, you will remain a poor lonely soul, vowed to your books, your deserted garret and your friendless brasseries! The eyes of the Galician were full of big tears.

As he reached the gate of the cemetery, he stopped short and stood gravely on the threshold.

Outside, in front of the door, two carriages faced each other, against the pavement. In the first, a private coupé with sober harness, were settled Zozé, Chambannes and Gerald, all three. Into the other—a black undertake carriage—young Boerzell was climbing beside the Raindal family.

The drivers started simultaneously. The two carriages turned in opposite directions, one going back to the elegance of the Right Bank, the other driving again into the studious district of the Left Bank.

Schleifmann followed them both alternately with his glance. Ah! if his good old Cyprien had been there to see that!

Gradually, the carriages grew dim at the two ends of the boulevard. He could hardly distinguish their vanishing silhouettes, one massive and without reflection, like a block of black crêpe, the other smart and light under the sparkle of a new coat of varnish.

Schleifmann smiled with melancholy pride.

THE END.

Milton Keynes UK
Ingram Content Group UK Ltd.
UKHW041943181124
451360UK00008B/909

9 789362 511539